THE
PASTA GOURMET

SUNNY BAKER
MICHELLE SBRAGA

Avery Publishing Group
Garden City Park, New York

Text Illustrator: John Wincek
Interior Color Photographs: Amy Reichman
Cover Photograph: Envision, New York, NY
Cover Design: William Gonzalez and Rudy Shur
In-House Editor: Lisa James
Typesetter: Bonnie Freid

Cataloging-in-Publication Data

Baker, Sunny.
    The pasta gourmet: creative pasta recipes from appetizers to
desserts / by Sunny Baker and Michelle Sbraga.
      p. cm.
      Includes index.
      ISBN 0-89529-663-2

    1. Cookery (Pasta)   I. Sbraga, Michelle.   II. Title.

TX809.M17B35   1995   641.8'22
                                        QBI95-20325

Printed in the United States of America

10   9   8   7   6   5   4   3   2   1

Contents

Acknowledgments,   vii

Preface,   ix

Introduction,   1

Part One   Introduction to Pasta

1. Pasta Basics,   5

2. Cooking With Pasta,   11

Part Two   The Pasta Machine

3. Choosing and Using a Hand-Cranked Machine,   17

4. Choosing and Using an Electric Extrusion Machine,   31

Part Three   Making Pastas

5. Basic Pastas,   45

6. Vegetable and Herb Pastas,   61

7. Flavors-You-Never-Thought-Of Pastas,   101

8. Fruit and Dessert Pastas,   123

9. Munchies,   137

Part Four Pasta Sauces and Dishes

10. Traditional Sauces,   153

11. Light Sauces,   171

12. International Sauces,   181

13. Dessert Toppings,   193

14. Pasta Dishes,   199

    Index,   225

To Michael and Kim

Acknowledgments

No book is ever completed by the authors alone. We would like to thank all the companies that provided us with the pasta-making equipment used in this book: VillaWare Manufacturing Company; Waring Products; Maverick Industries, Inc.; Creative Technologies Corporation; Cuisinarts Corporation; and Lello Appliances Corporation. Without their support, we would have never been able to produce so much wonderful pasta.

You have no idea of the room it takes to test seven different pasta machines. Besides the machines, you have the cooks, the illustrator, the taste testers, and the clean-up brigade. Our special thanks goes to Jan Warren Davies, who graciously let us use her spacious kitchen while she was away. The fact that she sold the house after her return has nothing to do with the amount of flour used.

Preface

Pasta—that wonderfully simple combination of flour, water, and (sometimes) eggs—has been enjoyed for countless generations by people around the world. Pasta and related noodles are universal foods that came into being wherever people had to invent uses for the grains they had at hand. Because of its simplicity, pasta goes with almost any topping, sauce, or spice to make hearty meals, elegant side dishes, or even unique desserts.

Inexpensive and nutritious, pasta has long been a staple of the American diet. But there has been a willingness of late to see pasta as a gourmet food, well worthy of kitchen artistry and creativity. Food retailers have taken note of this trend. As a result, the pasta chef has an ever-increasing number of options to explore, from a wider assortment of imported and domestic dried pasta to packaged fresh pasta, in an ever-expanding variety of flavors.

For the pasta lover who wants to go all out, there are also a number of good pasta machines on the market. From traditional hand-cranked machines to technologically sophisticated electric extrusion models, pasta machines allow you to create your own fresh, delicious pasta.

As dedicated pasta lovers, we've written this book to share with you both our passion for pasta and our long experience as pasta chefs. In Part One, we give you some general information—including an overview of the different pasta shapes—and some tips for both buying and cooking pasta. In Part Two, we teach you all about pasta machines, from how to choose one to how to use one. In Part Three, we tell you how to produce an almost endless variety of flavors using your pasta machine. We also tell you how to make other delicious goodies, such as breadsticks and won tons, using the special dies that come with some of the more sophisticated machines. And in Part Four, we give you recipes for sauces suited to every taste, from traditional to international. We also give you recipes for tasty dishes using pasta.

Sound good? Then read on—and learn how to become a pasta gourmet.

Introduction

$\mathcal{I}$s there anyone who doesn't like pasta? It has been a staple food around the world for centuries. But recently, chefs have looked at the humble noodle in a new light—as a gourmet food. Our goal in writing this book is to give you all the information you'll need to whip up gourmet pasta creations. We encourage you to try varied noodle and sauce combinations, and to find your personal favorites. To this end, we have provided diverse recipes for sauces and dishes to inspire you. We also encourage you to buy your own pasta machine and experiment with different shapes and flavors. We hope that you will enjoy gourmet pasta as much as we do.

We have based our recipes on a number of pasta-making traditions. To the surprise of many Americans, pasta is not the domain of Italy alone. In Asia, middle-eastern Europe, and Africa, pasta-like noodles are just as important to the local cuisines as they are to that of Italy. In fact, almost every cuisine around the world uses egg noodles in some shape or form. However, most knowledge of pasta in the United States comes from Italy, where pasta has been made since before the time of the ancient Romans.

THE THOROUGHLY MODERN VIEW OF PASTA

Pasta smothered in tomato sauce and Parmesan cheese is now a mainstay of family cooking in this country. We grew up on spaghetti prepared this way, so it wasn't until we started cooking for ourselves that all the other pasta possibilities were revealed to us. Though we still enjoy a meal of spaghetti with a good tomato sauce as much as we did when we were kids, we've discovered that there are many other pasta-and-sauce combinations to explore and enjoy.

Starting in the 1970s, many cooks, in their quest for fresher tastes and healthier cuisines, rediscovered the possibilities of pasta. And pasta is healthy, despite what you may have heard. A cup of cooked, unsauced pasta has about 200 calories. These calories are mostly in the form of complex carbohydrates, which nutritionists now see as the basis of a healthy diet. Pasta is also a good source of protein. The bad-health knock comes from high-calorie sauces, which this book avoids.

Some cooks prefer packaged pasta. Go to any

health food store today and you'll find pasta made from whole wheat, buckwheat, and other flours. It's not uncommon to find spinach-, tomato-, artichoke-, or herb-flavored pastas in ordinary supermarkets. There are also varieties of fresh pasta in gourmet shops and the freezer sections of most food stores.

USING HOMEMADE PASTA

Other cooks, like us, use pasta machines, the better to experiment with pasta in different flavors and textures. We love homemade pasta, but before you spend a few hundred dollars on a state-of-the-art machine, you should know that homemade pasta is different from the packaged pastas. Homemade pasta does offer more variety and flavor choices. But do not expect your homemade noodles and shapes to have the smoothness, lightness, compactness, or polish of packaged pasta.

Even the most expensive electric extrusion machines designed for home use will not produce pasta that looks like the manufactured varieties. In the United States, manufactured pasta is almost always made with semolina flour ground from durum wheat. In Italy, all pastas are made from durum wheat by law. Only a factory has the kind of machine able to knead and extrude the hard granular durum wheat flours, like semolina, into perfectly formed, polished pasta. You can use semolina flour in your own machine (see page 52). But the results, though tasty, will still not be the perfectly consistent, shiny pastas you can buy in the supermarket.

We hope the differences in shape and texture won't keep you from enjoying your pasta fresh. Dried, manufactured pasta is consistent, but fresh pasta, especially if it's homemade, does offer more possibilities. Fresh pasta has a different taste and consistency, one we savor and enjoy. With the subtleties of tastes available, we think you'll learn to love it as much as we do.

It's clear that pasta is not just a fad. It's been around for a long time. Pasta is a wholesome food with lots of possibilities and, with a good machine, it's easy to make. But enough talk. Now that we've whet your appetite and stirred your cravings, let's get acquainted with the wonderful world of pasta.

PART ONE

Introduction to Pasta

Before we get started, we thought it would be nice to take a quick look at pasta in general, from its origins to the best ways to prepare it. There's so much to learn about this delicious and versatile food!

We start out in Chapter 1 by looking at some of pasta's colorful history. We then check out pasta's nutritional value—we think you'll be pleased to find out how something that tastes so good can be so good for you. We then help you find your way around the pasta section of your local food store with a guide to some of the available shapes and

flavors, and introduce you to one of the great questions of our time—do you prefer your pasta fresh or dry? Finally, we give a couple of pointers for buying pasta.

In Chapter 2, we help you prepare a memorable pasta meal, from matching the sauce with the shape to cooking pasta the right way—and there is a little more to it than just putting pasta into boiling water. We also advise you on the best way to serve pasta, including a short guide to cheeses. We finish up with some tips for storing leftover cooked pasta.

1

Pasta Basics

Where did pasta first come from? No one really knows, since pasta has been a part of cuisines around the world for centuries. But we do know some of the history of this remarkable food, a history that we share with you in this chapter. We also explain why pasta is healthy, despite its earlier reputation to the contrary.

Have you ever stood, bewildered, in front of a supermarket shelf filled with a confusing variety of pasta shapes and flavors? Then you'll want to read our descriptions of the different types of pasta. You'll also appreciate our tips on how to buy pasta, if you prefer to not make it yourself.

PASTA—A UNIVERSAL FOOD FOR THE AGES

Pasta was the food of our ancestors; it has been made for centuries. In the Western world we tend to think of pasta as an Italian mainstay, although almost every culture features pasta and related noodles as a significant component of the local cuisine. There is documentation that the Chinese and Japanese were making noodles, their version of pasta, more than five thousand years ago. Scholars have discovered references to noo-

dles from the Etruscans, who lived in Italy before the rise of the Romans, that date from the fourth century B.C.

The ancient Italian noodles, called *laganum*—the Latin word that became "lasagna" in modern Italian—were probably something like the flat noodles we now call tagliatelle or fettuccine. References to laganum go back more than two thousand years, with stories of Cicero (106–43 B.C.), the great Roman orator, diplomat, and philosopher, enjoying his laganum cooked in fatty broth and covered with cheese and spices.

You may have heard the traditional story that, in the thirteenth century, Marco Polo brought noodles back to Italy after extensive travels in China. This is probably only partly true. Ancient records disclose that the Sicilian town of Trabia had a pasta factory several hundred years before then. Most scholars believe that Marco Polo simply brought back the information that the Chinese were eating noodles similar to those enjoyed by the Italians of the period.

In central and northern Italy, references to fresh egg pasta date from the Middle Ages. Large-scale pasta factories began springing up in Italy in the early nineteenth century, and dried pasta became popular early in the twentieth century. The traditional hard pasta, attributed to Italy and likely invented centuries ago in the southern part of the country, has become a standard.

Egg noodles are also common in Asian cooking. Frequently, Asian egg noodles are called "Chinese noodles" in recipes, but they are often the product of other Asian countries, including Malaysia, Thailand, Hong Kong, and Japan. Noodles made of brown rice flour are also popular thoughout Asia.

PASTA AS HEALTH FOOD

Pasta not only tastes good—it's good for you. In the not-so-distant past, pasta had a reputation as an unhealthy, high-calorie food with little nutritional redemption. Misinformed nutritionists berated starches, and maligned pasta as a key offender in the fattening of America. Unfounded fears mandated that it be banned from our diets. Those were dark days for pasta lovers. There was less guilt about eating a bowl of ice cream than snitching a few forkfuls of our beloved spaghetti or lasagna.

Pasta in itself is quite nutritious. It is simply what you put on the pasta that makes it either healthful or unhealthful. Thankfully, we've come a long way in expanding our knowledge and revising our opinions about pasta. Now, both traditional cooks and modern health food aficionados are singing its praises. If pasta's benefits are still not clear, here are some nutritional facts that every pasta gourmet should know:

• **Pasta is a valuable source of protein.** Though the amount of protein varies, depending on the type of flour used and whether or not eggs are included in the dough, all pastas offer a good distribution of the essential amino acids, the building blocks of protein. The average plain spaghetti offer a protein content of about 13 percent. Egg noodles consist of up to 14 percent protein.

• **Pasta is a rich source of complex carbohydrates.** Nutritionists now recommend that 55 percent of our daily food intake consist of complex carbohydrates. Because complex carbohydrates stay in the body longer, they help keep energy up and hunger at bay. Because they are digested at a moderate rate, they provide a sense of fullness that prevents the return of hunger too soon

after a meal. This is why professional athletes "carbo load" on pasta the night before an event to provide the fuel needed to keep their bodies running longer.

• **Pasta is relatively low in calories.** By itself, sitting naked on your plate, pasta contains approximately 400 calories for a two-cup serving. Of course, the exact calories vary based on type of flour used and whether eggs or oil are used. But in general, expect about 200 calories per cup of prepared, unsauced pasta.

• **Pasta is highly digestible.** Nutritionists determine how digestible a food is by comparing the nutrients consumed with the nutrients excreted. This is called the digestibility coefficient. The average digestibility coefficient of the carbohydrate in pasta is 98 percent; of the protein, 85 percent; and of the fat, 90 percent. These high digestibility coefficients mean that the nutrients in pasta are being absorbed and processed.

• **Pasta is as delicious with low-fat sauces as it is with high-fat sauces.** The greatest potential hazard to your health from pasta comes from covering it with too much fat and oil. Consider Alfredo sauce. Few people can afford the high price paid in calories, fat, and cholesterol that regular indulgence in a classic Fettuccine Alfredo—made with eggs, butter, heavy cream, and Parmesan cheese—demands. But a light Alfredo sauce with similar taste and texture can be made from soy milk and tofu, flavored with low-fat Parmesan and thickened with a bit of arrowroot powder. The resulting delight reduces the calories and fat by more than half. (The recipe is on page 177.)

TYPES OF PASTA

It used to be that deciding what type of pasta to buy was simple. You bought either spaghetti to go with your meatballs or elbow macaroni to go with your cheese sauce. Now, you have more choices to make, choices involving shape, flavor, and dry pasta versus fresh.

Pasta Shapes for Every Occasion

Part of pasta's appeal comes from its almost endless variety of shapes and sizes. Although most of the shapes we will be dealing with come from Italy, there is a rich noodle-making tradition in other parts of the world as well. The two non-Italian noodles we use most often, udon and soba, come from Japan. Both are thick round noodles, like very fat spaghetti. For you pasta machine users, we give directions on how to make both udon and soba noodles in Chapter 7.

In Italy, the terms for pasta shapes vary by manufacturer and province. For example, the terms *fettuccine* and *agnolotti*, used in Rome, become *tagliatelle* and *ravioli* in Bologna. This section provides an overview of the terms you are likely to encounter in your pasta adventures. Italian shapes fall into three basic categories: long, short, and fanciful.

Long Pastas

Some of the common long shapes include:

- **Bucatini.** This spaghetti is shaped like a thin tube.

Bucatini

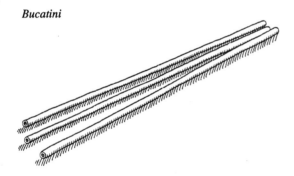

- **Capellini.** This is the thinnest of the spaghetti shapes, and is also called angel hair. It is often used in soup.

Capellini

- **Fettuccine.** This flat noodle is wider than linguine, but narrower than lasagna. It is also called tagliatelle.

Fettuccine

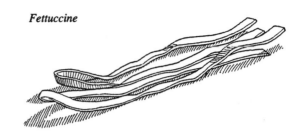

- **Lasagna.** This is a wide, flat noodle. Commercially produced lasagna has wavy edges. Homemade lasagna can be either flat or wavy.

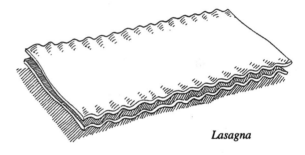

Lasagna

- **Linguine.** This noodle is flat, but thin.

Linguine

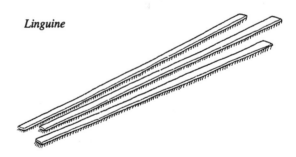

- **Long Fusilli.** This is a fat, solid spiral spaghetti.

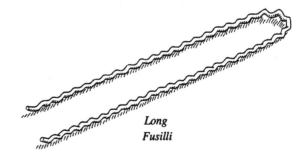

Long Fusilli

• **Spaghetti.** This is easily the most recognized shape. It comes in several different thicknesses.

Spaghetti

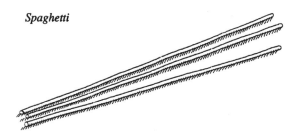

Short Pastas

Some of the common short pasta shapes include:

• **Ditali.** This is a short, tubular macaroni. It is often used in soups and salads.

Ditali

• **Mostaccioli.** This "small mustache" shape is similar to penne.

Mostaccioli

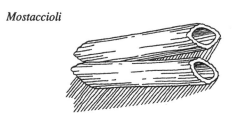

• **Orzo.** This rice-like shape is often used in soups and pilafs.

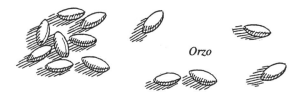

Orzo

• **Penne.** This tubular shape, available either grooved or plain, is about 1½ inches in length. The ends are cut diagonally to resemble a quill or a pen point. The ridged version may be called rigati.

Penne

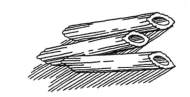

• **Rigatoni.** This is a very large, grooved, tubular pasta.

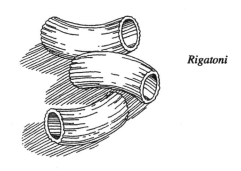

Rigatoni

• **Short Fusilli.** This short, fat screwlike pasta is also called rotelle.

*Short
Fusilli*

• **Ziti.** This is a large, tubular, slightly curved macaroni. Ziti are also called bridegrooms—your guess as to why is as good as ours.

Ziti

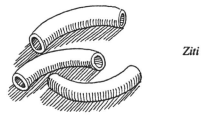

Fancifully Shaped Pastas

Some of the common fanciful pasta shapes include:

• **Cavatelli.** This is a short, curled noodle resembling a ruffled shell.

Cavatelli

• **Conchiglie.** This is a large shell shape, available either grooved or plain.

Conchiglie

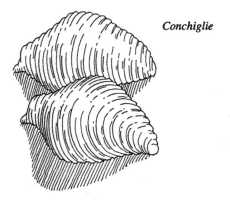

• **Conchigliette.** This is a small shell shape.

Conchigliette

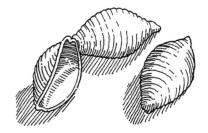

• **Farfelle.** This pasta is also referred to as bowties or butterflies.

Farfelle

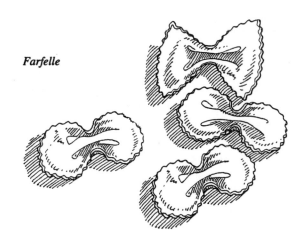

A World of Flavors

Pasta doesn't come in quite as many flavors as it does shapes, but there are certainly more than enough flavors to keep even the most dedicated pasta enthusiast experimenting for years. Obviously, the sauce or topping is a big part of the final taste of the meal. But the pasta itself makes no small contribution.

Part of pasta's flavor comes from the flour. Most Italian-style pasta is made from semolina, which is a specific grind of a hard winter wheat called durum. Many homemade pastas are made with unbleached white flour, the standard flour for most kinds of home cooking and baking. These flours are similar in taste.

Other flours are used to impart different tastes and textures to pasta. Whole wheat and oat flours give pasta a nuttier flavor, as does buckwheat flour. Brown rice flour gives pasta a mildly sweet flavor. Corn meal is also used to lend the flavor of corn to pasta.

Pasta can also be flavored with vegetables, such as broccoli or spinach; herbs, such as basil or oregano; spices, such as curry or saffron; and fruit, such as strawberries or lemons. We give directions in Part Three for making pasta with all these flavorings and more, and such flavors are now becoming common in gourmet shops and supermarkets.

Pasta Fresh and Dry

So—you've decided what pasta shape you want and what pasta flavor you would like to try. But you're not finished. You still have to decide whether you want your pasta fresh or dry.

Dry pasta is the easiest to find. Almost every kind of food store carries some kind of dry pasta, and many dedicate half an aisle or more to it. Dry pasta is very consistent in texture when cooked, and is available in the greatest variety of shapes. It is also becoming available in more and more flavors.

Fresh pasta, either store-bought or homemade, provides the greatest variety of flavors. A number of stores now stock fresh pasta, which is available in both refrigerated and frozen forms. The flavors of homemade pasta are limited only by your machine's ability to process a variety of flavoring agents. For example, your machine may not handle fruit pastas very well because fruit tends to make pasta very sticky, and some fruits have small seeds that can clog the mechanism.

You should realize that fresh pasta will not have the same texture when cooked as dry pasta does. Fresh pasta is softer and chewier, and takes less time to cook. But don't let these differences stop you from trying fresh pasta—our favorite kind!

TIPS FOR BUYING PASTA

By now, you're probably asking, "Well, what should I buy? What do I look for?" We offer the following information to guide you.

Dry Pasta

Dry pasta comes in more than 100 shapes and sizes, and can be found everywhere from the corner grocery store to fancy mail-order catalogs. No one place carries every shape, and confusion abounds when trying to figure out what a certain pasta is called. As we've mentioned, the same pasta is known by different names in different regions of Italy. Names can also change based on changes in size (short fusilli versus long fusilli) and whether there are ridges on the outside or not (penne versus mostaccioli). And pasta manufacturers add to the confusion by using different names for similar products, or by changing the spelling on the package ("linguine" versus "linguini"). Phew!

The good news is that many pasta shapes are interchangable. See Chapter 2 for some pointers on matching shapes to sauces, but feel free to experiment.

The other big decision in choosing a dried pasta is imported versus domestic. Until a few years ago, neither one of us would ever be caught buying dried pasta that wasn't imported from Italy. Domestic pasta never turned out right—it would either be too hard in the middle or too mushy. No amount of variation in cooking time helped.

Today, there is almost no difference between most of the imported and domestic brands. To be certain you are getting the best product available, look for the words "durum wheat" or "semolina flour" in the ingredient list. This foolproof method only takes a second, and will ensure that you are getting the best dried pasta available.

Fresh Pasta

Many supermarkets and gourmet shops now carry fresh pasta. It is best when bought in small amounts. When examining the package, make sure the pasta does not look dried out, and check for an expiration date. After purchasing, store the pasta in the refrigerator. We recommend using it as soon as possible, to ensure the best quality.

If you're used to either dried or homemade pasta, you may find that some of the store-bought fresh pastas, such as the fettuccine, may be somewhat thicker and chewier than you're used to. This is done to keep the pasta fresher for a longer time, and to cut down on breakage during shipping.

Some of these pastas are now being paired with their own sauces. We think it is just as easy to whip up your own sauce. We may be slightly biased, but store-bought sauce, to us, is never as good as homemade.

2
Cooking With Pasta

It's true. Of all the great foods in the world, pasta is probably the easiest to cook. Remember Jack Lemmon in *The Apartment*, in the scene where he used a tennis racket as a spaghetti strainer? But, really, there is a right way to cook pasta. We tell you how to do it. We also give you tips on matching sauces to shapes, and suggestions for serving your pasta, including a word on cheeses. And, if you do wind up with leftovers, we give you instructions for properly storing and reheating leftover cooked pasta.

MATCHING THE SAUCE TO THE SHAPE

Pasta is always the same but always different, depending on the flavorings you put in it and sauce you put on it. Part Three gives instructions for making pasta doughs in various flavors, if making pasta interests you. Part Four has sauce recipes for every taste, from traditional to exotic. Both parts contain information on what pasta flavors go best with what sauces.

But matching flavors is only part of the story. You will also want to match the sauce to the shape of your pasta. Does a big shape, such as ziti, demand a chunky sauce? What do you do with a tiny shape, such as orzo?

First, we'll look at Italian tradition. Then, we'll tell you what we think.

Pasta and Sauce, Italian Style

We are eclectic in our use of pasta, but you may find that the Italians are not. In matching a sauce to a specific pasta shape, they can be very specific. The delicate capellini requires a lighter sauce than the thick ciriole. Small pastine, such as grandinine and stelline, and short tubular pasta, including ditalini, avemarie, and small farfalline, are traditionally used in broths or soups, never in main dishes. Thin spaghetti is served with seafood sauces. Cream sauces demand the thicker regular spaghetti. Pestos are served on flat, narrow noodles, such as trenette. Anyway, that's what the Italians think. We think it is entirely possible to interchange shapes, so long was the exchange yields a similar cooked volume.

Going Beyond Authentic

Because pasta and noodles are international in scope, we don't believe there is one "right" way to enjoy them.

This is not a book about "authentic" presentations of pasta, though many of our recipes are derived from those of traditional chefs from around the world. There is no need to make pasta the classic Italian way, unless you want to. Pasta and noodles can be used in new ways to add dimension and personality to casseroles, salads, soups, and stews. Feel free to experiment with your pasta and sauce combinations.

That being said, we do agree that certain pastas seem right with certain sauces. But these preferences are our own, and may differ from yours. We use tubular shapes, like ziti, and envelope shapes, like conchiglie, when the sauce has bits of vegetables or fish to be caught in the spaces. Fine, slender noodles seem best to us with thin sauces that are accented with spices. For a cold pasta salad, a thicker pasta is our preference. Orzo can be used in place of rice, either in soups or as a side dish. But remember, there is no wrong way to eat pasta. Use the shapes you prefer—the ones that seem "right" with certain sauces should be decided by your cravings and the pasta on hand.

HOW TO COOK PERFECT PASTA EVERY TIME

The taste of pasta depends just as much on how it is cooked as on the ingredients it is made with. There is nothing worse than overcooked, mushy pasta that falls apart on the plate.

Here are the steps we recommend for cooking perfect pasta. If you've bought dried rice noodles at an Asian market, you should first soak them in cold water according to the directions on the package.

1. Place 4 to 5 quarts of water in a spaghetti cooker or other large pot for each pound of pasta you want to cook. Bring the water to a vigorous boil. Make sure that the pot is large enough, or it will boil over. Pasta needs a lot of boiling water to keep it from sticking together and forming clumps.

2. If you want to, salt the water lightly. We recommend the use of sea salt, if you really feel that salt is necessary. Add no more than 1 tablespoon of salt for each 4 to 5 quarts of water.

3. Add all of the pasta to the rapidly boiling water.

Stir vigorously as the pasta is added to make sure it is all under water.

4. Cover the pot until the water comes back to a boil. Remove the cover and test the pasta for doneness with your teeth. It should be tender, yet firm—*al dente*, which is Italian for "to the tooth." If the pasta was made fresh within the past hour, it may be ready at this point.

5. Test the pasta every 15 to 30 seconds thereafter, as necessary. It is difficult to say exactly how long it will take for the pasta to cook. Cooking time will vary depending on whether the pasta is dry or fresh. Remember, the fresher the pasta, the shorter the cooking time. Fresh pasta will take approximately 2 to 3 minutes to cook after the water starts to boil again. Dried pasta can take anywhere from 4 to 15 minutes to cook; frozen pasta may take a bit more time than that. Also, thickness is a factor, with thicker pastas taking approximately 4 to 6 minutes longer than thinner pastas. For most dishes, it is best to undercook the pasta slightly.

6. When the pasta is done, remove up to one-half cup of the cooking water and set it aside. Immediately remove the pasta from the heat, and drain in a colander. If you're using a spaghetti cooker, the removable colander is built in; just lift the colander out and place it in the sink. Do not rinse the pasta unless it is to be used in a cold salad.

7. Add a ladle or two of sauce to the pasta, or a tablespoon of oil, and mix well. This keeps the pasta from sticking together during serving. If the sauce is too thick, or if the pasta keeps sticking together, add a small amount of the reserved cooking water to the pasta. This works especially well with oil-based sauces. If you prefer not to add the cooking water, small amounts of additional olive oil may be used. Vegetable broth can also be used.

8. If you are making a cold salad, rinse the pasta with cold water and drain thoroughly. Shake the pasta in the colander until all the excess water is drained. This allows the sauce to cling better. Either cover the pasta with the sauce or mix the sauce in with the pasta, as appropriate.

9. Unless you're making a cold dish, serve the pasta immediately, with additional sauce on the side.

You will notice that our cooking instructions do not require adding salt or oil to the cooking water. Salt is not necessary, and only adds extra sodium to the recipe. Adding oil will only be necessary if you are using homemade pasta that is somewhat sticky. In that case, add a tablespoon of oil to the boiling water. This will keep the pasta from sticking together during cooking.

SERVING SUGGESTIONS FOR A SUPERB PASTA MEAL

Serve pasta in large, shallow bowls. When put into deep bowls, the sauce falls to the bottom and leaves the top dry. Large, flat plates will work also, but things can get messy if either the pasta or the sauce falls over the edge.

When serving pasta as a main dish, it is always advisable to keep the accompaniments as simple as possible. A tossed salad and plenty of fresh bread (or breadsticks made with your pasta machine) will usually fill up even the hungriest diner. Pasta salads are becoming more and more popular, both as main meals and as side dishes. Pasta as a side dish can accompany any meal. It is a welcome change from potatoes or rice.

Pasta is an easy and economical addition to parties, cookouts, and picnics. Pasta salads can be made ahead of time, then covered and kept in the refrigerator until needed. If you are taking the salad to another location, make sure there's a spot in the refrigerator or picnic cooler. Just mix the salad thoroughly before serving. Hot dishes, such as Baked Ziti (page 205), require a little more effort. When making the dish, we recommend that you undercook the pasta itself by a few minutes, so that it doesn't get mushy when reheated. After the dish has been made, it can be covered and left on the counter to cool. If it is going to be at least several hours before serving time, pop the dish in the refrigerator until needed—this will also make it easier to transport (no burned hands!). Before using, place the covered dish in the oven or microwave, and heat until the cheese is bubbly. Keep some extra sauce on hand, as the cooling and reheating can absorb all the liquid.

CHEESE AND PASTA TIPS

Don't sprinkle cheese on every dish just because it is pasta. Cheese is not used on all pasta, and it is never used on pasta dishes that contain any kind of fish. There are several kinds of cheese that can be used.

Parmesan Cheese

This hard cheese is used for grating, although some can be eaten in slices. Made from cow's milk, Parmesan has a tangy taste that goes well with pasta. If up to now you have used only cardboard shakers of Parmesan, buy a wedge of real Parmesan, and get ready for a treat.

Parmesan should never be grated ahead of time. Keep a whole piece of cheese, wrapped in damp cheesecloth, in a plastic container. Kept in the refrigerator, this cheese will last for months. If mildew starts to form, just cut that portion off. Parmesan can also be frozen, either in chunks or already grated.

Romano Cheese

Known as Pecorino in Italy, this is another hard cheese used for grating. It is made from sheep's milk, and has a sharper taste than Parmesan. Romano cheese should be stored in the same manner as Parmesan.

Other Cheeses

Cheddar, feta, Swiss, or almost any other cheese can be used on pasta, if you use common sense. We especially like a good sharp cheddar or an aged gouda on whole-grain pastas. Experiment!

STORING AND USING LEFTOVER COOKED PASTA

In the unlikely event that there are leftovers, cooked pasta can be kept for several days in the refrigerator. Use an airtight container. If only a small portion of sauce is also left, it can be mixed with the pasta. Large amounts of sauce should be kept separate from the pasta. This way, you can use as much sauce as you need for the leftovers, and use the rest the next time you make pasta. Cooked sauce can be stored for about a week.

To reheat, put the leftover pasta and the sauce in a baking dish, cover with foil, and bake at 325°F for 15 to 20 minutes, or until heated through. You can also heat it in the microwave. Cover the pasta with plastic wrap, and put on high heat for 1 to 2 minutes. Uncover and stir. If it is still not heated, return it to the microwave for 15 seconds. Repeat until the pasta is heated through.

One of the tastiest ways to use leftover cooked pasta without sauce is to make it with eggs. Coat a skillet with a nonstick cooking spray and add the pasta. Cook over medium heat for 1 to 2 minutes, or until the pasta is heated through. Add several lightly beaten eggs or an egg substitute to the skillet, and cook until the eggs are done. Serve immediately. If you have a small amount of tomato sauce on hand, you can serve it on the side.

PART TWO

The Pasta Machine

If you would rather buy your pasta and just concentrate on making the sauce, that's fine. Skip ahead to Part Four for sauce recipes. But the very best pasta, in our opinion, is that which you make yourself. When pasta is homemade, you and you alone maintain the quality, the texture, and the ultimate goodness and taste of the meal.

Pasta can be made by hand, but with a machine it's faster, and easier to control the thickness of the results. There are two general types of pasta machines on the market: hand-cranked models and electric models. The hand-cranked machines are fed dough that has been mixed on a board or in a food processor. The dough is then either cut on a roller machine into long or flat noodles, or forced through a die in an extrusion machine to make the desired shape. Electric extrusion machines do almost everything, from mixing to extruding, in one machine. Some machines even incorporate a blow dryer to dry the dough as it is extrudes.

What kind of machine should you get? That will depend on several factors. These include time, since the hand-cranked models take longer to use, and cost, since electric machines are generally more expensive. It also depends on what shapes you want to make. Roller machines are limited to making flat or round spaghetti and noodles, while extrusion machines are limited by the dies available for each particular model. See Chapter 3 for information on hand-cranked machines and Chapter 4 for information on electric extrusion machines.

3

Choosing and Using a Hand-Cranked Machine

*O*f you're an old-fashioned sort who doesn't go in for the latest in kitchen technology, but you would like a little assistance in making pasta, then a hand-cranked pasta machine is the perfect choice for you. Using a hand-cranked machine does take longer, as opposed to using one of the electric models. But we find that an afternoon spent mixing and cutting pasta on our trusty Atlas is a wonderful way to forget about the cares and worries of the week. It's also a link to the past, to the way that Grandma used to do it.

In this chapter, we list the advantages and disadvantages of choosing a hand-cranked machine, and review the two most popular machines. We also let you know what other kinds of utensils you'll find handy in your quest for homemade pasta.

After helping you choose a machine, we help you use it, by giving detailed steps for mixing, cutting, and extruding pasta dough. And since we're a little sentimental for the old days, we finish up with a description of how to cut dough by hand.

ADVANTAGES AND DISADVANTAGES OF A HAND-CRANKED MACHINE

There are several advantages to buying a hand-cranked machine:

• **Price.** A decent hand-cranked machine can be had for between $30 and $50, or at least $100 less than a decent mid-range electric machine.

• **Cleaning.** Because the dough used by a hand-cranked machine is kneaded into an elastic ball, the machine tends to stay clean, without a lot of dough getting stuck in nooks and crannies.

• **Dough Handling.** While a hand-cranked machine does require dough of a certain consistency, it is less likely than an electric machine to become balky if fed dough that is not of perfect consistency. Use of a hand-cranked machine also makes it easier to correct dough that isn't of the proper consistency.

• **Noise.** Electric machines can be noisy things, depending on the model. But a hand-cranked machine is quiet. This can be a real consideration if you live in relatively close quarters with others, such as in an apartment building.

Then again, there are disadvantages:

- **Time.** This is the main disadvantage. First, you have to mix the dough, which will take 10 to 15 minutes by hand or 5 minutes with a food processor. Then, you have to knead the dough for 2 minutes and let it rest for 5 minutes. Finally, you have to either roll and cut the dough, which can take 1 hour or more, or extrude the dough, which will take about 20 minutes. This may be more time than you can spare, especially during the week.
- **Variety.** A hand-cranked roller machine only makes long pasta. A hand-cranked extrusion machine only makes shaped pasta. If you want to use the roller machine to make long pasta, you still have to buy another machine—either hand-cranked or electric—to make shaped pasta.
- **Space.** To operate a roller machine, you'll need about 2 feet by 4 feet of space, plus a table or counter to mix and knead the pasta. That can be a problem if you live in a very small space.

TWO HAND-CRANKED PASTA MACHINES

The two hand-cranked models we looked at both come from Italy. The following topics are included in the evaluation of each machine: a list of standard features that are included in the basic purchase price; optional accessories, if any; storage requirements; a description of what material is covered in the instruction booklet; and information on using the machine, including mixing the dough, cutting or extruding the shapes, problems you may encounter, and cleaning requirements.

Atlas
Manufactured by OMC Marcato in Italy
Distributed in the United States by:
VillaWare Manufacturing Company
1420 East 36th Street
Cleveland, OH 44114
Telephone: (216) 391-6650

The classic Atlas is a shiny chrome, hand-cranked roller machine, probably similar to the one that Grandma may have used. Sturdy and dependable, it makes great flat noodles in a wide variety of widths, from delicate angel hair to 6-inch strips. We recommend this machine, or one like it, for every kitchen—even if you decide to go high-tech with one of the electric extrusion systems.

Except for the spaghetti attachment, which does make a rounded product, only flat noodles can be made with the Atlas. If you want shaped pasta, it has to be made either by hand, on a companion hand-cranked extrusion machine such as the Regina Atlas, or in an electric extrusion machine.

We also use a Bialetti, purchased in the early 1980s for about $100, which is an electric roller machine that works in a similar fashion as the Atlas. The Bialetti, still available in specialty stores, rolls and cuts the dough in the same fashion as the manual machine, and the cutters that come with the machine make the same kind of pasta. The Bialetti is a bit noisy. In our trials with the machine, there didn't seem to be much speed advantage to using the electric Bialetti over the hand-cranked Atlas. It does work well, though. So if you come across a Bialetti or own one already, you may want to consider it as an alternative to the Atlas.

Hand-Cranked Roller Machine

Standard Features

The Atlas's standard features are:

- Adjustable dough roller, 6 inches wide
- Cutting attachments for $\frac{1}{16}$-inch spaghetti and $\frac{1}{4}$-inch fettuccine
- Crank
- Table clamp

Optional Accessories

Seven additional cutting attachments are available: angel hair (1 mm), a flat noodle called trenette ($\frac{1}{8}$ inch), spaghetti ($\frac{1}{8}$ inch, round), two kinds of lasagna (a $\frac{1}{2}$-inch noodle and a 2-inch noodle, both with a zigzag edge), ravioli, and cannelloni.

Storage Requirements

When stored in its box, the Atlas requires a space measuring $8\frac{1}{4}$ inches long by 8 inches wide by $6\frac{1}{4}$ inches high. It weighs about 5 pounds. The additional cutting attachments each weigh less than a pound. Stored in their boxes, each individual attachment requires a space measuring 7 inches long by 3 inches wide by 2 inches high.

Instruction Booklet

The instruction manual for the Atlas, printed in four languages, may seem a little daunting. Read it over several times before starting. The instructions are written in steps that correspond to color pictures. There are four recipes included in the booklet for dishes made with noodles.

In this book we provide more detailed instructions for making dough and rolling out pasta with the Atlas machine—and almost all of the pasta dough recipes in this book can be used to make spaghetti or long, flat noodles with the Atlas.

Using the Machine

To use the Atlas, you will need a counter or table with a free edge, and enough room to crank the machine and roll out the pasta. We recommend a space at least 2 feet by 4 feet to effectively handle dough and machine. Before using, the Atlas must be securely clamped to the table or counter.

The dough must be made by hand or in the food processor. Pieces of dough are then shaped into long ribbons by passing them through dough rollers while the machine is cranked by hand. A knob with settings from 1 through 7 regulates the thickness of the rolled dough. After the dough is rolled, it is dipped lightly in flour on each side. The flour-dipped dough is folded in thirds before it is rolled through the machine at the next setting. As the numbers get larger on the setting knob, the dough rolls out thinner, and the ribbon of dough becomes longer. As the dough comes through the roller, it should be caught with the hand and pulled forward so it doesn't stick to itself. We provide illustrated, step-by-step instructions for this process on page 25.

When the dough has been rolled to the desired thickness, the cutting attachment is attached to the machine by sliding it over the indicated grooves. The rolled dough is then fed through the cutting attachment while the machine is cranked by hand.

The thickness desired is a matter of individual taste, and of the type of flour and other ingredients being used in the pasta dough. For example, you'll likely find that dough containing semolina flour can be rolled thinner than dough containing whole wheat flour.

It is often necessary to experiment with the different settings when rolling out the dough. Keep a pencil and paper nearby to write down your preferences for specific dough mixtures. Store your list with the machine so the settings will be handy for next time.

When making wide, flat noodles, such as lasagna, we preferred the dough rolled to the thickness indicated by setting 5, although strips used to make ravioli worked better when rolled to setting 6. Pasta rolled to the number 7 setting is very thin and tears easily, but we found this setting useful when making angel hair pasta and fine fettuccine.

We discovered one trick to getting more consistent results with the Atlas—setting the dough aside on a lightly floured towel for 5 to 20 minutes before cutting. This gives the dough a chance to dry. Don't allow the dough to sit too long, however, or it will become too dry and will crack when put through the cutters.

At first, you may find it difficult to feed the end of the dough into the cutting attachment. If you have trouble, just pinch the end and turn the handle until the dough catches. Once it catches, the dough will feed through the cutting attachment and come out in front of the machine. Just catch it in your free hand, stretch it out to the desired length, cut it, and set it aside on a lightly floured towel.

If the pasta does not easily separate into individual strands as it's cut, there is not enough flour on the dough before it goes through the cutting attachment. Remember that each time the dough is put through the rollers or cutting attachment, it must be dipped in flour (or sprinkled with flour). If the dough sticks together, the piece should be rerolled. You only have to work with one or two pieces to get a feel for the appropriate look and texture of properly rolled dough.

It's very easy to adapt different types of pasta recipes to this machine. Because the dough must be made by hand or with a food processor, it is easy to experiment with different flours, liquids, and textures. It's also possible to make pasta using fresh whole herbs with this machine—see pages 90 and 92.

Remember, the Atlas pasta machine should never be put into soap and water. Because the dough is not sticky when it goes through the cutting attachment, there is rarely any dough left in the machine. If some dough is caught, it can be removed with a toothpick or a soft brush. The dough roller and base assembly should be cleaned with a soft brush or wiped down with a cloth, and stored in its box.

Regina Atlas
Manufactured by OMC Marcato in Italy
Distributed in the United States by:
VillaWare Manufacturing Company
1420 East 36th Street
Cleveland, OH 44114
Telephone (216) 391-6650

This hand-cranked extrusion pasta machine is an inexpensive, capable machine that uses dough mixed either in a food processor or by hand. It does not offer as many die options as the more sophisticated electric machines, but it is easy to clean and operate. The dough

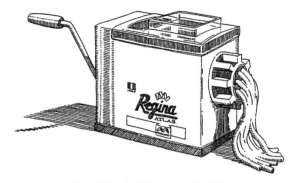

Hand-Cranked Extrusion Machine

consistency is not as critical for extruding with this machine as it is for most electric machines.

Standard Features

The Regina's standard features are:

• Five dies: rigatoni, macaroni, little macaroni, bucatini, and fusilli
• Die holder
• Die holder wrench
• Hand crank
• Table clamp
• Soft cleaning brush
• Small wooden sticks for cleaning the dies

Optional Accessories

None

Storage Requirements

The Regina Atlas requires a space measuring $10\frac{1}{2}$ inches long by 6 inches wide by 7 inches high when stored in its box. It weighs about 3 pounds. The dies are stored inside the machine.

Instruction Booklet

The instruction booklet for the Regina is printed in eight languages, including English. Very basic instructions on how to prepare the dough, extrude the pasta, change the dies, and clean the machine are provided, and correspond to colored pictures in the booklet. There are no special recipes or suggestions on how to use the pasta.

Using the Machine

Like the Atlas, the Regina Atlas is clamped to the table and hand cranked. Because this machine does not make long, rolled noodles, it does not require as much counter space as the Atlas. The dough for this machine must also be made separately by hand or in a food processor. Once the dough is made, you use one hand to feed it into the hopper while using the other hand to turn the crank. The machine extrudes the dough through a die, after which you cut it with a scissors or a knife to the desired length, and set it aside on a floured towel.

Sticky dough can be a problem when using this machine. If the dough is too moist, it will simply stick to the extrusion chamber and fail to be forced out of the die. We had a particular problem using semolina dough, which is naturally stickier than whole wheat or unbleached white flour dough. The instruction booklet says that if the pasta ends stick together during extrusion, you should sprinkle the whole piece of dough with flour before putting it into the hopper. We did so, and it helped.

The thinner shapes are easier to extrude with this machine. Pasta made with the larger dies, such as the tube-like rigatoni and macaroni dies, is tricky to cut. The shapes tend to close together or become flat. We found that dipping a sharp knife in flour before each cut helped solve the problem. The tube-like pasta shapes seem a little thicker and a bit chewier than the same shapes made with the electric extrusion machines. The thinner shapes were comparable to those made with the best of the electric machines.

Dough is difficult to extrude through the Regina Atlas if adequate flour is not used. In general, to successfully extrude the shapes, the dough used in the Regina Atlas must be drier than that used in the Atlas. Because the dough must be made by hand or with a food processor, it is easy to experiment with flours, liquids, and textures. Herb pastas can be made with this machine, providing that the herbs are finely chopped.

The Regina Atlas can be washed by hand in warm soap and water. A toothpick or wire brush can be used to clean the holes in the dies. The base assembly should be wiped down with a cloth, and stored in its box.

OTHER EQUIPMENT YOU'LL NEED

No matter what hand-cranked machine you use, there are a few additional accessories you will probably need to create pasta masterpieces. Here are the basic tools and equipment we recommend for anyone who is serious about making pasta.

Food Processor

A food processor is an indispensable kitchen tool whether or not you are making pasta. We depend on our trusty Cuisinart DLC-7 to mix the dough used to make pasta with the hand-cranked machines. The food processor is also necessary for puréeing or liquefying the vegetables, herbs, and fruits used in some of our pasta recipes.

With few exceptions, a blender is *not* a good substitute for a food processor, at least not when it comes to making pasta. A blender's narrow container and relatively small blades do not allow it to mix dough. Also, material at the bottom of a blender may liquefy before material at the top starts to move. You can use a blender to chop small amounts of herbs, or to liquefy tomatoes in small batches. But in general, we recommend the use of a food processor.

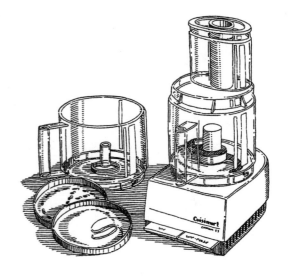

Sample Food Processor (Cuisinart)

Drying Rack

A drying rack is a rack used to dry flat or round noodles for long-term storage.

Drying Rack

Pastry Board

A pastry board is a large wooden board used to roll out pasta dough. You can use a countertop, but a pastry board is portable and easier to clean.

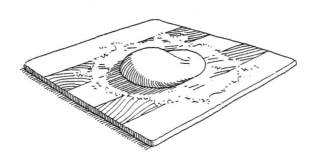

Pastry Board

Pasta Cutters and Pasta Wheels

Pasta cutters and wheels are devices used to cut various shapes of pasta, such as ravioli and lasagna, when making pasta by hand. Some can be used to both cut and seal ravioli.

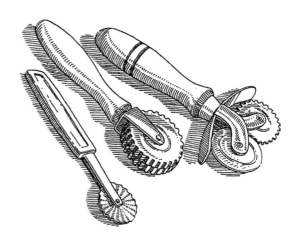

Various Pasta Cutters and Wheels

Pastry Scraper

A pastry scraper is a thin, stainless steel blade used to scrape up excess dough that may stick to the pastry board when mixing dough by hand.

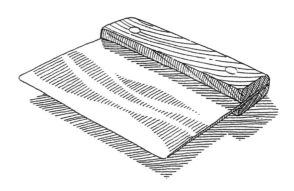

Pastry Scraper

Ravioli Rolling Pin

A ravioli rolling pin is similar to a regular rolling pin, except that it has indentations. These indentations mark out perfectly-sized ravioli squares when the pin is rolled over a sheet of dough. Filling is placed in the squares on half the sheet, after which the other half of the sheet is folded over. The dough is then cut along the lines with a knife, and sealed.

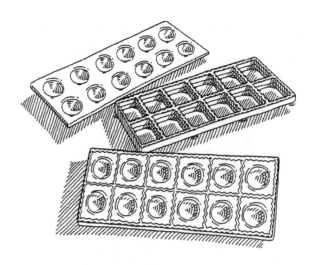

Various Ravioli Trays

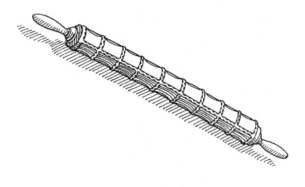

Ravioli Rolling Pin

Ravioli Trays

Another way of making ravioli at home is with a ravioli tray. VillaWare and other manufacturers produce wonderful trays for making ravioli and other filled pasta shapes by hand. Their use is more fully described in the ravioli recipe on page 209, but basically, a sheet of dough is laid over the tray, and pressed down. Filling is then placed in the center of each marked ravioli, and then a second sheet of dough is laid across the first sheet. The whole affair is then gone over with a rolling pin to cut and seal the ravioli.

If you use a dough strips from a hand-cranked machine, the width will be just about right for the trays. You can use ravioli dough strips extruded from an electric machine as well, though a strip will only cover half of the tray at a time. Making ravioli or other stuffed goodies with the trays is a quick and easy process—and the results look as good or better than those of the best Italian restaurant.

Tortellini Stamp

A tortellini stamp is a cookie cutter-like stamp used to cut out the dough for tortellini. A round cookie cutter works just as well, as does the rim of a glass dipped in flour.

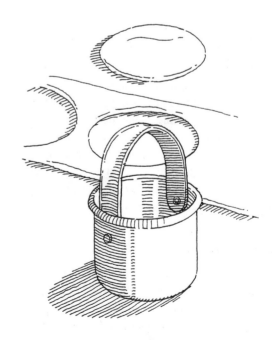

Tortellini Stamp

Standard Rolling Pin

As shown in the illustration below, rolling pins come in a couple of different shapes. They also come in a variety of materials, such as wood, marble, or plastic.

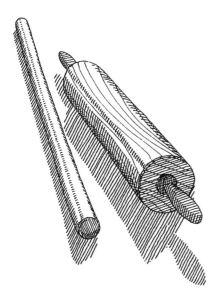

Standard Rolling Pins

USING A HAND-CRANKED MACHINE

We will admit that using a hand-cranked machine is not as easy as putting flour and liquid into one of the electric machines and just cutting the pasta off the die as it extrudes. For one thing, the dough must be made beforehand. But many cooks think of this as an advantage because of the sense of satisfaction they derive from handling the dough themselves. This section gives instructions for mixing dough, and for either cutting or extruding it into pasta.

Mixing the Dough

There are two ways to mix the dough for a hand-cranked pasta machine: by hand or with a food processor. Keep in mind that the amount of liquid used may have to be adjusted to account for such things as heat, humidity, and the type of flour used.

Mixing Dough by Hand

You can mix the dough by hand using the following procedure. It takes from 10 to 15 minutes.

1. Mound the flour on a pastry board or a work surface. Using your fingers, made a well in the center of the mound, keeping the sides of the well high. The flour can also be placed in a bowl to reduce the mess.

2. Add the liquid to the well. If using eggs, break them into the well and beat them with a fork, along with any other liquid used in the recipe. Slowly start to incorporate the flour on the sides of the well. Be careful not to let the sides of the mound collapse, or the liquid will escape.

3. As more flour is incorporated into the liquid, the dough will become very sticky and cling to the fork. At this point, discard the fork and continue to mix the dough using your fingers. Don't bother flouring your hands—they'll get sticky no matter what.

4. When all the flour has been incorporated into the liquid, form the dough into a ball. Begin to knead the dough by pushing down hard on the ball with the heel of your hand. Push the dough away from your body. Fold it in half and give it a one-quarter turn. If cutting the dough by hand, continue this process for 20 minutes, adding additional flour if the dough is still sticky. If the dough is going to be run through rollers on a machine like the Atlas, only 2 minutes of kneading is necessary. The action of the rollers will finish the kneading process.

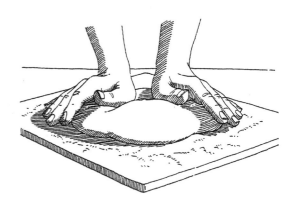

Pushing the Dough

Folding the Dough

5. After kneading, the ball will be smooth and shiny. Wrap the ball in plastic wrap and let it rest for 5 minutes on the counter, or refrigerate it for up to 2 days.

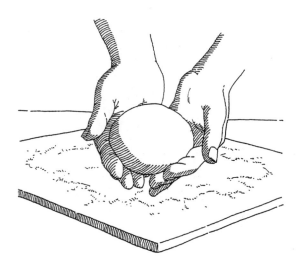

Finished Dough

Mixing Dough With a Food Processor

The time needed to make pasta dough by hand can be cut in half by using a food processor. Here are the steps.

1. Attach the processor's metal blade.

2. Add the flour to the work bowl and close the lid. With the machine running, slowly add the liquid through the feed tube, and pulse the machine until a ball begins to form (about 10 to 15 seconds). If the dough does not form a ball, it is too dry. Add 1 teaspoon of water and process for 1 additional minute. Repeat as necessary. If the dough is too sticky, add 1 tablespoon of flour and process for 1 additional minute. Repeat as necessary.

3. Place the dough on a lightly floured pastry board or work surface and knead it for 2 minutes, incorporating additional flour as necessary to make a smooth, shiny ball. More kneading time is not necessary because the food processor has done most of the work.

4. Cover the dough with plastic wrap and let it rest for 5 minutes on the counter, or refrigerate it for up to 2 days.

Hand-Cranked Cutting

Using a hand-cranked roller machine such as the Atlas takes from 1 to 2 hours after making the dough, depending on your level of experience. When time permits, we really enjoy the serenity of using a hand-cranked roller machine. It is a wonderfully satifsying feeling to produce and cut yards of fresh, delicious pasta ribbons. The following steps will give you the best results.

1. Attach the pasta machine to the counter or table with the clamp provided.

2. Uncover the ball of dough, made previously by hand or in a food processor, and cut off a small slice about ½-inch thick. Rewrap the remaining dough.

3. Set the regulating knob on the machine to position number 1 and insert the hand crank into the appropriate slot.

4. Feed the dough into the rollers from the top while turning the handle. This will flatten the dough.

Flattening the Dough

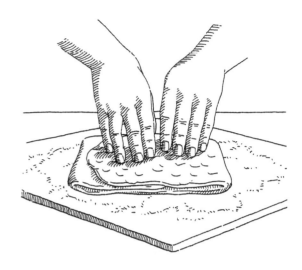

Folding the Dough

5. Catch the dough with your free hand as it comes through the back of the machine. This is especially important as the dough begins to thin, since it may stick to itself. If that happens, the dough should be sprinkled with flour and rerolled.

6. Add flour to the sheet of dough, and fold the top third down, toward your body. Then fold the bottom third up, away from your body. Put the dough through the rollers again at the same setting.

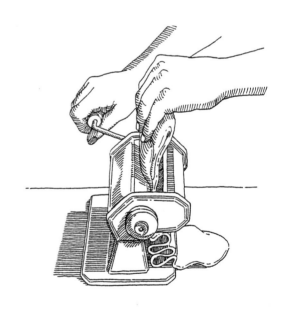

Rolling the Folded Dough

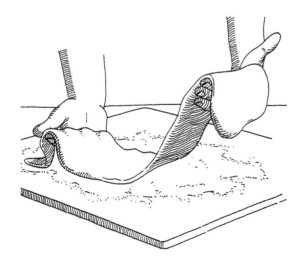

Dough after Flattening

7. Continue this process, gradually turning the regulating knob higher and rerolling the dough until it reaches the desired thickness, which you will learn to determine by experience. The higher the number on the regulating knob, the thinner the dough. The trick to this step is to continue adding

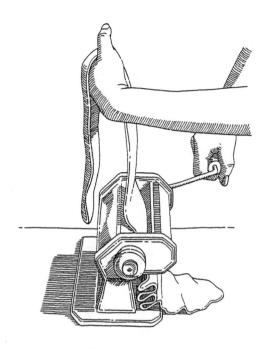

Thinning the Dough

Cutting the Dough

flour to the sheet of pasta if it feels even slightly sticky. If the dough is sticky, the cutting attachment will not completely cut through the dough.

8. When the dough reaches the desired thickness, set it aside to dry, uncovered, for 5 minutes while you prepare the next piece. The drying dough will take on a slightly leathery look.

9. After rolling two or three sheets and letting them dry, insert the crank into the slot in the cutting attachment.

10. Feed the dough through the cutting attachment. It may be necessary to pinch the end to allow it to feed through properly. Catch the cut dough in your hand as it comes out of the cutting attachment, or else it will bunch up under the machine.

11. Cut the pasta to the desired length with a knife or scissors as it comes out of the machine. Or, lay the full length of noodles on a work surface and cut with a knife. This second method will ensure that all the pasta is cut to the same length.

12. After the noodles are cut, lay them out straight on a lightly floured kitchen towel to dry, or over the back of a chair covered with a towel, or on a pasta drying rack.

13. We recommend allowing the pasta to dry for at least 1 hour before using. This will help remove any stickiness, and help keep the pasta from clumping while it cooks. If you don't plan to use the pasta right away, you can dry it for storage according to the instructions on page 47.

Cutting Machine-Rolled Dough Into Hand-Formed Shapes

Sometimes you may want to cut your flat, rolled pasta dough into shapes for ravioli, tortellini, wide lasagna, or other special purposes. Clear plenty of counter space and follow this procedure.

1. Cut the rolled dough into the desired shape. You can use either a sharp knife or one of the pasta-cutting implements described on pages 22 and 23.

2. Lay the pieces out straight on a lightly floured kitchen towel to dry, or over the back of a chair covered with a towel, or on a pasta drying rack until you're ready to use them.

3. Stuff or fill the pasta according to the directions in the recipe.

4. We recommend allowing the pasta to dry for at least 1 hour before using, or freezing the stuffed pasta shapes for long-term storage. You should refrigerate stuffed pasta during the drying process, especially in the summer.

Hand-Cranked Extrusion

A hand-cranked extrusion machine can cut at least 40 minutes, if not more, off the time it takes to make pasta with a roller machine. Follow these instructions to make perfect shapes.

1. Attach the pasta machine to the counter or table with the clamp provided.

2. Uncover the ball of dough, made previously by hand or in a food processor, and cut it in half. Rewrap the remaining dough.

3. Insert the hand crank into the slot.

4. Place the dough in the hopper of the machine and turn the crank. It may be necessary to push the dough down with your fingers (don't worry, they won't get caught). As the crank turns, the dough will be extruded into the desired shape. If the dough is sticky when extruded, coat the outside of the dough with flour, put it back into the hopper, and extrude again.

5. Using a sharp knife, cut the pasta into the desired length and lay it on a lightly floured towel. Repeat the process with the remaining dough.

6. We recommend allowing the pasta to dry for at least 1 hour before using. Or dry the pasta for storage according to the instructions on page 47.

CUTTING DOUGH BY HAND

Now *this* is old-fashioned pasta—Grandma would be so proud. You'll need plenty of counter space and plenty of flour. Ready?

1. Lay the ball of dough, made previously by hand or in a food processor, on a lightly floured pastry board or counter. If the available counter space is small, cut the ball of dough in half or in quarters before starting to roll. It's more work, but the pieces are more managable.

2. Using a floured rolling pin, firmly press down on the dough and start rolling it out, from the center to the edge. Roll the dough into a rectangular shape. As the dough starts to thin out, turn it over. If it starts to stick, loosen the dough with a pastry scraper and add a small amount of flour to the surface. Dust the rolling pin with additional flour if necessary.

3. Continue rolling the dough, using lighter strokes as it starts to thin. Roll the dough until it is almost paper thin, approximately $\frac{1}{16}$-inch thick. You should be able to almost see through it. If the sheet becomes too large, cut the dough in half and continue rolling each sheet separately until the required thickness is achieved.

4. If the dough seems a little sticky, dust it with some flour. Then fold the bottom half up, away from your body. Continue folding in half until the dough is about 4 to 6 inches wide.

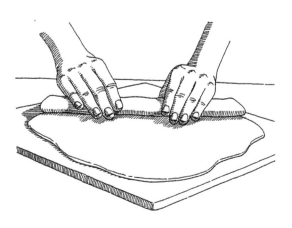

Folding the Dough

5. Using a sharp knife, slice the dough into strips. For linguine, make the strips about ⅛-inch wide. For fettuccine, make them about ¼-inch wide. For lasagna, make them about 2 to 3 inches wide.

finished pasta out straight on a lightly floured towel to dry, or over the back of a chair draped with a floured towel, or on a pastry drying rack.

Cutting the Dough

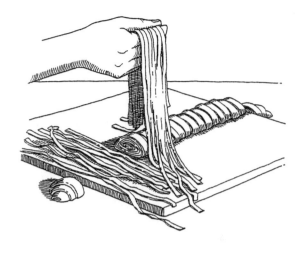

Unrolling the Strands

6. After you've finished cutting, unroll the strands and cut them to the desired length. Lay the

7. We recommend allowing the pasta to dry for at least 1 hour before using. Or dry it for storage according to the instructions on page 47.

4

Choosing and Using an Electric Extrusion Machine

lectric extrusion pasta machines for home use were first introduced in the 1970s, but until recently, we would never have recommended an electric machine to anyone. Michelle had one of the early electric extrusion machines. It was not a pleasant experience. The dough would never reach the right consistency and was hard to extrude, and the finished product never tasted right. You get the picture. Needless to say, that machine spent the rest of its life hidden away in the back of a dark cabinet.

All of that has changed. The new electric machines have revolutionized the possibilities for homemade pasta. Most are versatile and easy to use. Almost before you can say *"Mamma Mia,"* you'll have fresh, delicious, nutritious pasta ready to cook and serve. Though we still prefer our older hand-cranked roller machine for making large, flat noodles for lasagna and ravioli, the best of the electric extrusion machines are unrivaled for both speed of production and the number of shapes that can be extruded with ease.

In this chapter, we first look at the advantages and disadvantages of choosing an electric pasta machine. We then review five popular models, and give a list of features you should look for when you go shopping. Finally, we give you some pointers on using your pasta machine.

ADVANTAGES AND DISADVANTAGES OF AN ELECTRIC EXTRUSION MACHINE

There are several advantages to buying an electric extrusion machine:

• **Time.** This is right at the top of the list, and for good reason: while it can take from 30 minutes to 2 hours to make pasta with a hand-cranked machine, depending on how you mix and process the dough, it only takes about 15 to 20 minutes with an electric machine. That means you can easily whip up a batch of pasta anytime, even after a hectic day at work.

• **Variety.** An electric machine can make a wide variety of pasta shapes, from macaroni to spaghetti to ziti, depending on the model. By contrast, a hand-cranked roller model only makes flat, long noodles. Some of the electric machines also come with attachments for such items as breadsticks and cookies.

• **Space.** If you've got a kitchen table, you can make pasta with an electric machine. By contrast, the hand-cranked roller and extrusion machines both require space to make the dough, and the hand-cranked roller machine requires space to operate the machine itself.

An electric machine also has its disadvantages:

• **Price.** You can get a cheap electric machine for less than $100. However, as with everything else in life, you get what you pay for, and you can expect to pay from $130 to $250 for a decent mid-range machine, and from $250 to over $400 for a high-end machine. Of course, there are always sales.

• **Cleaning.** The time saved in making pasta with an extrusion machine can be lost in cleaning the machine's parts. Today's electric extrusion machines have it all over the models from the 1970s in the time it takes to clean them, but it still takes time and some patience. Some machines require more elbow grease than others to get the dough out of the nooks and crannies.

• **Dough Handling.** An electric pasta machine requires dough of a certain consistency, a consistency that varies from machine to machine. If the dough is too dry or too wet, it will not extrude, and can gum up the machine. Hand-cranked machines, whether they roll the pasta or extrude it, are much more forgiving of inconsistencies in the dough than are most electric machines.

• **Noise.** Some electric pasta machines behave like a quiet houseguest. Others sound like a garbage disposal trying to digest an unripe grapefruit. One of the noisy ones will not win you friends among your neighbors.

FIVE ELECTRIC EXTRUSION MACHINES

We looked at five electric extrusion machines. There are more, but these are among the most popular. The following topics are included in the evaluation of each machine: a list of standard features that are included in

Sample Electric Extrusion Machine (Simac PastaMatic)

the basic purchase price; optional accessories, if any; storage requirements; a description of what material is covered in the instruction booklet; and information on using the machine, including mixing the dough, cutting or extruding the shapes, problems you may encounter, cleaning requirements, and safety features.

Primo Pasta
Manufactured and distributed by:
Waring Products
Box 349
283 Main Street
New Hartford, CT 06057
Telephone: (203) 379-8573

The Waring Primo Pasta is a relatively new entry among the electric extrusion machines on the market. It can make up to $1\frac{1}{2}$ pounds of pasta at one time, and unlike some extrusion models, it is easy to make and extrude half batches of pasta—a nice feature for small families.

Standard Features

The Primo Pasta's standard features are:

• Ten dies: spaghetti, thin spaghetti, large spaghetti, fettuccine, linguine, egg noodle, lasagna, rigatoni, macaroni/ziti, and breadstick/pretzel

- Liquid measuring cup
- Flour measuring cup
- Cleaning tool
- Die holder wrench
- Cleaning brush
- Three packages of ready-to-use pasta dough mix (with deluxe model only)

Optional Accessories

None

Storage Requirements

The Primo Pasta requires a space measuring 14 inches long by $10 \frac{5}{8}$ inches wide by 14 inches high when stored in its box. It weighs just under 10 pounds.

Instruction Booklet

The instruction booklet contains information on assembling, operating, disassembling, and cleaning the machine, with corresponding drawings of all the parts and dies. The booklet also includes recipes for making regular and specialty pastas, such as those flavored with broccoli, oranges, or herbs. There are hints for using other flours and liquids, and tips on cooking pasta.

Using the Machine

This machine comes with its own measuring cups for both flour and liquid. To mix the dough, the extrude/mix control knob is turned to the mix position and the correct measure of flour is added to the machine's work bowl. The cover is closed and locked into place, and the power switch turned on. The liquid mixture is slowly and carefully poured through slots in the cover of the machine. Although the cup is marked for a measure of required liquid, you should be aware that the exact amount of liquid needed will vary slightly depending on the type of flour being used.

Two minutes after pouring in all of the liquid, the power switch is turned off and the cover lifted to test the consistency of the dough. The dough is ready for extrusion when it has a moist granular consistency, similar to that of coffee grounds. If the dough is too dry or too wet, more liquid or flour should be added slowly, 1 tablespoon at a time, and the machine left to run for 1 minute after each addition. These steps are repeated as necessary, until the dough is the right consistency. At that point, the control knob is turned to the extrude position. The pasta will start appearing from the die in a minute or two.

The consistency of the dough is critical when using this machine. If the consistency is not correct, a clicking sound alerts the user that something is wrong. The machine should then be turned off immediately. At this point, the extrusion chamber needs to be cleaned before the pasta-making process can continue. You will want to quickly learn the correct consistency for dough extrusion, because this machine is not that easy to take apart when the chamber is filled with an unsuitable mixture.

To remove the work bowl, the entire bowl unit is pulled out of the base of the machine when the work bowl release lever is pushed. (In theory, anyway. The lever on our machine did not have a smooth release.) Once the bowl is removed, the dough pusher can be pulled out of the extrusion chamber. The instruction booklet does not recommend returning extruded pasta to the work bowl, so expect to waste some dough until you learn what you're doing with this machine.

After reassembling the system, improperly prepared dough needs to be adjusted as mentioned before, with either with 1 tablespoon of flour if the dough is too wet or 1 tablespoon of liquid if too dry. The dough is then remixed for 1 minute. This process is repeated as necessary until the dough is the correct consistency. When it's finally right, the knob is again turned to the extrude position.

The Primo Pasta is not a good choice if you want to extrude herb-flavored pastas that involve coarse textures. It does best with finely ground flours and smooth doughs.

This machine is relatively easy to clean. All the removable parts are dishwasher safe (with the heated dry cycle turned off). The housing should only be cleaned with a damp cloth; the main mechanism should never be immersed in water. The manufacturer recommends cleaning the dies with the cleaning tool provided. They then can be rinsed in warm water or washed in the dishwasher.

The Primo Pasta has an interlock mechanism for safety. If the lid is opened during extrusion, the machine turns off.

Pasta-Del-Giorno
Manufactured and distributed by:
Maverick Industries, Inc.
265 Raritan Center Parkway
Edison, NJ 08837
Telephone: (908) 417-9666

This machine makes approximately 1½ pounds of fresh pasta at a time. Measurements are provided for the flour required to make half a batch, but no half-batch liquid markings are given on the measuring cup provided with the machine, so the user must figure out liquid proportions (which are closer to 60 percent of the full-batch amounts, rather than 50 percent). The machine is a generally good performer, though a noisy one.

Standard Features

The Pasta-Del-Giorno's standard features are:

• Eleven dies: spaghetti, linguine, small macaroni, large macaroni, lasagna, fettuccine, vermicelli, gnocchi, bagels, breadsticks/pretzels, and cookies
• Measuring cup (one used for both flour and liquid)
• Push pin for cleaning the dies

Optional Accessories

None

Storage Requirements

The Pasta-Del-Giorno requires a space measuring 19 inches long by 14 inches wide by 12½ inches high when stored in its box. It weighs about 17 pounds.

Instruction Booklet

The instruction booklet includes information on ma-

chine safeguards, assembly and disassembly, machine operation, cooking instructions, making fresh pasta, and cleaning the machine, along with helpful hints. The booklet has a picture of the machine disassembled and labeled, and has text and pictures showing the assembly process. Eight recipes for using fresh pasta are also included. This machine comes with dies for gnocchi, cookies, bagels, and breadsticks/pretzels, but there are no instructions given for using these dies or recipes for making these foods in the instruction booklet. (We do provide recipes for gnocchi, breadsticks, and pretzels within our book.)

Using the Machine

The Pasta-Del-Giorno comes with its own measuring cup. The same cup is used for both flour and liquid, and contains detailed markings for the flour needed to make full and half batches of pasta. Half batches of pasta are made with half the amount of flour, but the liquid required is 60 percent of the amount called for in the full batch.

The setup of the Pasta-Del-Giorno is a bit different from some of the other machines. This machine divides the work bowl into two areas that are separated by a mixing wall. After the flour is placed in the mixing area, the die is inserted, and the lid is closed. The liquid is added very slowly through a slot in the top of the lid. When the dough is the proper consistency, you will still see a few small flecks of flour. The dough will look crumbly, with moist small pea or peanut-sized lumps. When this consistency is reached, the wall is removed and the dough is pushed forward into the extrusion area, where it is forced against the back side of the die and extruded. This differs from other machines, where the dough is forced downward into an extrusion chamber and then pushed forward.

We had no problem getting the correct dough consistency with this machine. Even testing our own concoctions was not a problem, once we understood the correct consistency needed for the dough. If the dough was not of the correct consistency as it extruded, we just moved it back into the other chamber, added 1 tablespoon of flour or water as needed, and remixed for 1 minute. The face plate pulls off the front of the machine to allow easy removal of incorrectly mixed dough from the extrusion chamber. According to the instruction booklet, extruded dough that has been improperly mixed can be put back into the mixing chamber. We tried it, and the dough extruded successfully.

As the dough extrudes, it passes in front of a built-in dryer in the base of the machine. This dryer helps remove any stickiness. It also helps keep the pasta from clumping together before cooking. If the pasta doesn't clump together before cooking, it is less likely to stick together while cooking.

The Pasta-Del-Giorno instruction booklet has a great tip that can be used with any machine. It states that only 90 percent of the liquid should be poured into the flour and mixed before checking the consistency. At this point, the decision can be made to add more liquid if necessary. This technique can ensure that the dough never becomes too wet. Another good tip given is to put the die into the freezer for 30 to 40 minutes before cleaning with a toothpick or the push pin.

All removable parts of this machine are dishwasher safe in the top rack. The main body and the motor base and knobs can be wiped off with a damp cloth. Never put these parts into water. It is also recommended by the manufacturer that water be kept out of the dryer fan and the on/off switch areas.

The Pasta-Del-Giorno is equipped with two safety features. There is an overload device that automatically shuts off the motor if the latter is straining hard and begins to overheat. This may happen if the machine has made several loads in rapid succession. If this happens, the machine needs to be allowed to cool off for 30 minutes. This machine is also equipped with an interlock mechanism on the cover, which will immediately shut off the machine if the cover is removed.

PastaExpress X3000

Manufactured and distributed by:
Creative Technologies Corporation
170 53rd Street
Brooklyn, NY 11232-4319
Telephone: (718) 492-8400
Customer service number: (800) 282-5240

The PastaExpress makes $1\frac{1}{2}$ pounds of pasta at a time. No instructions are given for half batches. The instruction booklet states that 2 teaspoons of oil should be included in all pasta recipes to achieve the best dough consistency for this machine. It you want to make 100 percent fat-free pasta, this machine is not the best choice.

Standard Features

The PastaExpress X3000's standard features are:

- Twelve dies: spaghetti, linguine, small macaroni, large macaroni/ziti, large macaroni/rigatoni, lasagna, vermicelli, fettuccine, gnocchi, pretzel/breadstick, bagel, and cookie
- Measuring cup (one used for both flour and liquid)
- Instructional video tape
- Gourmet pasta flour

Optional Accessories

None

Storage Requirements

The PastaExpress requires a space measuring $13\frac{1}{4}$ inches long by $9\frac{3}{4}$ inches wide by $12\frac{1}{4}$ inches high when stored in its box. It weighs about 13 pounds.

Instruction Booklet

The instruction booklet includes information on assembling and disassembling the machine, along with drawings of the machine parts. There is also information on machine operation, dough consistency, dies, and flour variations, along with directions for making and cooking pasta. There are twelve recipes for using the pasta, and for making gnocchi, pretzels, bagels, and cookies.

Using the Machine

The PastaExpress comes with one measuring cup that is used for both flour and liquid. None of the recipes indicate the amounts of ingredients to be used for half batches of pasta. Logically, a half batch would be one cup of flour in the PastaExpress measuring cup, since a full batch uses two cups, plus half of the liquid indicated in the recipe. The liquid portion would have be estimated. Once you are familiar with the machine and know the consistency required for making pasta, adding liquid for a half batch should not be a problem.

After the flour is added, the machine is turned on. The instructions state that one third of the liquid should be added at a time. All the liquid should be added over a span of 3 to 3¼ minutes. The liquid-addition phase is much longer for this machine than for others.

Like the Pasta-Del-Giorno, the extrusion chamber for the PastaExpress is in the front of the machine, and the dough is pushed forward rather than extruded downward. There is only one chamber in the work bowl. The mixing blade rotates one way to mix the dough. When the extrude switch is turned on, the blade rotates in the opposite direction, forcing the dough into the extrusion chamber and through the die. This machine also has a built-in blower that dries the pasta as it extrudes.

The dough is ready when it has a pea-sized, crumbly consistency. We had no problem getting the correct consistency for the dough to extrude properly. If the dough is too dry or too wet, add 1 tablespoon of either liquid or flour, and remix for 1 minute. If there is a problem, the front face plate is very easy to remove. The instructions indicate that extruded dough can be put back into the work bowl.

The only problem we had during the extrusion process was that the dough seemed to accumulate in the right front corner of the work bowl. The machine had to be stopped and the dough redistributed several times before all the dough was extruded.

The die on the PastaExpress is flanked by the knobs that hold the face plate onto the machine. These knobs stick out in front of the die. This makes cutting the extruding pasta off the die more difficult than if the die was positioned in front of the knobs. It's not an impossible situation, but it does take some maneuvering.

There is a good tip listed in the helpful hints. The instructions with all pasta machines recommend soaking the die in warm water or hot oil before using. The PastaExpress booklet suggests soaking the die in water, and then spraying nonstick cooking spray or olive oil directly onto the die. This could help cut down on the oil used, and reduce fat and cholesterol (and result in less-greasy fingers and bowls).

The helpful hints included also state that the dies can be frozen and then be tapped on the counter for cleaning. This does work sometimes, but don't throw away your toothpick.

The removable parts of this pasta machine are not dishwasher safe. They are made of a nonstick polyester material that can be easily cleaned with a mild detergent and wiped dry.

This machine has two safety features. The off switch is in the middle of a movable plate with the mix position on one side and the extrude position on the other. To turn the machine on and mix, the plate must be moved down so the mix position can be activated. To move the switch to the extrude position, the machine must be in the off position and the plate moved up, because going from the mix position to the extrude position without stopping at the off position can cause damage to the motor. The machine also has a cover interlock mechanism that causes the motor to stop if the lid is opened during operation.

Cuisinart Deluxe Pasta Maker
Manufactured and distributed by:
Cuisinarts Corporation
1 Cummings Point Road
Stamford, CT 06904
Telephone (203) 975-4600
Customer Service (800) 726-0190

This is a solid, well-built machine. The five standard pasta dies are brass reinforced for durability. The two specialty dies (for gnocchi and breadsticks) are made of nylon.

No special measuring cups are needed for this machine. A full recipe yields 1½ pounds of fresh pasta, but the machine has the capacity to make 3 pounds of pasta at one time. A half batch can easily be made by cutting the ingredients in half.

Our only complaint about the machine is very minor. The extra dies available for the machine can only be bought as a set. Also, the die for linguine is considered an extra. This may not be a problem for some cooks, but we use the linguine noodle for many dishes.

As we said, very minor. We'll get over it and use the slightly wider fettuccine die instead.

Standard Features

The Deluxe Pasta Maker's standard features are:

- Seven dies: capellini, spaghetti, fettuccine, ribbed penne/ziti, lasagna, gnocchi, and breadsticks
- Die wrench
- Spatula

Optional Accessories

There is an optional three-pack of dies for linguine, macaroni, and shells.

Storage Requirements

The Deluxe Pasta Maker requires a space measuring 14¼ inches long by 10 inches wide by 13 inches high when stored in its box. It weighs about 15 pounds.

Instruction Booklet

The instruction booklet has easy-to-read information on the parts of the machine, and disassembly and assembly, as well as tips for making perfect pasta, all with corresponding black-and-white photographs. Other information includes tips on cleaning the machine, cooking and storing fresh pasta, and matching shapes to sauces. Recipes are included for making different types of pasta (including one with egg substitute), gnocchi, breadsticks, and four pasta sauces. All the recipes include nutritional information.

Using the Machine

The lid of the work bowl resembles that of the Cuisinart food processor in that it twists into place, rather than being hinged. Before starting the mixing process, a shutter slide must be pushed into the base of the machine to keep the flour and liquid from falling into the extrusion chamber during processing. All pasta recipes call for some oil. Rather than being mixed with the water or eggs, the oil is added to the work bowl with the flour. The top cover is locked into place and the machine is turned on.

The liquid is poured slowly but steadily into a small feed tube in the top of the lid. The dough is then mixed until moist, but not sticky, walnut-sized lumps are formed. This process should take between 3 and 9 minutes.

We had no trouble getting the right consistency for the dough. It is easy to tell the correct consistency, as the pieces of dough are large. It is also easy to correct dough that is too dry or too wet by adding 1 tablespoon of either liquid or flour. One thing we found when making full recipes is that the dough may look mixed on the top, but the bottom may still be dry. When you check the dough, also check it at the bottom of the work bowl.

The instructions recommend allowing two large walnut-sized lumps of dough to come through the opening of the extrusion chamber before fitting the die into place. This is a foolproof test of whether or not the dough is mixed correctly. The first time we made dough in the Deluxe Pasta Maker it looked like it was of the correct consistency. However, when we let a little of the dough extrude through the chamber, it was definitely too dry. All we had to do was put the shutter slide back in place and turn on the machine. All the dough was automatically expelled from the chamber. We just fed it back into the machine through the feed tube, added 1 tablespoon of water, and remixed. It came through perfectly the next time.

Once the dough comes through the extrusion chamber correctly, the selected die can then be set in place. When the pasta reaches the length desired, it is cut off flush with the surface of the die using the spatula provided.

The instructions for the Deluxe Pasta Maker included a good die-cleaning tip. Let the die sit at room temperature for 30 minutes with the plug of dough remaining on the back of the die. When the dough has dried out somewhat, gently pull it out of the die. A lot of the dough will come off this way. Pins or toothpicks should never be used to push dough through the openings of these dies. According to the booklet, the inner surfaces are polished to a mirror finish, and any scratches can impair their functioning.

The booklet states that after bits of dried dough are

brushed from the parts, they may be washed by hand or in the silverware basket of the dishwasher. The base of the machine should be wiped down with a damp cloth.

The Cuisinart Deluxe Pasta Maker has a thermostat that will automatically stop the machine if it begins to overheat. This may happen if the machine has been in continuous operation for 1 hour or more. If this happens, turn the machine off and allow it to cool for at least 30 minutes. The other safety feature is a cover interlock mechanism that shuts the machine off automatically if the cover is removed.

PastaMatic MX700
Manufactured by Simac in Italy
Distributed in the United States by:
Lello Appliances Corporation
355 Murray Hill Parkway
East Rutherford, NJ 07073
Telephone (201) 939-2555

This machine has been referred to as the Cadillac of pasta machines. The praise is well deserved. It has been on the market for several years and does almost everything well, from pasta to pizza dough to cookies. It handles nonstandard pasta mixtures with aplomb and exudes the most consistent shapes of all the machines we tried. Each recipe calls for one pound of flour (approximately 3¾ cups), which is measured with a regular measuring cup. The liquid measuring cup provided with the machine is clearly marked for full and half batches.

This machine is simple to use. Part of the reason for this is the well-organized instruction booklet, including a picture of what the pasta should look like after extrusion. The pictures are helpful because the finished product doesn't always look the same from one time to the next, especially the first few times the machine is used. Another feature we really liked was the large selection of dies. Most of the PastaMatic dies are made of brass for durability.

Standard Features

The PastaMatic MX700's standard features are:

• Eight dies: linguine, macaroni, capellini, small fettuccine, spaghetti, lasagna, bucato (a hollow spaghetti), and cookies

• Liquid measuring cup
• Die wrench

Optional Accessories

Sixteen additional dies are available: spaghettini (large spaghetti), chitarre (square spaghetti), small shells, pasta del contadino (farmer's pasta), tagliatella (a type of fettuccine), pappardella (large fettuccine), bucatino (hollow spaghetti), bucatino regato (hollow ridged spaghetti), fili d'oro (golden threads), maccheroni quadrati (square maccheroni), penne (ziti), maccheroni quadrifoglio (clover maccheroni), sfoglia large per ravioli (wide-width dough for ravioli), gnocchi, pizza dough, and breadsticks.

Storage Requirements

The PastaMatic requires a space measuring 12 inches long by 10½ inches wide by 11 inches high when stored in its box. It weighs about 18 pounds.

The PastaMatic has one feature that no other electric machine has. There is a storage compartment in the back of the machine with space for eight dies, the measuring cup, and the electrical cord. This keeps everything together in one neat package.

Instruction Booklet

The instruction booklet contains information on machine parts, general procedures, assembly and disassembly, and cleaning. The easy-to-follow text corresponds to many colorful pictures. There are many pasta recipes, including those made with different flours and vegetables. This informative booklet also contains recipes for things you might never have thought could be made with a pasta machine, such as won ton skins, tortilla chips, and spicy wafers from India called papadums. Also included are recipes for an assortment of sauces, toppings, and dressings to go with your creations.

Using the Machine

Making pasta with the PastaMatic is slightly different than making pasta with the other machines. Instead of providing a flour measuring cup or a specific flour measurement, the instructions call for one pound of flour. The instructions do point out that one pound of flour is somewhere between $3\frac{1}{2}$ and $3\frac{3}{4}$ cups. It is recommended that you weigh the flour before use. Not everyone has a scale, and even with the exact amount called for, the liquid will vary because of such things as the humidity and type of flour used. If you can't weigh the flour, pick a constant amount and use it consistently, adjusting the amount of liquid needed. Once that decision is made, the machine is a breeze to use.

After the flour is added and the lid is closed, the machine is turned on and the liquid is added very slowly. The instructions state that it should take 1 full minute to add all the liquid to the flour. The machine is then left to run for 2 full minutes while kneading the dough. At this point, the cover is removed and the consistency of the dough is checked. It should be in moist, but not sticky, walnut-size lumps. If dough is too dry, 1 teaspoon of water is added and the machine is left to run for another minute. If the dough is too wet, 1 tablespoon of flour is added to the bowl and the machine is left to run for another minute. Either process is repeated as necessary.

Here is where the tricky part comes in. Once the dough reaches the correct consistency, the machine needs to run for a certain amount of time as indicated by the recipe. The time it takes for the dough to reach the desired consistency is subtracted from the kneading time stated in the recipe. It took us a minute or two, going back and forth between the recipe and the general procedure information, before the mental light clicked on (well, it was late). All the information is in the booklet, but you have to do some page-turning to get the whole story.

Like the Cuisinart Deluxe Pasta Maker, the PastaMatic completes the dough processing cycle without the extrusion die in place. When the dough is ready, the shutter slide is pulled open and the dough is allowed into the extrusion chamber. As soon as it begins coming through the opening, the machine is stopped, and the dough is cut off and placed back in the mixing bowl. Again, this is a good final test of whether or not the dough is the correct consistency. If it is too wet or dry, the shutter slide is closed and the machine is turned on. The dough will be pushed out of the extrusion chamber. It can then be added back into the work bowl and remixed. When the dough is ready, the die is inserted to begin the extrusion process.

Although the base and the bowl are not dishwasher safe, cleaning them is easy. The dough just wipes right off. A toothpick can be used in grooves and crevices. The cleaning instructions indicate that if the dough is left to dry in the die it is easier to loosen. Instructions for other machines say the same thing, but this was the only one in which all the dried dough fell off when the die was gently tapped on the counter.

The lid of this machine contains an interlock mechanism that will turn the machine off if the lid is removed.

WHAT TO LOOK FOR WHEN YOU GO SHOPPING

We put the machines you've just read about through their paces in a variety of pasta-making situations, something like the engineers at *Consumer Reports* might do. Of the machines we tested, even the poorest model performed adequately, though we had to watch that the dough didn't freeze the motor—one machine actually started smoking. On the other hand, the most expensive and apparently toughest machine performed flawlessly using the same batch of dough that choked the lesser system. We also experienced the agony and the ecstasy of trying to clean each machine. We certainly learned a lot about what you should look for before taking possession of any pasta machine.

When shopping, you must weigh price against performance. Look to see how easy or difficult it is to remove dough residue from the machine's mixing and extrusion chambers. Look for positive switch action (a click or some other sign that the switch was turned on or off), solid mating of surface against surface, and quality knobs and locks. The overall impression should be one of a well-built appliance.

New pasta machines and improved versions of older models are coming out on the market all the time. If you don't have a machine, or want to upgrade from an older style, there are a few factors you should consider before you spend your money.

Performance

The most important component of an electric extrusion machine is its motor. The machine should be capable of churning and successfully delivering the thickest and most ineptly prepared dough. In our tests, the machines that were the most forgiving of improper dough consistency were the expensive ones. These machines were generally also the ones in which is was easiest to correct the dough.

Since there is no way of knowing the perseverance of a pasta machine before purchase, either get recommendations from fellow chefs or buy from a store with a liberal return policy.

Available Attachments

What dies are available for your machine? Some machines are bundled with a wide range of attachments for the most common applications. Others require the purchase of expensive dies and other components. You can't use one manufacturer's dies in another's machine, so the choice of machine locks you into that manufacturer's options.

Safety

The safest machines, from an electrical point of view, have three-pronged plugs to ground potential shocks through the plug instead of through you. (Of course, if you live in a house without grounded outlets, this feature won't protect you.) At the very least, make sure the machine is UL approved.

Instructions

We've given you an idea of what's in the instruction booklets for the machines we tested. If you're looking at another brand, don't feel bashful about sitting down with the booklet and reading it cover to cover in the store. Look for the following things:

- Easy-to-understand instructions
- Adequate pictures or illustrations, including a clear picture of what the dough should look before extrusion

- Clear recipes
- Information on how to use the pasta
- Safety features
- Helpful hints

Noise

If noise is a discomforting factor in your kitchen, test each machine before purchase. Just turning the empty machine on in the store will give you an indication of its noise level. Remember that once the machine is loaded with dough, it will doubtlessly become louder. Also remember that the noise will persist until all of the pasta is extruded, which could be as long as 15 to 20 minutes.

Cleaning

The machine should be durable and easy to clean, without a lot of tunnels and plastic seams that trap hard-to-remove dough. Try to get a machine with dies that are easy to clean—although no matter what machine you get, some of the included dies will be easier to clean than others. If you use a dishwasher, look for dishwasher-safe plastic components. Placing all elements from a machine (except the motor/electrical portion) in the dishwasher is an expedient clean-up technique. If the removable parts are not specifically listed as dishwasher safe in the literature, they may melt in the heat of mechanical dish washing systems.

Storage Space

Everything needs its own space. We recommend storing any pasta machine in its box. The weights and dimensions for the machines we tested are in the previous section. Figure out where the machine will be stored and look at the machine's size and weight before you get it home (and only then realize that it will have to sit in the middle of the kitchen floor).

USING AN ELECTRIC EXTRUSION MACHINE

This is pasta the easy way: no kneading, no rolling, no flour, flour everywhere. But simple as it is, there are still a couple of things you should keep in mind before you start.

Choosing the Die

The hardest thing about using an electric extrusion machine is deciding what shape you want to make. That decision partially depends on the sauce being served, a topic we discussed in Chapter 2. It also depends on the flour being used, since doughs made with whole-grain flours tend to extrude more easily when a large-shape die is used.

The choice of a die also depends on the mood you're in. Are you feeling trendy (blue corn fettuccine with Confetti Sauce), or traditional (spaghetti with Chunky Marinara Sauce), or somewhere in between (Vegetable Lasagna With White Sauce)? There are so many choices!

Dough Consistency

The amount of liquid used with the different machines varies considerably. Generally, electric machines use less liquid than the hand-cranked models, because the dough in an electric machine is mixed into a loose consistency instead of a solid mass. One thing to remember is that the amount of liquid used in the same recipe on any given day will vary because of differences in heat, humidity, altitude, the specific brand and grind of flour, the time of day the pasta is being made, and whether or not the moon is full.

Well, the moon may not have anything to do with it, but almost everything else does. The idea we're trying to get across is that you must become familiar with the texture needed for your specific pasta machine. You'll need to create this texture regardless of the amount of flour and liquid called for in the directions.

So exactly how much flour and liquid is needed for the various machines? Many of the extrusion machines come with a measuring cup for either flour, or liquid, or both. These cups give precise measurements for each specific machine. If you have a brand of pasta machine not reviewed in this chapter, we recommend that you carefully figure out the flour and liquid needed. Once you have that information, write it down somewhere

safe, maybe on the lid of the box. This way, if the measuring cups are lost or misplaced, you will be able to measure out the amounts as needed.

One manufacturer recommends pouring only 90 percent of the liquid into the machine before checking the consistency. This way, the dough never becomes too wet. Clearing a machine of wet, sticky dough can be a time-consuming chore.

Extruding the Dough

Once the die is in place and the dough has reached the correct consistency, it's time to extrude. If you have ever struggled through making pasta by hand, you'll find that the use of an electric machine is a real treat. Just flip a switch or slide a shutter, or do whatever your particular machine calls for, and just watch the shapes start to come through.

If you are having trouble getting the dough to extrude properly, here are a few tips:

• Don't skip the step about putting the die in either hot water or oil—check your instruction booklet—before placing it on the pasta machine. It really does help make the extrusion process easier. One manufacturer recommends spraying nonstick cooking spray or olive oil on the die before extruding. Try it on your machine if you have trouble getting the pasta to extrude smoothly.

• If the dough has ragged edges, or won't come out at all, it is probably too dry. Add water per your machine's instructions, and remix for a minute before rechecking the consistency. Follow the directions for your particular machine. You may have to take the extrusion chamber apart and clean it out before you can begin again.

• If the dough is very sticky when extruding, or if it is sticking to the mixing arm, it's probably too wet. Add flour per your machine's instructions, and remix for a minute before rechecking the consistency.

• If the dough being extruded is only slightly sticky, it will usually extrude with no problems. To keep the pasta from sticking together before cooking, dust it with wheat flour or corn meal. When cooked in boiling water (as opposed to a soup or stew), the flour or meal will sink to the bottom of the pot and won't mix with the cooking pasta.

• When using a die for a fine pasta, such as a very thin spaghetti or angel hair, a pasta dough that is just slightly more moist helps the extrusion process.

• Check your instruction booklet for noises the pasta machine may make to get your attention during the extrusion process. The Primo Pasta has a clicking sound that goes off if the dough is not mixed correctly, and the Pasta-Del-Giorno and the Deluxe Pasta Maker have safety overload devices that shut the motor off if it begins to overheat from the strain.

As the dough extrudes, have a bowl or plate handy to catch the pasta and cut it at the desired length. Or, catch the ends of the pasta in your hands as it extrudes. Cut the pasta to the desired length and lay it flat on a floured kitchen towel until needed. (We like the second method better.) The pasta cooks evenly if all the pieces are dried evenly.

When all the pasta dough has been processed, it can immediately be placed in a pot of boiling water (see the cooking instructions on page 12). Our preference is to lay the pasta flat as it extrudes and let it dry for 1 hour before cooking. The cooking process takes a minute or two longer, but we both think the slight drying improves the flavor and texture of the pasta. It also reduces the pasta's tendency to clump while cooking.

Don't ever let the pasta-making process get so frustrating that you never use your pasta machine. All of the major manufacturers have customer service telephone numbers for your convenience. Don't hesitate to call them when something just won't go right. Look at all the fun you will be missing if your pasta machine just sits on the shelf, collecting dust.

PART THREE

Making Pastas

There it is—your brand-new pasta machine, sitting in the middle of your kitchen table. As you open the box, visions of delicious pasta dinners fill your head. You take out the equipment, you look at the instructions.

Now what?

First things first: *The importance of understanding your machine before using it can't be stressed enough.* Make sure you understand the functions of the various parts, and how the machine comes apart and goes back together. It is absolutely necessary that you familiarize yourself with the basic components and operation of your pasta machine before you make your first batch of dough. Once you understand how the machine works, see Part Two for information on mixing and checking the dough, adjusting ingredient amounts, and producing the pasta.

In these chapters, we give you directions for making a wide variety of pastas. Before moving on to the specialty pastas in Chapters 6 through 8, you should master the basic pastas in Chapter 5. Chapter 5 also has information on flours and on pasta storage. Chapter 9 contains directions for making other treats, such as breadsticks or pizza, with your pasta machine.

The pasta directions in these chapters are based on the following considerations:

• All directions call for $3\frac{1}{2}$ cups of flour. This approximates the amount of flour required by all the machine manufacturers.

• All the pastas listed here use liquid amounts called for in the instructions for Simac's PastaMatic MX700, our preferred machine. The recipes will generally work without modification with the Cuisinart Deluxe Pasta Maker as well. For other machines, you will need to adjust the recipes through experimentation, using the guidelines provided in both Part Two and the instruction booklet for your machine. Most of the required adjustments will be minor.

• Each set of directions gives steps for both electric extrusion machines and hand-cranked machines. The hand-cranked machine directions use a food processor to make the dough. If you want to cut the dough by hand, increase the kneading time to 20 minutes, and see page 28.

• Most of these directions use whole eggs. It is possible to use any of the liquid variations given in the pasta directions in Chapter 5, or to use an egg substitute instead of the whole egg.

• Many of the pasta directions in this book, as well as those in the instruction booklets with the various pasta machines, call for the addition of oil to the dough. This gives the dough a silky feel, and makes cutting or extruding the dough easier. The oil can be increased by a tablespoon or two, or it can be eliminated entirely. If you adjust the amount of oil used, don't forget to also adjust the total amount of liquid used. Note that the instruction booklet for the Cuisinart Deluxe Pasta Maker calls for the oil to be added in with the flour, instead of mixed into the liquid. Olive oil is specified when its flavor would enhance that of the pasta (see page 155), while canola oil is specified when a blander oil is desired. Any other vegetable oil except olive oil can be substituted for canola.

• The one thing we don't add to any of our pastas—or any of our sauces, for that matter—is salt. Salt has traditionally been used to both enhance flavor and preserve food. We believe that taste can be better enhanced through the use of herbs and spices, and by not overcooking food. And since you can make fresh pasta whenever you want, there is no reason to use salt as a preservative. If you must add salt, we recommend using sea salt. Keep in mind that pasta made without salt is more tender.

You will notice that each set of directions in Chapters 6 through 8 contains a Take a Chance section. This section gives you some tips on how to creatively manipulate each pasta to create new tastes and textures. Each set of directions in Chapters 6 through 8 also contains a Suggested Sauces section, which gives you tips for matching each pasta flavor with specific sauces from Part Four. These are by no means all the combinations you can create—they are suggestions cast in pasta dough, not in concrete! So go ahead and experiment.

5

Basic Pastas

A little flour, a little water, maybe some egg or oil–
what can be simpler, or more satisfying, than basic pasta?
We strongly recommend that you start out making the basic pastas
described in this chapter before moving on to the flavored pastas
covered in following chapters.

Before getting started, we would advise you to read
the inset on the following pages–*Know Your Flours and
Storage Methods*–which discusses the flours used in basic pasta
and storage methods for homemade pasta.

For each flour described in the inset, the chapter contains a set of directions
for using this flour along with plain water to make delicious pasta.
Variations make the same pasta using whole eggs; egg yolks;
egg whites; and eggs, oil, and water. Six flours with
five variations each–that's thirty pastas, and we haven't even
gotten to the flavored pastas yet!

Know Your Flours and Storage Methods

WORKING WITH FLOURS

Flour doesn't just mean all-purpose white anymore. Flours made from different grains will give your pasta a variety of tastes and textures. It is important to know that some shapes work better than others, depending on the flour used. We've found that dough made with whole grain flours is better rolled into wider noodles or extruded though dies with larger openings.

Unbleached White Flour

This has become the standard baking flour, found on supermarket and pantry shelves everywhere. It is made from red winter wheat. "Unbleached" means that it has been through less processing than bleached flour. Although not as nutritious as whole grain flour, it is lighter and easier to work with, especially for the pasta-making novice. Most of the instructions in the manufacturers' booklets call for unbleached flour, but you can substitute other flours as desired.

Whole Wheat Flour

Whole wheat flour is made from whole grains of wheat, including the outer covering or husk of the grain. As a result, it provides more vitamins and fiber than unbleached flour. Whole wheat flour is available in a number of grinds, from very coarse to very fine. All grinds can be substituted in equal measure for unbleached flour in most recipes.

Whole wheat pasta will be slightly heavier in texture and nuttier in flavor than unbleached flour pasta. Additional water (typically, from a teaspoon to a tablespoon for a full batch) is required when using whole wheat flour. Coarser grinds require slightly more water. Coarser whole-wheat pastas

should be rolled into flat noodles, such as fettuccine or lasagna. Pasta made from finely ground whole wheat flour, sometimes called pastry flour in the health food stores, can be made into any shape.

Semolina Flour

Semolina flour is a fine grind of hard durum winter wheat. It is rich in gluten, which is a protein that makes dough elastic. Semolina dough has more strength than dough made with regular flour, and thus can easily be formed into many shapes. Most packaged pastas are made from semolina flour. Semolina flour can be used in electric extrusion machines, but a pure semolina dough is too sticky to be hand-rolled. Because of the doughy texture of pasta made entirely with semolina flour, we recommend mixing it with unbleached white flour (or finely ground whole wheat flour) in equal amounts.

Buckwheat Flour

This heavy flour is milled from toasted buckwheat seeds (groats). It has a heavy, nutty flavor. Buckwheat pasta dough is tender and gritty, and is similar in its handling properties to coarsely ground whole wheat flour. Buckwheat flour can be mixed with unbleached white flour or finely ground whole wheat flour for a lighter taste and smoother texture. Buckwheat flour is best for wide, thick noodles, but not good for thin shapes, as the dough breaks apart easily.

Brown Rice Flour

This mildly sweet flour is made from brown rice, which is rice from which only the inedible hull has been removed. It is high in fiber. Dough made from brown rice flour is slightly stickier than that made with whole wheat flour, but otherwise similar in its handling properties. Brown rice flour is best used in flat noodles.

Oat Flour

This fiber-filled flour can be found in most well-stocked health food stores. It can also be made at home with quick-cooking rolled oats and a blender. It can be used in most pasta recipes in the same way as coarsely ground whole wheat flour. We use oat flour in one of our favorite dessert pastas, Oatmeal Cookie Pasta (page 127).

Corn Meals

Yellow, white, and blue corn meals can add flavor and nutrition to many pasta recipes. Corn meal must always be mixed with other flours. Use it sparingly, as the grainy texture of doughs that contain meal make them difficult to extrude or roll. Corn meal is best used in flat noodles.

STORING YOUR PASTA

If you get a little carried away, you will want to know how to properly store your pasta. Pasta can be stored either fresh or dry.

Storing Fresh Pasta

To store fresh pasta, put it in an airtight container or a sealed plastic bag and keep it in the refrigerator. To take the best advantage of its wonderful flavor, use within two to three days, although it will keep a week or longer. Fresh pasta can also be frozen for up to two months. It can go right from the freezer to a boiling pot of water. Adjust the cooking time accordingly, since frozen pasta takes longer to cook.

Dough made for one of the hand-cranked pasta machines can be wrapped in plastic after kneading and stored in the refrigerator for two to three days. While the dough can be frozen, we don't recommend it. The thawing process can make it mushy. Dough made in an electric extrusion machine can also be stored after the kneading process, but it will then have to be cut by hand or on a hand-cranked machine because it will not be of the consistency required by an electric machine.

Drying Pasta

There are several ways to dry pasta. The easiest way is to lay it flat on a lightly floured towel. This ensures that the pasta will dry evenly. When it is bunched up, it dries quickly in some areas, while other areas may take up to a day longer. We also found that we liked pasta that had been dried for at least 1 hour before cooking. It seems to taste better. This is our personal preference.

Long pasta can be hung over a chair covered with a lightly floured towel, or put on a drying rack (see page 22). It can be tricky to pick pasta up that has been dried this way. It tends to break, especially the thinner pastas such as angel hair.

Long pasta such as angel hair can be dried in nests, in which the pasta is folded upon itself. If you choose this method, make certain that the pasta is not sticky, or it will clump together. When drying the pasta, keep checking that the underside of the nest is also drying, and turn it over if necessary. Otherwise, the whole nest may mold. It is best to use this method of drying for very thin pastas.

The drying times for various pastas will vary, according to their size, shape, and thickness, and the temperature and humidity. It will take from several hours to one day. When dry, the pasta will look a little like leather. Once the pasta is dry, place it in an airtight container and store at room temperature for several months. Be careful when picking up the pasta, since it will break easily.

Simple Homemade Pasta With Water

Preparation Time: *Varies with the equipment used*
Yield: *1½ Pounds*

3½ cups unbleached white flour

1 cup water

The simplest homemade pasta is that made with unbleached white flour. This flour produces a light yet firm dough that's easy for the beginning pasta chef to work with. Therefore, we recommend that you master the use of this dough—with all its variations in liquid ingredients—if this is your first try at making pasta.

FOR ELECTRIC EXTRUSION MACHINES:

1. Place the flour in the pasta machine. With the machine running, slowly add the water. Process until the dough reaches the consistency specified in the instruction booklet. If the dough is too dry or too wet, add more water or flour per the instruction booklet.

2. Extrude the pasta, following the directions in instruction booklet.

FOR HAND-CRANKED MACHINES:

1. Place the flour in the food processor. With the machine running, slowly add the water. Pulse until a ball begins to form, about 10 to 15 seconds.

2. If the dough is too dry when all the water has been added, add 1 teaspoon of water, and pulse until a ball begins to form. If the dough is too wet, add 1 tablespoon of flour, and pulse until a ball begins to form. Repeat either process as necessary.

3. Remove the dough from the food processor and place it on a lightly floured pastry board or work surface. Knead the dough, incorporating additional flour into the ball of dough until it becomes smooth and shiny. The dough should be kneaded for 2 minutes.

4. Cover the dough with plastic wrap and let it rest for 5 minutes on the counter, or refrigerate it for up to 2 days.

5. Cut or extrude the dough according to the instructions on pages 25 or 28.

COOKING INSTRUCTIONS:

At this point, you can cook the pasta immediately. However, we recommend drying it for 1 hour beforehand to improve both the taste and the texture. Cook the pasta in 4 to 5 quarts of vigorously boiling water. Add all of the pasta at once, covering the pot until the water returns to a rapid boil. After uncovering the pot, test the pasta for doneness by biting into a piece. It should be tender, yet firm. If the

pasta's not done, test every 15 to 30 seconds thereafter. Total cooking time will depend on how fresh and how thick the pasta is—the drier and thicker it is, the longer it will take.

Variations

• To make Simple Homemade Pasta with Eggs, place 4 large eggs in a measuring cup, and beat lightly with a fork. Add enough water to make 1 cup of liquid.

• To make Simple Homemade Pasta with Egg Yolks, place 7 large egg yolks in a measuring cup, and beat lightly with a fork. Add enough water to make 1 cup of liquid. If using an electric machine, see the instruction booklet. If using a hand-cranked machine, increase the kneading time to 10 minutes, and let the dough rest for at least 1 hour before using.

• To make Simple Homemade Pasta with Egg Whites, place 6 large egg whites in a measuring cup, and beat lightly with a fork. Add enough water to make 1 cup of liquid.

• To make Simple Homemade Pasta with Eggs, Oil, and Water, place 2 or 3 large eggs in a measuring cup, and beat lightly with a fork. Add 1 tablespoon olive oil, and mix well. Add enough water to make 1 cup of liquid.

Whole Wheat Pasta With Water

Preparation Time: *Varies with the equipment used*
Yield: *1¹/₂ Pounds*

2¹/₂ cups whole wheat flour

1 cup unbleached white flour

1 cup water

Whole wheat flour makes a much stiffer dough than unbleached white does. To facilitate handling, and to avoid an overly grainy taste, always mix whole wheat flour with unbleached white flour. Start by using the mixture of flours given below. Then, experiment—as little as ¹/₂ cup or as much as 1¹/₂ cups of unbleached white can be mixed in with the whole wheat.

Depending on how much whole wheat flour is used, it may be necessary to adjust the amount of liquid used. After mastering the basic water directions, you can also experiment with the different liquid variations listed.

FOR ELECTRIC EXTRUSION MACHINES:

1. Place the flours in the pasta machine. With the machine running, slowly add the water. Process until the dough reaches the consistency specified in the instruction booklet. If the dough is too dry or too wet, add more water or flour per the instruction booklet.

2. Extrude the pasta, following the directions in instruction booklet.

FOR HAND-CRANKED MACHINES:

1. Place the flours in the food processor, and pulse 3 times to mix. With the machine running, slowly add the water. Pulse until a ball begins to form, about 10 to 15 seconds.

2. If the dough is too dry when all the water has been added, add 1 teaspoon of water, and pulse until a ball begins to form. If the dough is too wet, add 1 tablespoon of flour, and pulse until a ball begins to form. Repeat either process as necessary.

3. Remove the dough from the food processor and place it on a lightly floured pastry board or work surface. Knead the dough, incorporating additional flour into the ball of dough until it becomes smooth and shiny. The dough should be kneaded for 2 minutes.

4. Cover the dough with plastic wrap and let it rest for 5 minutes on the counter, or refrigerate it for up to 2 days.

5. Cut or extrude the dough according to the instructions on pages 25 or 28.

COOKING INSTRUCTIONS:

At this point, you can cook the pasta immediately. However, we recommend drying it for 1 hour beforehand to improve both the taste and the texture. Cook the pasta in 4 to 5 quarts of vigorously boiling

water. Add all of the pasta at once, covering the pot until the water returns to a rapid boil. After uncovering the pot, test the pasta for doneness by biting into a piece. It should be tender, yet firm. If the pasta's not done, test every 15 to 30 seconds thereafter. Total cooking time will depend on how fresh and how thick the pasta is—the drier and thicker it is, the longer it will take.

Variations

• To make Whole Wheat Pasta with Eggs, place 4 large eggs in a measuring cup, and beat lightly with a fork. Add enough water to make 1 cup of liquid.

• To make Whole Wheat Pasta with Egg Yolks, place 7 large egg yolks in a measuring cup, and beat lightly with a fork. Add enough water to make 1 cup of liquid. If using an electric machine, see the instruction booklet. If using a hand-cranked machine, increase the kneading time to 10 minutes, and let the dough rest for at least 1 hour before using.

• To make Whole Wheat Pasta with Egg Whites, place 6 large egg whites in a measuring cup, and beat lightly with a fork. Add enough water to make 1 cup of liquid.

• To make Whole Wheat Pasta with Eggs, Oil, and Water, place 2 or 3 large eggs in a measuring cup, and beat lightly with a fork. Add 1 tablespoon olive oil, and mix well. Add enough water to make 1 cup of liquid.

Semolina Pasta With Water

Preparation Time: *Varies with
the equipment used*
Yield: *1½ Pounds*

2 cups semolina flour

1½ cups unbleached white flour

1 cup water

Pasta imported from Italy is made from semolina, a coarse grind of durum wheat. Like whole wheat flour, semolina produces a stiff dough, and is best mixed with unbleached white flour. Pasta made from semolina flour alone also tends to be very doughy and somewhat sticky—another good reason for mixing it with unbleached white flour. Once you are comfortable with the feel of this dough, you can try experimenting with different proportions of unbleached white to semolina.

Depending on how much semolina flour is used, it may be necessary to adjust the amount of liquid used. After mastering the basic water directions, you can also experiment with the different liquid variations listed.

FOR ELECTRIC EXTRUSION MACHINES:

1. Place the flours in the pasta machine. With the machine running, slowly add the water. Process until the dough reaches the consistency specified in the instruction booklet. If the dough is too dry or too wet, add more water or flour per the instruction booklet.

2. Extrude the pasta, following the directions in instruction booklet.

FOR HAND-CRANKED MACHINES:

1. Place the flours in the food processor, and pulse 3 times to mix. With the machine running, slowly add the water. Pulse until a ball begins to form, about 10 to 15 seconds.

2. If the dough is too dry when all the water has been added, add 1 teaspoon of water, and pulse until a ball begins to form. If the dough is too wet, add 1 tablespoon of flour, and pulse until a ball begins to form. Repeat either process as necessary.

3. Remove the dough from the food processor and place it on a lightly floured pastry board or work surface. Knead the dough, incorporating additional flour into the ball of dough until it becomes smooth and shiny. The dough should be kneaded for 2 minutes.

4. Cover the dough with plastic wrap and let it rest for 5 minutes on the counter, or refrigerate it for up to 2 days.

5. Cut or extrude the dough according to the instructions on pages 25 or 28.

COOKING INSTRUCTIONS:

At this point, you can cook the pasta immediately. However, we recommend drying it for 1 hour beforehand to improve both the taste and the texture. Cook the pasta in 4 to 5 quarts of vigorously boiling water. Add all of the pasta at once, covering the pot until the water returns to a rapid boil. After uncovering the pot, test the pasta for doneness by biting into a piece. It should be tender, yet firm. If the pasta's not done, test every 15 to 30 seconds thereafter. Total cooking time will depend on how fresh and how thick the pasta is—the drier and thicker it is, the longer it will take.

Variations

• To make Semolina Pasta with Eggs, place 4 large eggs in a measuring cup, and beat lightly with a fork. Add enough water to make 1 cup of liquid.

• To make Semolina Pasta with Egg Yolks, place 7 large egg yolks in a measuring cup, and beat lightly with a fork. Add enough water to make 1 cup of liquid. If using an electric machine, see the instruction booklet. If using a hand-cranked machine, increase the kneading time to 10 minutes, and let the dough rest for at least 1 hour before using.

• To make Semolina Pasta with Egg Whites, place 6 large egg whites in a measuring cup, and beat lightly with a fork. Add enough water to make 1 cup of liquid.

• To make Semolina Pasta with Eggs, Oil, and Water, place 2 or 3 large eggs in a measuring cup, and beat lightly with a fork. Add 1 tablespoon olive oil, and mix well. Add enough water to make 1 cup of liquid.

Buckwheat Pasta With Water

Preparation Time: *Varies with the equipment used*
Yield: *1¹/₂ Pounds*

2 cups buckwheat flour

1¹/₂ cups unbleached white flour

1 cup water

Buckwheat flour is very heavy and gritty. This dough becomes thin very quickly when being rolled on a hand-cranked roller machine. It should always be mixed with unbleached white flour. You can experiment with different unbleached white-to-buckwheat ratios after you are comfortable with these directions.

Depending on how much buckwheat flour is used, it may be necessary to adjust the amount of liquid used. After mastering the basic water directions, you can also experiment with the different liquid variations listed.

FOR ELECTRIC EXTRUSION MACHINES:

1. Place the flours in the pasta machine. With the machine running, slowly add the water. Process until the dough reaches the consistency specified in the instruction booklet. If the dough is too dry or too wet, add more water or flour per the instruction booklet.

2. Extrude the pasta, following the directions in instruction booklet.

FOR HAND-CRANKED MACHINES:

1. Place the flours in the food processor, and pulse 3 times to mix. With the machine running, slowly add the water. Pulse until a ball begins to form, about 10 to 15 seconds.

2. If the dough is too dry when all the water has been added, add 1 teaspoon of water, and pulse until a ball begins to form. If the dough is too wet, add 1 tablespoon of flour, and pulse until a ball begins to form. Repeat either process as necessary.

3. Remove the dough from the food processor and place it on a lightly floured pastry board or work surface. Knead the dough, incorporating additional flour into the ball of dough until it becomes smooth and shiny. The dough should be kneaded for 2 minutes.

4. Cover the dough with plastic wrap and let it rest for 5 minutes on the counter, or refrigerate it for up to 2 days.

5. Cut or extrude the dough according to the instructions on pages 25 or 28.

COOKING INSTRUCTIONS:

At this point, you can cook the pasta immediately. However, we recommend drying it for 1 hour beforehand to improve both the taste and the texture. Cook the pasta in 4 to 5 quarts of vigorously boiling

water. Add all of the pasta at once, covering the pot until the water returns to a rapid boil. After uncovering the pot, test the pasta for doneness by biting into a piece. It should be tender, yet firm. If the pasta's not done, test every 15 to 30 seconds thereafter. Total cooking time will depend on how fresh and how thick the pasta is—the drier and thicker it is, the longer it will take.

Variations

• To make Buckwheat Pasta with Eggs, place 4 large eggs in a measuring cup, and beat lightly with a fork. Add enough water to make 1 cup of liquid.

• To make Buckwheat Pasta with Egg Yolks, place 7 large egg yolks in a measuring cup, and beat lightly with a fork. Add enough water to make 1 cup of liquid. If using an electric machine, see the instruction booklet. If using a hand-cranked machine, increase the kneading time to 10 minutes, and let the dough rest for at least 1 hour before using.

• To make Buckwheat Pasta with Egg Whites, place 6 large egg whites in a measuring cup, and beat lightly with a fork. Add enough water to make 1 cup of liquid.

• To make Buckwheat Pasta with Eggs, Oil, and Water, place 2 or 3 large eggs in a measuring cup, and beat lightly with a fork. Add 1 tablespoon olive oil, and mix well. Add enough water to make 1 cup of liquid.

Brown Rice Pasta With Water

Preparation Time: *Varies with the equipment used*
Yield: *1½ Pounds*

2 cups brown rice flour

1½ cups unbleached white flour

1 cup water

Brown rice flour has its own distinctive taste. It makes an interesting pasta for spaghetti, and is great in soups. Once you are comfortable working with these directions, you can start to experiment with the ratio of unbleached white flour to brown rice flour.

Depending on how much brown rice flour is used, it may be necessary to adjust the amount of liquid used. After mastering the basic water directions, you can also experiment with the different liquid variations listed.

FOR ELECTRIC EXTRUSION MACHINES:

1. Place the flours in the pasta machine. With the machine running, slowly add the water. Process until the dough reaches the consistency specified in the instruction booklet. If the dough is too dry or too wet, add more water or flour per the instruction booklet.

2. Extrude the pasta, following the directions in instruction booklet.

FOR HAND-CRANKED MACHINES:

1. Place the flours in the food processor, and pulse 3 times to mix. With the machine running, slowly add the water. Pulse until a ball begins to form, about 10 to 15 seconds.

2. If the dough is too dry when all the water has been added, add 1 teaspoon of water, and pulse until a ball begins to form. If the dough is too wet, add 1 tablespoon of flour, and pulse until a ball begins to form. Repeat either process as necessary.

3. Remove the dough from the food processor and place it on a lightly floured pastry board or work surface. Knead the dough, incorporating additional flour into the ball of dough until it becomes smooth and shiny. The dough should be kneaded for 2 minutes.

4. Cover the dough with plastic wrap and let it rest for 5 minutes on the counter, or refrigerate it for up to 2 days.

5. Cut or extrude the dough according to the instructions on pages 25 or 28.

COOKING INSTRUCTIONS:

At this point, you can cook the pasta immediately. However, we recommend drying it for 1 hour beforehand to improve both the taste and the texture. Cook the pasta in 4 to 5 quarts of vigorously boiling water. Add all of the pasta at once, covering the pot until the water returns to a rapid boil. After uncovering the pot, test the pasta for doneness by biting into a piece. It should be tender, yet firm. If the pasta's not done, test every 15 to 30 seconds thereafter. Total cooking time will depend on how fresh and how thick the pasta is—the drier and thicker it is, the longer it will take.

Variations

• To make Brown Rice Pasta with Eggs, place 4 large eggs in a measuring cup, and beat lightly with a fork. Add enough water to make 1 cup of liquid.

• To make Brown Rice Pasta with Egg Yolks, place 7 large egg yolks in a measuring cup, and beat lightly with a fork. Add enough water to make 1 cup of liquid. If using an electric machine, see the instruction booklet. If using a hand-cranked machine, increase the kneading time to 10 minutes, and let the dough rest for at least 1 hour before using.

• To make Brown Rice Pasta with Egg Whites, place 6 large egg whites in a measuring cup, and beat lightly with a fork. Add enough water to make 1 cup of liquid.

• To make Brown Rice Pasta with Eggs, Oil, and Water, place 2 or 3 large eggs in a measuring cup, and beat lightly with a fork. Add 1 tablespoon olive oil, and mix well. Add enough water to make 1 cup of liquid.

Oat Pasta With Water

Preparation Time: *Varies with the equipment used*
Yield: *1½ Pounds*

2 cups oat flour

1½ cups unbleached white flour

1 cup water

Oat flour provides another interesting variation in taste and texture. Become comfortable with this recipe before experimenting with the unbleached white-to-oat ratio.

Depending on how much oat flour is used, it may be necessary to adjust the amount of liquid used. After mastering the basic water directions, you can also experiment with the different liquid variations listed.

FOR ELECTRIC EXTRUSION MACHINES:

1. Place the flours in the pasta machine. With the machine running, slowly add the water. Process until the dough reaches the consistency specified in the instruction booklet. If the dough is too dry or too wet, add more water or flour per the instruction booklet.

2. Extrude the pasta, following the directions in instruction booklet.

FOR HAND-CRANKED MACHINES:

1. Place the flours in the food processor, and pulse 3 times to mix. With the machine running, slowly add the water. Pulse until a ball begins to form, about 10 to 15 seconds.

2. If the dough is too dry when all the water has been added, add 1 teaspoon of water, and pulse until a ball begins to form. If the dough is too wet, add 1 tablespoon of flour, and pulse until a ball begins to form. Repeat either process as necessary.

3. Remove the dough from the food processor and place it on a lightly floured pastry board or work surface. Knead the dough, incorporating additional flour into the ball of dough until it becomes smooth and shiny. The dough should be kneaded for 2 minutes.

4. Cover the dough with plastic wrap and let it rest for 5 minutes on the counter, or refrigerate it for up to 2 days.

5. Cut or extrude the dough according to the instructions on pages 25 or 28.

COOKING INSTRUCTIONS:

At this point, you can cook the pasta immediately. However, we recommend drying it for 1 hour beforehand to improve both the taste and the texture. Cook the pasta in 4 to 5 quarts of vigorously boiling water. Add all of the pasta at once, covering the pot until the water returns to a rapid boil. After uncovering the pot, test the pasta for doneness by biting into a piece. It should be tender, yet firm. If the

pasta's not done, test every 15 to 30 seconds thereafter. Total cooking time will depend on how fresh and how thick the pasta is—the drier and thicker it is, the longer it will take.

Variations

• To make Oat Pasta with Eggs, place 4 large eggs in a measuring cup, and beat lightly with a fork. Add enough water to make 1 cup of liquid.

• To make Oat Pasta with Egg Yolks, place 7 large egg yolks in a measuring cup, and beat lightly with a fork. Add enough water to make 1 cup of liquid. If using an electric machine, see the instruction booklet. If using a hand-cranked machine, increase the kneading time to 10 minutes, and let the dough rest for at least 1 hour before using.

• To make Oat Pasta with Egg Whites, place 6 large egg whites in a measuring cup, and beat lightly with a fork. Add enough water to make 1 cup of liquid.

• To make Oat Pasta with Eggs, Oil, and Water, place 2 or 3 large eggs in a measuring cup, and beat lightly with a fork. Add 1 tablespoon olive oil, and mix well. Add enough water to make 1 cup of liquid.

6

Vegetable and Herb Pastas

Vegetables and herbs give pasta a whole different look and flavor. Only your own taste will limit the vegetables and herbs you may try, although some vegetables work better than others. For example, some vegetables, such as crookneck squash, don't impart much flavor.

Some tips for making vegetable and herb pastas:

&. Put your juice extractor to good use on your vegetables. Vegetable juice works just like water in these recipes. Juice is also helpful in trying to keep the dies clean of vegetable fibers.

&. Even with vegetables chopped very fine or puréed, be prepared to pick out fibrous strands from the die. The pasta may extrude unevenly because of strands caught in the die.

&. When making these pastas, keep in mind that the color will fade on very thin shapes, such as thin noodles or spaghetti. These directions work better with wider noodles such as fettuccine or lasagna, or with the bigger shaped pastas.

&. Let your imagination run wild with different vegetable and herb combinations. We include a few of our favorite combinations.

Garlic Pasta

Preparation Time: *Varies with the equipment used*
Yield: *1½ Pounds*

4 large eggs

Water

8 garlic cloves, crushed

3½ cups unbleached white flour

As if we don't get enough garlic, we went and put it into our pasta. But it certainly does taste good there! Use this pasta in Spinach Lasagna Noodle Soup (page 202), Pasta e Fagioli (page 203), Baked Ziti (page 205), or Lasagna Roll-Ups With Chunky Marinara Sauce (page 213).

FOR ELECTRIC EXTRUSION MACHINES:

1. Place the eggs in a large measuring cup, and beat lightly. Add enough water to make 1 cup of liquid.

2. Place the garlic and flour in the pasta machine. With the machine running, slowly add the liquid. Process until the dough reaches the consistency specified in the instruction booklet. If the dough is too dry or too wet, add more water or flour per the instruction booklet.

3. Extrude the pasta, following the directions in instruction booklet.

FOR HAND-CRANKED MACHINES:

1. Place the eggs in a large measuring cup, and beat lightly. Add enough water to make 1 cup of liquid.

2. Place the garlic and flour in the food processor, and pulse 3 times to mix. With the machine running, slowly add the liquid. Pulse until a ball begins to form, about 10 to 15 seconds.

3. If the dough is too dry when all the liquid has been added, add 1 teaspoon of water, and pulse until a ball begins to form. If the dough is too wet, add 1 tablespoon of flour, and pulse until a ball begins to form. Repeat either process as necessary.

4. Remove the dough from the food processor and place it on a lightly floured pastry board or work surface. Knead the dough, incorporating additional flour into the ball of dough until it becomes smooth and shiny. The dough should be kneaded for 2 minutes.

5. Cover the dough with plastic wrap and let it rest for 5 minutes on the counter, or refrigerate it for up to 2 days.

6. Cut or extrude the dough according to the instructions on pages 25 or 28.

COOKING INSTRUCTIONS:

At this point, you can cook the pasta immediately. However, we recommend drying it for 1 hour beforehand to improve both the taste and the texture. Cook the pasta in 4 to 5 quarts of vigorously boiling

water. Add all of the pasta at once, covering the pot until the water returns to a rapid boil. After uncovering the pot, test the pasta for doneness by biting into a piece. It should be tender, yet firm. If the pasta's not done, test every 15 to 30 seconds thereafter. Total cooking time will depend on how fresh and how thick the pasta is—the drier and thicker it is, the longer it will take.

Take a Chance:

- Make Garlic Chive Pasta by omitting the crushed garlic cloves and adding ½ cup finely chopped fresh garlic chives. Or leave in the garlic cloves and add ½ cup of finely chopped regular chives.
- Add 1 to 2 teaspoons black pepper.
- Add 4 crushed garlic cloves to any of the herb pastas.

Suggested Sauces:

- This pasta can be served with any of the sauces in Chapters 10, 11, and 12.

Using Garlic

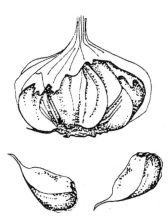

Always use fresh garlic. The head should be firm, without any green sprouts. Never refrigerate garlic—store it in a cool, dry place away from the sun.

Minced garlic, in either oil or water, is available commercially. But preserving your own garlic in oil is simple. Just peel the cloves and place them in a covered glass jar containing 2 cups of extra virgin olive oil. Cover the jar tightly and store in a cool, dry place for 1 week. Remove the garlic cloves as needed. The oil will pick up the rich taste of the garlic. It can be used in any recipe calling for olive oil. This oil will keep almost indefinitely, as long as you are constantly using both the cloves and the oil. If you don't use the garlic often, put it in a shallow container and store in the refrigerator.

Pesto Pasta

Preparation Time: *Varies with the equipment used*
Yield: *1½ Pounds*

3 eggs

2 tablespoons olive oil

Water

½ cup fresh basil leaves

3 cups unbleached white flour

½ cup freshly grated Parmesan cheese

1 tablespoon finely ground pine nuts

This pasta almost doesn't need a sauce, since the sauce is built in. For a special experience, use it in Traditional Lasagna (page 206).

FOR ELECTRIC EXTRUSION MACHINES:

1. Place the eggs in a large mixing cup, and beat lightly. Add the oil, and mix well. Add enough water to make 1 cup of liquid. Set aside.

2. Chop the basil very finely, either by hand or with a food processor. If you use a food processor, you still may have to finish chopping by hand to get pieces that are fine enough to not clog the die.

3. Place the flour, cheese, pine nuts, and basil in the pasta machine. With the machine running, slowly add the liquid. Process until the dough reaches the consistency specified in the instruction booklet. If the dough is too dry or too wet, add more water or flour per the instruction booklet.

4. Extrude the pasta, following the directions in instruction booklet.

FOR HAND-CRANKED MACHINES:

1. Place the eggs in a large mixing cup, and beat lightly. Add the oil, and mix well. Add enough water to make 1 cup of liquid. Set aside.

2. Place the basil in the food processor and pulse 3 to 5 times, or until the basil is finely chopped.

3. Add the flour, cheese, and pine nuts to the food processor, and pulse 3 times to mix. With the machine running, slowly add the liquid. Pulse until a ball begins to form, about 10 to 15 seconds.

4. If the dough is too dry when all the liquid has been added, add 1 teaspoon of water, and pulse until a ball begins to form. If the dough is too wet, add 1 tablespoon of flour, and pulse until a ball begins to form. Repeat either process as necessary.

5. Remove the dough from the food processor and place it on a lightly floured pastry board or work surface. Knead the dough, incorporating additional flour into the ball of dough until it becomes smooth and shiny. The dough should be kneaded for 2 minutes.

6. Cover the dough with plastic wrap and let it rest for 5 minutes on the counter, or refrigerate it for up to 2 days.

7. Cut or extrude the dough according to the instructions on pages 25 or 28.

COOKING INSTRUCTIONS:

At this point, you can cook the pasta immediately. However, we recommend drying it for 1 hour beforehand to improve both the taste and the texture. Cook the pasta in 4 to 5 quarts of vigorously boiling water. Add all of the pasta at once, covering the pot until the water returns to a rapid boil. After uncovering the pot, test the pasta for doneness by biting into a piece. It should be tender, yet firm. If the pasta's not done, test every 15 to 30 seconds thereafter. Total cooking time will depend on how fresh and how thick the pasta is—the drier and thicker it is, the longer it will take.

Take a Chance:

• Make Mint Pesto Pasta by omitting the basil and using ½ cup fresh mint leaves.

Suggested Sauces:

• Serve hot with the following sauces: Chunky Marinara (page 158), Slow-Cooked Spaghetti With Chicken (page 162), Arrabbiata (page 161), Red Clam (page 165), White Clam (page 164), Herbed Butter (page 166), or Wild Mushroom (page 186).

• Serve cold with the following sauces or dressings: Aglio e Olio (page 154), Quick Olive (page 156), Sinless Summer Cheese (page 168), Uncooked Tomato (page 173), Spicy Steamed Vegetable (page 178), or Green Yogurt (page 188).

Spinach Pasta

Preparation Time: *Varies with the equipment used*
Yield: *1½ Pounds*

3 large eggs

½ cup cooked, drained, and finely chopped spinach (reserve cooking water)

3½ cups unbleached white flour

This is the most popular vegetable noodle in the world. Use this pasta in Spinach Lasagna Noodle Soup (page 202), Baked Ziti (page 205), any of the lasagna recipes (pages 206, 208, and 213), Classic Cheese Ravioli (page 209), or Tortellini With Fresh Spinach Filling (page 217).

FOR ELECTRIC EXTRUSION MACHINES:

1. Place the eggs in a large measuring cup, and beat lightly. Add enough reserved cooking water to make 1 cup of liquid.

2. Place the spinach and flour in the pasta machine. With the machine running, slowly add the liquid. Process until the dough reaches the consistency specified in the instruction booklet. If the dough is too dry or too wet, add more water or flour per the instruction booklet.

3. Extrude the pasta, following the directions in instruction booklet.

FOR HAND-CRANKED MACHINES:

1. Place the eggs in a large measuring cup, and beat lightly. Add enough reserved cooking water to make 1 cup of liquid.

2. Place the spinach and flour in the food processor, and pulse 3 times to mix. With the machine running, slowly add the liquid. Pulse until a ball begins to form, about 10 to 15 seconds.

3. If the dough is too dry when all the liquid has been added, add 1 teaspoon of water, and pulse until a ball begins to form. If the dough is too wet, add 1 tablespoon of flour, and pulse until a ball begins to form. Repeat either process as necessary.

4. Remove the dough from the food processor and place it on a lightly floured pastry board or work surface. Knead the dough, incorporating additional flour into the ball of dough until it becomes smooth and shiny. The dough should be kneaded for 2 minutes.

5. Cover the dough with plastic wrap and let it rest for 5 minutes on the counter, or refrigerate it for up to 2 days.

6. Cut or extrude the dough according to the instructions on pages 25 or 28.

COOKING INSTRUCTIONS:

At this point, you can cook the pasta immediately. However, we recommend drying it for 1 hour beforehand to improve both the taste and the texture. Cook the pasta in 4 to 5 quarts of vigorously boiling

water. Add all of the pasta at once, covering the pot until the water returns to a rapid boil. After uncovering the pot, test the pasta for doneness by biting into a piece. It should be tender, yet firm. If the pasta's not done, test every 15 to 30 seconds thereafter. Total cooking time will depend on how fresh and how thick the pasta is—the drier and thicker it is, the longer it will take.

Take a Chance:

• Shape the pasta into fettuccine noodles. Mix with an equal amount of egg fettuccine noodles to make Straw and Hay.

• Make into any small shape and create a tri-colored hot or cold dish along with egg pasta and a red pasta, such as Beet (page 73), Tomato (page 77), or Tomato Chili (page 112).

• Serve as a side dish with the cheese sauce from Festive Macaroni and Cheese (page 207).

Suggested Sauces:

• Serve hot with the following sauces: Sautéed Garlic and Bread Crumbs (page 155), Slow-Cooked Spaghetti With Chicken (page 162), Italian Cheese Medley (page 169), Onion Raisin (page 173), Creamy Natural Tomato (page 176), Garden Fresh Primavera (page 180), Wild Mushroom (page 186), Verde (page 190), or Curry With Chicken (page 184).

• Serve hot or cold with Pesto Sauce (page 159).

• Serve cold with Uncooked Tomato Sauce (page 173) or Spicy Ginger Sauce (page 189).

Whole Wheat Spinach Pasta

Preparation Time: *Varies with the equipment used*
Yield: *1 1/2 Pounds*

3 large eggs

1/4 cup cooked, drained, and finely chopped spinach (reserve the cooking water)

2 cups whole wheat flour

1 1/2 cups unbleached white flour

There are several brands of whole wheat spinach pasta in the health food stores that are very good, but none of them compare to what you can make at home. Because of the density of whole wheat flour, 1 additional teaspoon of water may be needed before the dough reaches the desired consistency.

FOR ELECTRIC EXTRUSION MACHINES:

1. Place the eggs in a large measuring cup, and beat lightly. Add enough reserved cooking water to make 1 cup of liquid.

2. Place the spinach and the flours in the pasta machine. With the machine running, slowly add the liquid. Process until the dough reaches the consistency specified in the instruction booklet. If the dough is too dry or too wet, add more water or flour per the instruction booklet.

3. Extrude the pasta, following the directions in instruction booklet.

FOR HAND-CRANKED MACHINES:

1. Place the eggs in a large measuring cup, and beat lightly. Add enough reserved cooking water to make 1 cup of liquid.

2. Place the spinach and the flours in the food processor, and pulse 3 times to mix. With the machine running, slowly add the liquid. Pulse until a ball begins to form, about 10 to 15 seconds.

3. If the dough is too dry when all the liquid has been added, add 1 teaspoon of water, and pulse until a ball begins to form. If the dough is too wet, add 1 tablespoon of flour, and pulse until a ball begins to form. Repeat either process as necessary.

4. Remove the dough from the food processor and place it on a lightly floured pastry board or work surface. Knead the dough, incorporating additional flour into the ball of dough until it becomes smooth and shiny. The dough should be kneaded for 2 minutes.

5. Cover the dough with plastic wrap and let it rest for 5 minutes on the counter, or refrigerate it for up to 2 days.

6. Cut or extrude the dough according to the instructions on pages 25 or 28.

COOKING INSTRUCTIONS:

At this point, you can cook the pasta immediately. However, we recommend drying it for 1 hour beforehand to improve both the taste and the texture. Cook the pasta in 4 to 5 quarts of vigorously boiling

water. Add all of the pasta at once, covering the pot until the water returns to a rapid boil. After uncovering the pot, test the pasta for doneness by biting into a piece. It should be tender, yet firm. If the pasta's not done, test every 15 to 30 seconds thereafter. Total cooking time will depend on how fresh and how thick the pasta is—the drier and thicker it is, the longer it will take.

Take a Chance:

• Change the ratio of wheat flour to unbleached flour. Don't use whole wheat flour alone, or the pasta will be very grainy.

Suggested Sauces:

• Serve hot with the following sauces: Sautéed Garlic and Bread Crumbs (page 155), Slow-Cooked Spaghetti With Chicken (page 162), Italian Cheese Medley (page 169), Onion Raisin (page 173), Creamy Natural Tomato (page 176), Garden Fresh Primavera (page 180), Wild Mushroom (page 186), Verde (page 190), or Curry With Chicken (page 184).

• Serve hot or cold with Pesto Sauce (page 159).

• Serve cold with Uncooked Tomato Sauce (page 173) or Spicy Ginger Sauce (page 189).

Broccoli Pasta

Preparation Time: *Varies with the equipment used*
Yield: *1½ Pounds*

2 large eggs

1 tablespoon olive oil

¼ cup steamed and finely chopped broccoli (reserve the cooking water)

3½ cups unbleached white flour

Even broccoli haters won't be able to pass up this treat. Use it in Versatile Vegetable and Pasta Stew (page 204), Baked Ziti (page 205), Vegetable Lasagna With White Sauce (page 208), and Lasagna Roll-Ups With Chunky Marinara Sauce (page 213).

FOR ELECTRIC EXTRUSION MACHINES:

1. Place the eggs in a large measuring cup, and beat lightly. Add the oil, and mix well. Add enough reserved cooking water to make 1 cup of liquid.

2. Place the broccoli and flour in the pasta machine. With the machine running, slowly add the liquid. Process until the dough reaches the consistency specified in the instruction booklet. If the dough is too dry or too wet, add more water or flour per the instruction booklet.

3. Extrude the pasta, following the directions in instruction booklet.

FOR HAND-CRANKED MACHINES:

1. Place the eggs in a large measuring cup, and beat lightly. Add the oil, and mix well. Add enough reserved cooking water to make 1 cup of liquid.

2. Place the broccoli and flour in the food processor, and pulse 3 times to mix. With the machine running, slowly add the liquid. Pulse until a ball begins to form, about 10 to 15 seconds.

3. If the dough is too dry when all the liquid has been added, add 1 teaspoon of water, and pulse until a ball begins to form. If the dough is too wet, add 1 tablespoon of flour, and pulse until a ball begins to form. Repeat either process as necessary.

4. Remove the dough from the food processor and place it on a lightly floured pastry board or work surface. Knead the dough, incorporating additional flour into the ball of dough until it becomes smooth and shiny. The dough should be kneaded for 2 minutes.

5. Cover the dough with plastic wrap and let it rest for 5 minutes on the counter, or refrigerate it for up to 2 days.

6. Cut or extrude the dough according to the instructions on pages 25 or 28.

COOKING INSTRUCTIONS:

At this point, you can cook the pasta immediately. However, we recommend drying it for 1 hour beforehand to improve both the taste and the texture. Cook the pasta in 4 to 5 quarts of vigorously boiling water. Add all of the pasta at once, covering the pot until the water returns to a rapid boil. After uncovering the pot, test the pasta for doneness by biting into a piece. It should be tender, yet firm. If the pasta's not done, test every 15 to 30 seconds thereafter. Total cooking time will depend on how fresh and how thick the pasta is—the drier and thicker it is, the longer it will take.

Take a Chance:

• Add either 1 tablespoon lemon zest (page 175) or ¼ cup diced red bell pepper.

• Serve as a side dish with the cheese sauce from Festive Macaroni and Cheese (page 207).

Suggested Sauces:

• Serve hot with the following sauces: Quick Olive (page 156), Slow-Cooked Spaghetti With Chicken (page 162), Italian Cheese Medley (page 169), Herbed Butter (page 166), Spicy Steamed Vegetable (page 178), Carbonara (page 176), Creamy Natural Tomato (page 176), Garden Fresh Primavera (page 180), Gingered Chickpeas With Garlic (page 191), or Curry With Chicken (page 184).

• Serve hot or cold with Lavender-Scented Roasted Garlic Sauce (page 172).

• Serve cold with Aglio e Olio (page 154) or Pesto Sauce (page 159), either alone or with 1 cup shredded cooked chicken and ½ cup diced red bell pepper added.

Bugs's Carrot Pasta

Preparation Time: *Varies with the equipment used*
Yield: *1½ Pounds*

½ cup fresh carrot juice

½ cup water

3½ cups unbleached white flour

The flavor of carrot juice is sometimes better than that of the whole vegetable itself. This pasta can have a very strong taste, and should be dressed very simply. Use it in Vegetable Lasagna With White Sauce (page 208).

FOR ELECTRIC EXTRUSION MACHINES:

1. Place the juice and water in a measuring cup, and mix well.

2. Place the flour in the pasta machine. With the machine running, slowly add the liquid. Process until the dough reaches the consistency specified in the instruction booklet. If the dough is too dry or too wet, add more water or flour per the instruction booklet.

3. Extrude the pasta, following the directions in instruction booklet.

FOR HAND-CRANKED MACHINES:

1. Place the juice and water in a measuring cup, and mix well.

2. Place the flour in the food processor. With the machine running, slowly add the liquid. Pulse until a ball begins to form, about 10 to 15 seconds.

3. If the dough is too dry when all the liquid has been added, add 1 teaspoon of water, and pulse until a ball begins to form. If the dough is too wet, add 1 tablespoon of flour, and pulse until a ball begins to form. Repeat either process as necessary.

4. Remove the dough from the food processor and place it on a lightly floured pastry board or work surface. Knead the dough, incorporating additional flour into the ball of dough until it becomes smooth and shiny. The dough should be kneaded for 2 minutes.

5. Cover the dough with plastic wrap and let it rest for 5 minutes on the counter, or refrigerate it for up to 2 days.

6. Cut or extrude the dough according to the instructions on pages 25 or 28.

COOKING INSTRUCTIONS:

At this point, you can cook the pasta immediately. However, we recommend drying it for 1 hour beforehand to improve both the taste and the texture. Cook the pasta in 4 to 5 quarts of vigorously boiling water. Add all of the pasta at once, covering the pot until the water returns to a rapid boil. After uncovering the pot, test the pasta for doneness by biting into a piece. It should be tender, yet firm. If the

pasta's not done, test every 15 to 30 seconds thereafter. Total cooking time will depend on how fresh and how thick the pasta is—the drier and thicker it is, the longer it will take.

Take a Chance:

• Omit the carrot juice. Instead, place ¼ cup puréed cooked carrots in a large measuring cup. Add water to make 1 cup of liquid. Mix the ingredients well.

Suggested Sauces:

• Serve hot with Slow-Cooked Spaghetti Sauce With Chicken (page 162), Herbed Butter Sauce (page 166), Creamy Natural Tomato Sauce (page 176), Gingered Chickpeas With Garlic (page 191), or just a dash of lemon juice.

• Serve cold with Aglio e Olio (page 154) or Pesto Sauce (page 159).

Beet Pasta

Beets are used more for color than flavor. The color is a deep garnet color, rather than a tomato red.

Preparation Time: *Varies with the equipment used*
Yield: *1½ Pounds*

4 large eggs

¼ cup cooked, puréed, and strained beets (reserve the cooking water)

3½ cups unbleached white flour

FOR ELECTRIC EXTRUSION MACHINES:

1. Place the eggs in a large measuring cup, and beat lightly. Add enough reserved cooking water to make 1 cup of liquid.

2. Place the beets and flour in the pasta machine. With the machine running, slowly add the liquid. Process until the dough reaches the consistency specified in the instruction booklet. If the dough is too dry or too wet, add more water or flour per the instruction booklet.

3. Extrude the pasta, following the directions in instruction booklet.

FOR HAND-CRANKED MACHINES:

1. Place the eggs in a large measuring cup, and beat lightly. Add enough reserved cooking water to make 1 cup of liquid.

2. Place the beets and flour in the food processor, and pulse 3 times to mix. With the machine running, slowly add the liquid. Pulse until a ball begins to form, about 10 to 15 seconds.

3. If the dough is too dry when all the liquid has been added, add 1 teaspoon of water, and pulse until a ball begins to form. If the dough is too wet, add 1 tablespoon of flour, and pulse until a ball begins to form. Repeat either process as necessary.

4. Remove the dough from the food processor and place it on a lightly floured pastry board or work surface. Knead the dough, incorporating additional flour into the ball of dough until it becomes smooth and shiny. The dough should be kneaded for 2 minutes.

5. Cover the dough with plastic wrap and let it rest for 5 minutes on the counter, or refrigerate it for up to 2 days.

6. Cut or extrude the dough according to the instructions on pages 25 or 28.

COOKING INSTRUCTIONS:

At this point, you can cook the pasta immediately. However, we recommend drying it for 1 hour beforehand to improve both the taste and the texture. Cook the pasta in 4 to 5 quarts of vigorously boiling water. Add all of the pasta at once, covering the pot until the water returns to a rapid boil. After uncovering the pot, test the pasta for doneness by biting into a piece. It should be tender, yet firm. If the pasta's not done, test every 15 to 30 seconds thereafter. Total cooking time will depend on how fresh and how thick the pasta is—the drier and thicker it is, the longer it will take.

Take a Chance:

• Omit the cooked beets, and use a combination of reserved cooking water and either eggs or water to equal 1 cup liquid.

• Make into any small shape and create a tri-colored hot or cold dish along with egg pasta and Spinach Pasta (page 66).

Suggested Sauces:

• Serve hot with Herbed Butter Sauce (page 166) or Spicy Steamed Vegetable Sauce (page 178).

• Serve cold with Aglio e Olio (page 154) or Confetti Sauce (page 187).

Jalapeño Pepper Pasta

Like tomatoes, jalapeños are technically a fruit. They add a piquant taste to any pasta.

Preparation Time: *Varies with the equipment used*
Yield: *1½ Pounds*

3 large eggs

Water

6 red or green jalapeño peppers, seeded and either finely chopped or puréed

3½ cups unbleached white flour

FOR ELECTRIC EXTRUSION MACHINES:

1. Place the eggs in a large measuring cup, and beat lightly. Add enough water to make 1 cup of liquid.

2. Place the peppers and flour in the pasta machine. With the machine running, slowly add the liquid. Process until the dough reaches the consistency specified in the instruction booklet. If the dough is too dry or too wet, add more water or flour per the instruction booklet.

3. Extrude the pasta, following directions in the instruction booklet.

FOR HAND-CRANKED MACHINES:

1. Place the eggs in a large measuring cup, and beat lightly. Add enough water to make 1 cup of liquid.

2. Place the peppers and flour in the food processor, and pulse 3 times to mix. With the machine running, slowly add the liquid. Pulse until a ball begins to form, about 10 to 15 seconds.

3. If the dough is too dry when all the liquid has been added, add 1 teaspoon of water, and pulse until a ball begins to form. If the dough is too wet, add 1 tablespoon of flour, and pulse until a ball begins to form. Repeat either process as necessary.

4. Remove the dough from the food processor and place it on a lightly floured pastry board or work surface. Knead the dough, incorporating additional flour into the ball of dough until it becomes smooth and shiny. The dough should be kneaded for 2 minutes.

5. Cover the dough with plastic wrap and let it rest for 5 minutes on the counter, or refrigerate it for up to 2 days.

6. Cut or extrude the dough according to instructions on pages 25 or 28.

COOKING INSTRUCTIONS:

At this point, you can cook the pasta immediately. However, we recommend drying it for 1 hour beforehand to improve both the taste and the texture. Cook the pasta in 4 to 5 quarts of vigorously boiling water. Add all of the pasta at once, covering the pot until the water returns to a rapid boil. After uncovering the pot, test the pasta for doneness by biting into a piece. It should be tender, yet firm. If the

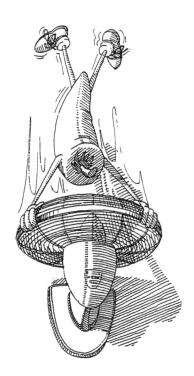

Hot, Hotter, Hottest Peppers

You'll notice that we like to spice things up with various kinds of hot pepper. The number of varieties of these peppers are almost endless. The crushed red pepper specified in a lot of our recipes is prepared commercially. For an even hotter flavor, buy a string of New Mexico peppers, known as a *ristra*. Cut off a pepper and pop it into the blender or food processor. Grind it into small flakes, and use according to the recipe instructions. That will get your tongue wagging!

Some of the other common varieties of chili peppers include:

• **Cayenne.** This is the variety used commercially in ground powder and hot sauces. This long, sharply pointed pod can also be bought fresh to add bite to salads and homemade sauces. On a heat scale of 1 to 10, this variety rates about an 8.

• **Habanero.** This lantern-shaped chili is considered to be the hottest chili around. The pod is about 3 inches long and 1 inch wide, and comes in colors ranging from light green and yellow to orange and bright red. The habenero gets a 10 on our heat scale.

• **Jalapeño.** This is one of the best-known chili peppers. It is most often seen in green or red, but also comes in purple. This variety rates about a 5 on the heat scale.

• **Poblano.** This heart-shaped pepper is from 4 to 6 inches long. It has a very dark green skin. Poblanos are mild, rating a 3 on our scale.

• **Serrano.** This thin, slightly curved pod is from 1 to 4 inches long. It comes in the same colors as the habenero, but is a little lower on the heat scale at about a 7.

• **Thai.** This pepper was developed in Thailand after peppers were brought to that country by traders in the early sixteenth century. These peppers, needle-thin and 2 to 3 inches long, rate about an 8 on the heat scale. If Thai peppers are not available, you can use serranos.

When handling hot peppers of any type, be *very* careful to not touch your eyes, on which pepper juice can have a devastating effect. When working with chili peppers, either use gloves, or give your hands a good washing with soap and water after handling.

For you hot food lovers: Much of the heat in a chili is in the seeds. If you really like it hot, leave the seeds in, unless you're making pasta in an electric extrusion machine.

pasta's not done, test every 15 to 30 seconds thereafter. Total cooking time will depend on how fresh and how thick the pasta is—the drier and thicker it is, the longer it will take.

Take a Chance:

• Eliminate the jalapeños and try other chili peppers, such as serranos, poblanos, or habaneros.

Suggested Sauces:

• Serve hot with the following sauces: Magnificent Mushroom (page 163), Italian Cheese Medley (page 169), Herbed Butter (page 166), Spicy Steamed Vegetable (page 178), Creamy Natural Tomato (page 176), Feathery Light Alfredo (page 177), Garden Fresh Primavera (page 180), Wild Mushroom (page 186), Verde (page 190), or Curry With Chicken (page 184).

• Serve warm with Fresh Lemongrass Sauce (page 185).

• Serve cold with Aglio e Olio (page 154), Uncooked Tomato Sauce (page 173), Confetti Sauce (page 187), or Spicy Ginger Sauce (page 189).

Tomato Pasta

Dare to be different—eat your tomatoes in your pasta rather than on it. Because the tomato paste is so thick, the dough may require additional water to reach the correct consistency. Use this pasta in Minestrone Soup (page 201) or Pasta e Fagioli (page 203).

Preparation Time: *Varies with the equipment used*
Yield: *1½ Pounds*

2 large eggs

1 tablespoon olive oil

4 tablespoons tomato paste

Water

3½ cups unbleached white flour

FOR ELECTRIC EXTRUSION MACHINES:

1. Place the eggs in a large measuring cup, and beat lightly. Add the oil and tomato paste, and mix well. Add enough water to make 1 cup of liquid.

2. Place the flour in the pasta machine. With the machine running, slowly add the liquid. Process until the dough reaches the consistency specified in the instruction booklet. If the dough is too dry or too wet, add more water or flour per the instruction booklet.

3. Extrude the pasta, following the directions in instruction booklet.

FOR HAND-CRANKED MACHINES:

1. Place the eggs in a large measuring cup, and beat lightly. Add the oil and tomato paste, and mix well. Add enough water to make 1 cup of liquid.

2. Place the flour in the food processor. With the machine running, slowly add the liquid. Pulse until a ball begins to form, about 10 to 15 seconds.

3. If the dough is too dry when all the liquid has been added, add 1 teaspoon of water, and pulse until a ball begins to form. If the dough is too wet, add 1 tablespoon of flour, and pulse until a ball begins to form. Repeat either process as necessary.

4. Remove the dough from the food processor and place it on a lightly floured pastry board or work surface. Knead the dough, incorporating additional flour into the ball of dough until it becomes smooth and shiny. The dough should be kneaded for 2 minutes.

5. Cover the dough with plastic wrap and let it rest for 5 minutes on the counter, or refrigerate it for up to 2 days.

6. Cut or extrude the dough according to the instructions on pages 25 or 28.

COOKING INSTRUCTIONS:

At this point, you can cook the pasta immediately. However, we recommend drying it for 1 hour beforehand to improve both the taste and the texture. Cook the pasta in 4 to 5 quarts of vigorously boiling water. Add all of the pasta at once, covering the pot until the water returns to a rapid boil. After uncovering the pot, test the pasta for doneness by biting into a piece. It should be tender, yet firm. If the pasta's not done, test every 15 to 30 seconds thereafter. Total cooking time will depend on how fresh and how thick the pasta is—the drier and thicker it is, the longer it will take.

Take a Chance:

• Make into any small shape and create a tri-colored hot or cold dish along with egg pasta and Spinach Pasta (page 66).

Suggested Sauces:

• Serve hot with the following sauces: Aglio e Olio (page 154), Slow-Cooked Spaghetti With Chicken (page 162), Italian Cheese Medley (page 169), Herbed Butter (page 166), Spicy Steamed Vegetable (page 178), Carbonara (page 176), Wild Mushroom (page 186), or Confetti (page 187).

• Serve cold with Pesto Sauce (page 159).

Corn Pasta

Corn meal mixed with the flour gives pasta a slightly crunchy, almost nutty taste. Use this pasta in any of the lasagna recipes (pages 206, 208, and 213) or Classic Cheese Ravioli (page 209).

Preparation Time: *Varies with the equipment used*
Yield: *1½ Pounds*

4 large eggs

1 tablespoon canola oil

Water

2 cups unbleached white flour

1½ cups yellow corn meal

FOR ELECTRIC EXTRUSION MACHINES:

1. Place the eggs in a large measuring cup, and beat lightly. Add the oil, and mix well. Add enough water to make 1 cup of liquid.

2. Place the flour and the corn meal in the pasta machine. With the machine running, slowly add the liquid. Process until the dough reaches the consistency specified in the instruction booklet. If the dough is too dry or too wet, add more water or flour per the instruction booklet.

3. Extrude the pasta, following the directions in instruction booklet.

FOR HAND-CRANKED MACHINES:

1. Place the eggs in a large measuring cup, and beat lightly. Add the oil, and mix well. Add enough water to make 1 cup of liquid.

2. Place the flour and the corn meal in the food processor, and pulse 3 times to mix. With the machine running, slowly add the liquid. Pulse until a ball begins to form, about 10 to 15 seconds.

3. If the dough is too dry when all the liquid has been added, add 1 teaspoon of water, and pulse until a ball begins to form. If the dough is too wet, add 1 tablespoon of flour, and pulse until a ball begins to form. Repeat either process as necessary.

4. Remove the dough from the food processor and place it on a lightly floured pastry board or work surface. Knead the dough, incorporating additional flour into the ball of dough until it becomes smooth and shiny. The dough should be kneaded for 2 minutes.

5. Cover the dough with plastic wrap and let it rest for 5 minutes on the counter, or refrigerate it for up to 2 days.

6. Cut or extrude dough according to instructions on pages 25 or 28.

COOKING INSTRUCTIONS:

At this point, you can cook the pasta immediately. However, we recommend drying it for 1 hour beforehand to improve both the taste and the texture. Cook the pasta in 4 to 5 quarts of vigorously boiling water. Add all of the pasta at once, covering the pot until the water returns to a rapid boil. After uncovering the pot, test the pasta for doneness by biting into a piece. It should be tender, yet firm. If the pasta's not done, test every 15 to 30 seconds thereafter. Total cooking time will depend on how fresh and how thick the pasta is—the drier and thicker it is, the longer it will take.

Take a Chance:

- Omit the yellow corn meal, and use white meal.

Suggested Sauces:

- Serve hot with the following sauces: Aglio e Olio (page 154), Magnificent Mushroom (page 163), Herbed Butter (page 166), Lavender-Scented Roasted Garlic (page 172), Onion Raisin (page 173), Spicy Steamed Vegetable (page 178), Hot Citrus (page 175), Creamy Natural Tomato (page 176), Cilantro Peanut Pesto (page 182), or Verde (page 190).

- Serve warm with Fresh Lemongrass Sauce (page 185).

- Serve cold with the following sauces or dressings: Pesto (page 159), Sinless Summer Cheese (page 168), Uncooked Tomato (page 173), Confetti (page 187), or Green Yogurt (page 188).

Blue Corn Pasta

Preparation Time: *Varies with the equipment used*
Yield: *1½ Pounds*

3 large eggs

1 tablespoon canola oil

Water

2 cups unbleached flour

1½ cups blue corn meal

Not neon blue, but, yes, blue pasta. Blue corn has a distinctive flavor and is very nutritious. Use this pasta in Classic Cheese Ravioli (page 209).

FOR ELECTRIC EXTRUSION MACHINES:

1. Place the eggs in a large measuring cup, and beat lightly. Add the oil, and mix well. Add enough water to make 1 cup of liquid.

2. Place the flour and the corn meal in the pasta machine. With the machine running, slowly add the liquid. Process until the dough reaches the consistency specified in the instruction booklet. If the dough is too dry or too wet, add more water or flour per the instruction booklet.

3. Extrude the pasta, following the directions in instruction booklet.

FOR HAND-CRANKED MACHINES:

1. Place the eggs in a large measuring cup, and beat lightly. Add the oil, and mix well. Add enough water to make 1 cup of liquid.

2. Place the flour and the corn meal in the food processor, and pulse 3 times to mix. With the machine running, slowly add the liquid. Pulse until a ball begins to form, about 10 to 15 seconds.

3. If the dough is too dry when all the liquid has been added, add 1 teaspoon of water, and pulse until a ball begins to form. If the dough is too wet, add 1 tablespoon of flour, and pulse until a ball begins to form. Repeat either process as necessary.

4. Remove the dough from the food processor and place it on a lightly floured pastry board or work surface. Knead the dough, incorporating additional flour into the ball of dough until it becomes smooth and shiny. The dough should be kneaded for 2 minutes.

5. Cover the dough with plastic wrap and let it rest for 5 minutes on the counter, or refrigerate it for up to 2 days.

6. Cut or extrude dough according to the instructions on pages 25 or 28.

COOKING INSTRUCTIONS:

At this point, you can cook the pasta immediately. However, we recommend drying it for 1 hour beforehand to improve both the taste and the texture. Cook the pasta in 4 to 5 quarts of vigorously boiling water. Add all of the pasta at once, covering the pot until the water returns to a rapid boil. After uncovering the pot, test the pasta for doneness by biting into a piece. It should be tender, yet firm. If the pasta's not done, test every 15 to 30 seconds thereafter. Total cooking time will depend on how fresh and how thick the pasta is—the drier and thicker it is, the longer it will take.

Take a Chance:

• Make Jalapeño Blue Corn Pasta by adding 6 red or green finely chopped jalapeño peppers to the flour.

Suggested Sauces:

• Serve hot with the following sauces: Aglio e Olio (page 154), Herbed Butter (page 166), Spicy Steamed Vegetable (page 178), Hot Citrus (page 175), Creamy Natural Tomato (page 176), Cilantro Peanut Pesto (page 182), or Verde (page 190).

• Serve warm with Fresh Lemongrass Sauce (page 185).

• Serve cold with the following sauces or dressings: Pesto (page 159), Sinless Summer Cheese (page 168), Lavender-Scented Roasted Garlic (page 172), Uncooked Tomato (page 173), Confetti (page 187), or Green Yogurt (page 188).

Basil Pasta

Preparation Time: *Varies with the equipment used*
Yield: *1½ Pounds*

4 large eggs

Water

½ cup fresh basil leaves

3½ cups unbleached white flour

Basil is one of the most popular herbs. Its fresh taste is just as good in pasta as it is on top of it. Use this pasta in Minestrone Soup (page 201), any of the lasagna recipes (pages 206, 208, and 213), or Classic Cheese Ravioli (page 209).

FOR ELECTRIC EXTRUSION MACHINES:

1. Place the eggs in a large measuring cup, and beat lightly. Add enough water to make 1 cup of liquid. Set aside.

2. Chop the basil very finely, either by hand or with a food processor. If you use a food processor, you still may have to finish chopping by hand to get pieces that are fine enough to not clog the die.

3. Place the basil and flour in the pasta machine. With the machine running, slowly add the liquid. Process until the dough reaches the consistency specified in the instruction booklet. If the dough is too dry or too wet, add more water or flour per the instruction booklet.

4. Extrude the pasta, following the directions in instruction booklet.

FOR HAND-CRANKED MACHINES:

1. Place the eggs in a large measuring cup, and beat lightly. Add enough water to make 1 cup of liquid. Set aside.

2. Place the basil in a food processor and pulse 3 to 5 times, or until the basil is finely chopped.

3. Add the flour to the food processor, and pulse 3 times to mix. With the machine running, slowly add the liquid. Pulse until a ball begins to form, about 10 to 15 seconds.

4. If the dough is too dry when all the liquid has been added, add 1 teaspoon of water, and pulse until a ball begins to form. If the dough is too wet, add 1 tablespoon of flour, and pulse until a ball begins to form. Repeat either process as necessary.

5. Remove the dough from the food processor and place it on a lightly floured pastry board or work surface. Knead the dough, incorporating additional flour into the ball of dough until it becomes smooth and shiny. The dough should be kneaded for 2 minutes.

6. Cover the dough with plastic wrap and let it rest for 5 minutes on the counter, or refrigerate it for up to 2 days.

7. Cut or extrude the dough according to the instructions on pages 25 or 28.

COOKING INSTRUCTIONS:

At this point, you can cook the pasta immediately. However, we recommend drying it for 1 hour beforehand to improve both the taste and the texture. Cook the pasta in 4 to 5 quarts of vigorously boiling water. Add all of the pasta at once, covering the pot until the water returns to a rapid boil. After uncovering the pot, test the pasta for doneness by biting into a piece. It should be tender, yet firm. If the pasta's not done, test every 15 to 30 seconds thereafter. Total cooking time will depend on how fresh and how thick the pasta is—the drier and thicker it is, the longer it will take.

Take a Chance:

• Omit the basil, and use ½ cup fresh oregano or marjoram leaves.

Suggested Sauces:

• Serve hot with the following sauces: Aglio e Olio (page 154), Chunky Marinara (page 158), Slow-Cooked Spaghetti With Chicken (page 162), Arrabbiata (page 161), Red Clam (page 165), White Clam (page 164), Herbed Butter (page 166), or Wild Mushroom (page 186).

• Serve cold with the following sauces or dressings: Quick Olive (page 156), Sinless Summer Cheese (page 168), Uncooked Tomato (page 173), Spicy Steamed Vegetable (page 178), or Green Yogurt (page 188).

Preserving Basil

Dried basil lacks the punch of its fresh counterpart. Keep fresh basil on hand all year long by packing whole leaves in olive oil. The oil must completely cover the basil, or the basil will mold. Even though the oil solidifies, we prefer to keep our basil in the refrigerator, where it will keep almost forever. Just remember to fill the container with new oil after taking out some basil leaves.

Whole Wheat Basil Pasta

Preparation Time: *Varies with the equipment used*
Yield: *11/2 Pounds*

4 eggs

Water

1/2 cup fresh basil leaves

21/2 cups whole wheat flour

1 cup unbleached white flour

Nutritious and delicious! Like regular basil pasta, you can use this in Minestrone Soup (page 201), any of the lasagna recipes (pages 206, 208, and 213), or Classic Cheese Ravioli (page 209).

FOR ELECTRIC EXTRUSION MACHINES:

1. Place the eggs in a large measuring cup, and beat lightly. Add enough water to make 1 cup of liquid. Set aside.

2. Chop the basil very finely, either by hand or with a food processor. If you use a food processor, you still may have to finish chopping by hand to get pieces that are fine enough to not clog the die.

3. Place the basil and the flours in the pasta machine. With the machine running, slowly add the liquid. Process until the dough reaches the consistency specified in the instruction booklet. If the dough is too dry or too wet, add more water or flour per the instruction booklet.

4. Extrude the pasta, following the directions in instruction booklet.

FOR HAND-CRANKED MACHINES:

1. Place the eggs in a large measuring cup, and beat lightly. Add enough water to make 1 cup of liquid. Set aside.

2. Place the basil in the food processor and pulse 3 to 5 times, or until the basil is finely chopped.

3. Add the flours to the food processor, and pulse 3 times to mix. With the machine running, slowly add the liquid. Pulse until a ball begins to form, about 10 to 15 seconds.

4. If the dough is too dry when all the liquid has been added, add 1 teaspoon of water, and pulse until a ball begins to form. If the dough is too wet, add 1 tablespoon of flour, and pulse until a ball begins to form. Repeat either process as necessary.

5. Remove the dough from the food processor and place it on a lightly floured pastry board or work surface. Knead the dough, incorporating additional flour into the ball of dough until it becomes smooth and shiny. The dough should be kneaded for 2 minutes.

6. Cover the dough with plastic wrap and let it rest for 5 minutes on the counter, or refrigerate it for up to 2 days.

7. Cut or extrude the dough according to the instructions on pages 25 or 28.

COOKING INSTRUCTIONS:

At this point, you can cook the pasta immediately. However, we recommend drying it for 1 hour beforehand to improve both the taste and the texture. Cook the pasta in 4 to 5 quarts of vigorously boiling water. Add all of the pasta at once, covering the pot until the water returns to a rapid boil. After uncovering the pot, test the pasta for doneness by biting into a piece. It should be tender, yet firm. If the pasta's not done, test every 15 to 30 seconds thereafter. Total cooking time will depend on how fresh and how thick the pasta is—the drier and thicker it is, the longer it will take.

Take a Chance:

• Make Whole Wheat Marjoram Pasta by omitting the basil and using ½ cup fresh marjoram leaves.

Suggested Sauces:

• Serve hot with the following sauces: Aglio e Olio (page 154), Chunky Marinara (page 158), Slow-Cooked Spaghetti With Chicken (page 162), Arrabbiata (page 161), Red Clam (page 165), White Clam (page 164), Herbed Butter (page 166), or Wild Mushroom (page 186).

• Serve cold with the following sauces or dressings: Quick Olive (page 156), Sinless Summer Cheese (page 168), Uncooked Tomato (page 173), Spicy Steamed Vegetable (page 178), or Green Yogurt (page 188).

Lemon Basil Pasta

Preparation Time: *Varies with the equipment used*
Yield: *1½ Pounds*

½ cup lemon juice, strained of pulp

½ cup warm water

½ cup fresh basil leaves

3½ cups unbleached white flour

We are very partial to the taste of lemons, and love it paired with basil. Using lemon juice can sometimes make a slightly sticky pasta. Air dry the pasta for at least 1 hour before cooking. Use it in Spinach Lasagna Noodle Soup (page 202).

FOR ELECTRIC EXTRUSION MACHINES:

1. Place the juice and water in a measuring cup, and mix well. Set aside.

2. Chop the basil very finely, either by hand or with a food processor. If you use a food processor, you still may have to finish chopping by hand to get pieces that are fine enough to not clog the die.

3. Place the basil and flour in the pasta machine. With the machine running, slowly add the liquid. Process until the dough reaches the consistency specified in the instruction booklet. If the dough is too dry or too wet, add more water or flour per the instruction booklet.

4. Extrude the pasta, following the directions in instruction booklet.

FOR HAND-CRANKED MACHINES:

1. Place the juice and water in a measuring cup, and mix well. Set aside.

2. Place the basil in the food processor and pulse 3 to 5 times, or until the basil is finely chopped.

3. Add the flour to the food processor, and pulse 3 times to mix. With the machine running, slowly add the liquid. Pulse until a ball begins to form, about 10 to 15 seconds.

4. If the dough is too dry when all the liquid has been added, add 1 teaspoon of water, and pulse until a ball begins to form. If the dough is too wet, add 1 tablespoon of flour, and pulse until a ball begins to form. Repeat either process as necessary.

5. Remove the dough from the food processor and place it on a lightly floured pastry board or work surface. Knead the dough, incorporating additional flour into the ball of dough until it becomes smooth and shiny. The dough should be kneaded for 2 minutes.

6. Cover the dough with plastic wrap and let it rest for 5 minutes on the counter, or refrigerate it for up to 2 days.

Top: Pasta e Fagioli (page 203)
Center: Traditional Lasagna (page 206)
Bottom: Italian Meatballs (page 158)
and Smooth Tomato Marinara Sauce
With Basil (page 160) over spaghetti
with Whole Wheat Breadsticks (page 138)

Top: *Udon Noodles (page 118)*
with Spicy Ginger Sauce (page 189)
Bottom: *Chicken Won Tons (page 146)*

7. Cut or extrude the dough according to the instructions on pages 25 or 28.

COOKING INSTRUCTIONS:

Because this pasta can be very sticky, we recommend drying it for 1 hour before cooking. This will not only improve both the taste and the texture, but will also reduce the tendency of the pasta to clump while cooking. Cook in 4 to 5 quarts of vigorously boiling water. Add all of the pasta at once, covering the pot until the water returns to a rapid boil. After uncovering the pot, test the pasta for doneness by biting into a piece. It should be tender, yet firm. If the pasta's not done, test every 15 to 30 seconds thereafter. Total cooking time will depend on how fresh and how thick the pasta is—the drier and thicker it is, the longer it will take.

Take a Chance:

• Make Lemon Dill Pasta by omitting the basil and using ¼ cup of the feathery leaves cut from fresh dill stalks that are then chopped as specified in the recipe. The taste of dill is very pronounced, which is why the amount used is reduced.

Suggested Sauces:

• Serve hot with the following sauces: Aglio e Olio (page 154), Chunky Marinara (page 158), Slow-Cooked Spaghetti With Chicken (page 162), Arrabbiata (page 161), Red Clam (page 165), White Clam (page 164), Herbed Butter (page 166), or Wild Mushroom (page 186).

• Serve cold with the following sauces or dressings: Quick Olive (page 156), Sinless Summer Cheese (page 168), Uncooked Tomato (page 173), Spicy Steamed Vegetable (page 178), or Green Yogurt (page 188).

Sage Thyme Pasta

Preparation Time: *Varies with the equipment used*
Yield: *1½ Pounds*

4 large eggs

Water

¼ cup fresh sage leaves

¼ cup fresh thyme leaves

3½ cups unbleached white flour

Sage and thyme combine to form a strong, clean taste. You can use this pasta in Versatile Vegetable and Pasta Stew (page 204) or Classic Cheese Ravioli (page 209).

FOR ELECTRIC EXTRUSION MACHINES:

1. Place the eggs in a large measuring cup, and beat lightly. Add enough water to make 1 cup of liquid. Set aside.

2. Chop the sage and thyme very finely, either by hand or with a food processor. If you use a food processor, you still may have to finish chopping by hand to get pieces that are fine enough to not clog the die.

3. Place the herbs and flour in the pasta machine. With the machine running, slowly add the liquid. Process until the dough reaches the consistency specified in the instruction booklet. If the dough is too dry or too wet, add more water or flour per the instruction booklet.

4. Extrude the pasta, following the directions in the instruction booklet.

FOR HAND-CRANKED MACHINES:

1. Place the eggs in a large measuring cup, and beat lightly. Add enough water to make 1 cup of liquid. Set aside.

2. Place the sage and thyme in the food processor and pulse 3 to 5 times, or until the herbs are finely chopped.

3. Add the flour to the food processor, and pulse 3 times to mix. With the machine running, slowly add the liquid. Pulse until a ball begins to form, about 10 to 15 seconds.

4. If the dough is too dry when all the liquid has been added, add 1 teaspoon of water, and pulse until a ball begins to form. If the dough is too wet, add 1 tablespoon of flour, and pulse until a ball begins to form. Repeat either process as necessary.

5. Remove the dough from the food processor and place it on a lightly floured pastry board or work surface. Knead the dough, incorporating additional flour into the ball of dough until it becomes smooth and shiny. The dough should be kneaded for 2 minutes.

6. Cover the dough with plastic wrap and let it rest for 5 minutes on the counter, or refrigerate it for up to 2 days.

7. Cut or extrude dough according to the instructions on pages 25 or 28.

COOKING INSTRUCTIONS:

At this point, you can cook the pasta immediately. However, we recommend drying it for 1 hour beforehand to improve both the taste and the texture. Cook the pasta in 4 to 5 quarts of vigorously boiling water. Add all of the pasta at once, covering the pot until the water returns to a rapid boil. After uncovering the pot, test the pasta for doneness by biting into a piece. It should be tender, yet firm. If the pasta's not done, test every 15 to 30 seconds thereafter. Total cooking time will depend on how fresh and how thick the pasta is—the drier and thicker it is, the longer it will take.

Take a Chance:

• Make Basil Oregano Pasta by omitting the sage and thyme leaves and using ¼ cup each basil and oregano leaves.

Suggested Sauces:

• Serve hot with the following sauces: Chunky Marinara (page 158), Slow-Cooked Spaghetti With Chicken (page 162), Magnificent Mushroom (page 163), Herbed Butter (page 166), Onion Raisin (page 173), Spicy Steamed Vegetable (page 178), Garden Fresh Primavera (page 180), Confetti (page 187), or Greek Tomato (page 183).

• Serve cold with Aglio e Olio (page 154), Uncooked Tomato Sauce (page 173), or Green Yogurt Dressing (page 188).

Parsley Pasta

Preparation Time: *Varies with the equipment used*
Yield: *1½ Pounds*

4 large eggs

Water

1 bunch fresh parsley, leaves only (flat parsley works best for hand-cranked cutting)

3½ cups unbleached white flour

To make the whole-leaf form of this pasta, a hand-cranked cutting machine must be used, or else the dough must be cut by hand (see page 28). If cutting by hand, knead the dough for 20 minutes instead of 2 minutes. In this form, whole herbs are put between two sheets of dough and rolled together. Use a wider cut of noodle, such as fettuccine or lasagna, to see the full effect of the whole leaves of parsley. If you are using an electric extrusion machine, you must chop the parsley finely before processing.

You can use this pasta in Minestrone Soup (page 201), Pasta e Fagioli (page 203), Versatile Vegetable and Pasta Stew (page 204), any of the lasagna recipes (pages 206, 208, and 213), or Classic Cheese Ravioli (page 209).

FOR ELECTRIC EXTRUSION MACHINES:

1. Place the eggs in a large measuring cup, and beat lightly. Add enough water to make 1 cup of liquid. Set aside.

2. Chop the parsley very finely, either by hand or with a food processor. If you use a food processor, you still may have to finish chopping by hand to get pieces that are fine enough to not clog the die.

3. Place the parsley and flour in the pasta machine. With the machine running, slowly add the liquid. Process until the dough reaches the consistency specified in the instruction booklet. If the dough is too dry or too wet, add more water or flour per the instruction booklet.

4. Extrude the pasta, following the directions in instruction booklet.

FOR HAND-CRANKED MACHINES:

1. Place the eggs in a large measuring cup, and beat lightly. Add enough water to make 1 cup of liquid.

2. Place the flour in the food processor. With the machine running, slowly add the liquid. Pulse until a ball begins to form, about 10 to 15 seconds.

3. If the dough is too dry when all the liquid has been added, add 1 teaspoon of water, and pulse until a ball begins to form. If the dough is too wet, add 1 tablespoon of flour, and pulse until a ball begins to form. Repeat either process as necessary.

4. Remove the dough from the food processor and place it on a lightly floured pastry board or work surface. Knead the dough, incorporating additional flour into the ball of dough until it becomes smooth and shiny. The dough should be kneaded for 2 minutes.

5. Cover the dough with plastic wrap and let it rest for 5 minutes on the counter, or refrigerate it for up to 2 days.

6. To cut the dough, follow the instructions for putting the dough through the rollers on page 25. The dough is thin enough when the number 6 is reached on the thickness knob.

7. Lay each ribbon of pasta on work surface, and let it dry for 5 minutes.

8. Firmly press the parsley leaves on one half of the dough, leaving a $\frac{1}{4}$-inch edge around the outside of the dough. Fold the plain half of the dough over the leaves, and press the edges together with your fingers.

9. Do not refold the dough, but run the ribbon through the rollers once again at the number 6 setting. This will help seal the parsley between the sheets of dough.

10. Run the ribbon of dough through the desired cutting attachment. Remove any parsley leaves that pull out of the dough during cutting.

COOKING INSTRUCTIONS:

At this point, you can cook the pasta immediately. However, we recommend drying it for 1 hour beforehand to improve both the taste and the texture. Cook the pasta in 4 to 5 quarts of vigorously boiling water. Add all of the pasta at once, covering the pot until the water returns to a rapid boil. After uncovering the pot, test the pasta for doneness by biting into a piece. It should be tender, yet firm. If the pasta's not done, test every 15 to 30 seconds thereafter. Total cooking time will depend on how fresh and how thick the pasta is—the drier and thicker it is, the longer it will take.

Take a Chance:

• Omit the parsley, and use the fresh herb of your choice.

• Make Whole Wheat Parsley Leaf Pasta by reducing the unbleached white flour to $1\frac{1}{4}$ cups, and adding $2\frac{1}{4}$ cups whole wheat flour.

Suggested Sauces:

• Serve hot with the following sauces: Chunky Marinara (page 158), Slow-Cooked Spaghetti With Chicken (page 162), Magnificent Mushroom (page 163), Italian Cheese Medley (page 169), Herbed Butter (page 166), Amatriciana (page 174), Carbonara (page 176), Bolognese-Style (page 179), Creamy Natural Tomato (page 176), Feathery Light Alfredo (page 177), or Confetti (page 187).

• Serve cold with Aglio e Olio (page 154), Quick Olive Sauce (page 156), Sinless Summer Cheese Sauce (page 168), or Spicy Steamed Vegetable Sauce (page 178).

Buckwheat Pasta With Cilantro

Preparation Time: *Varies with the equipment used*
Yield: *1½ Pounds*

4 large eggs

Water

1 bunch fresh cilantro, leaves only

2¼ cups buckwheat flour

1¼ cups unbleached white flour

Both the buckwheat and cilantro have distinct tastes that combine surprisingly well. To make the whole-leaf form of this pasta, a hand-cranked cutting machine must be used, or else the dough must be cut by hand (see page 28). If cutting by hand, knead the dough for 20 minutes, instead of the 2 minutes required by the machine. In this form, whole herbs are put between two sheets of dough and rolled together. Use a wider cut of noodle, such as fettuccine or lasagna, to see the full effect of the whole leaves of cilantro. If you are using an electric extrusion machine, you must chop the cilantro finely before processing.

You can use this pasta in Spinach Lasagna Noodle Soup (page 202).

FOR ELECTRIC EXTRUSION MACHINES:

1. Place the eggs in a large measuring cup, and beat lightly. Add enough water to make 1 cup of liquid. Set aside.

2. Chop the cilantro very finely, either by hand or with a food processor. If you use a food processor, you still may have to finish chopping by hand to get pieces that are fine enough to not clog the die.

3. Place the cilantro and the flours in the pasta machine. With the machine running, slowly add the liquid. Process until the dough reaches the consistency specified in the instruction booklet. If the dough is too dry or too wet, add more water or flour per the instruction booklet.

4. Extrude the pasta, following the directions in instruction booklet.

FOR HAND-CRANKED MACHINES:

1. Place the eggs in a large measuring cup, and beat lightly. Add enough water to make 1 cup of liquid.

2. Place the flours in the food processor, and pulse 3 times to mix. With the machine running, slowly add the liquid. Pulse until a ball begins to form, about 10 to 15 seconds.

3. If the dough is too dry when all the liquid has been added, add 1 teaspoon of water, and pulse until a ball begins to form. If the dough is too wet, add 1 tablespoon of flour, and pulse until a ball begins to form. Repeat either process as necessary.

4. Remove the dough from the food processor and place it on a lightly floured pastry board or work surface. Knead the dough, incorporating additional flour into the ball of dough until it becomes smooth and shiny. The dough should be kneaded for 2 minutes.

5. Cover the dough with plastic wrap and let it rest for 5 minutes on the counter, or refrigerate it for up to 2 days.

6. To cut the dough, follow the instructions for putting the dough through the rollers on page 25. The dough is thin enough when the number 6 is reached on the thickness knob.

7. Lay each ribbon of pasta on the work surface, and let it dry for 5 minutes.

8. Firmly press the cilantro leaves on one half of the dough, leaving a ¼-inch edge around the outside of the dough. Fold the plain half of the dough over the leaves, and press the edges together with your fingers.

9. Do not refold the dough, but run the ribbon through the rollers once again at the number 6 setting. This will help seal the cilantro between the sheets of dough.

10. Run the ribbon of dough through the desired cutting attachment. Remove any cilantro leaves that pull out of the dough during cutting.

COOKING INSTRUCTIONS:

At this point, you can cook the pasta immediately. However, we recommend drying it for 1 hour beforehand to improve both the taste and the texture. Cook the pasta in 4 to 5 quarts of vigorously boiling water. Add all of the pasta at once, covering the pot until the water returns to a rapid boil. After uncovering the pot, test the pasta for doneness by biting into a piece. It should be tender, yet firm. If the pasta's not done, test every 15 to 30 seconds thereafter. Total cooking time will depend on how fresh and how thick the pasta is—the drier and thicker it is, the longer it will take.

Take a Chance:

• Make Whole Wheat Cilantro Pasta by omitting the buckwheat flour and using whole wheat flour.

Suggested Sauces:

• Serve hot with the following sauces: Chunky Marinara (page 158), Slow-Cooked Spaghetti With Chicken (page 162), Magnificent Mushroom (page 163), Italian Cheese Medley (page 169), Herbed Butter (page 166), Amatriciana (page 174), Bolognese-Style (page 179), Creamy Natural Tomato (page 176), Feathery Light Alfredo (page 177), or Confetti (page 187).

• Serve cold with Aglio e Olio (page 154), Quick Olive Sauce (page 156), Sinless Summer Cheese Sauce (page 168), or Spicy Steamed Vegetable Sauce (page 178).

Spinach Basil Pasta

Preparation Time: *Varies with the equipment used*
Yield: *1¹/₂ Pounds*

2 large eggs

Water

¹/₄ cup fresh basil leaves

¹/₄ cup steamed and finely chopped fresh spinach

3¹/₂ cups unbleached white flour

This wonderfully green pasta is a great alternative to plain Spinach Pasta. Use it in Baked Ziti (page 205).

FOR ELECTRIC EXTRUSION MACHINES:

1. Place the eggs in a large measuring cup, and beat lightly. Add enough water to make 1 cup of liquid. Set aside.

2. Chop the basil very finely, either by hand or with a food processor. If you use a food processor, you still may have to finish chopping by hand to get pieces that are fine enough to not clog the die.

3. Place the spinach, basil, and flour in the pasta machine. With the machine running, slowly add the liquid. Process until the dough reaches the consistency specified in the instruction booklet. If the dough is too dry or too wet, add more water or flour per the instruction booklet.

4. Extrude the pasta, following the directions in instruction booklet.

FOR HAND-CRANKED MACHINES:

1. Place the eggs in a large measuring cup, and beat lightly. Add enough water to make 1 cup of liquid. Set aside.

2. Place the basil in the food processor and pulse 3 to 5 times, or until the basil is finely chopped.

3. Add the spinach and flour to the food processor, and pulse 3 times to mix. With the machine running, slowly add the liquid. Pulse until a ball begins to form, about 10 to 15 seconds.

4. If the dough is too dry when all the liquid has been added, add 1 teaspoon of water, and pulse until a ball begins to form. If the dough is too wet, add 1 tablespoon of flour, and pulse until a ball begins to form. Repeat either process as necessary.

5. Remove the dough from the food processor and place it on a lightly floured pastry board or work surface. Knead the dough, incorporating additional flour into the ball of dough until it becomes smooth and shiny. The dough should be kneaded for 2 minutes.

6. Cover the dough with plastic wrap and let it rest for 5 minutes on the counter, or refrigerate it for up to 2 days.

7. Cut or extrude the dough according to the instructions on pages 25 or 28.

COOKING INSTRUCTIONS:

At this point, you can cook the pasta immediately. However, we recommend drying it for 1 hour beforehand to improve both the taste and the texture. Cook the pasta in 4 to 5 quarts of vigorously boiling water. Add all of the pasta at once, covering the pot until the water returns to a rapid boil. After uncovering the pot, test the pasta for doneness by biting into a piece. It should be tender, yet firm. If the pasta's not done, test every 15 to 30 seconds thereafter. Total cooking time will depend on how fresh and how thick the pasta is—the drier and thicker it is, the longer it will take.

Take a Chance:

• Omit the chopped spinach. Add enough of the water the spinach has been cooked in to equal 1 cup of liquid when added to the eggs.

• Omit the basil and add ¼ teaspoon cinnamon.

Suggested Sauces:

• Serve hot with the following sauces: Sautéed Garlic and Bread Crumbs (page 155), Chunky Marinara (page 158), Slow-Cooked Spaghetti With Chicken (page 162), Arrabbiata (page 161), or Magnificent Mushroom (page 163).

• Serve cold with Aglio e Olio (page 154), Pesto Sauce (page 159), Sinless Summer Cheese Sauce (page 168), or Green Yogurt Dressing (page 188).

Tomato Oregano Pasta

Preparation Time: *Varies with the equipment used*
Yield: *1½ Pounds*

2 large eggs

1 tablespoon olive oil

4 tablespoons tomato paste

Water

½ cup fresh oregano leaves

3½ cups unbleached white flour

This pasta is an Italian-food lover's delight. The thickness of the tomato paste may require additional liquid in order to get dough of the proper consistency. Use this pasta in Pasta e Fagioli (page 203) or Baked Ziti (page 205).

FOR ELECTRIC EXTRUSION MACHINES:

1. Place the eggs in a large measuring cup, and beat lightly. Add the oil and tomato paste, and mix well. Add enough water to make 1 cup of liquid. Set aside.

2. Chop the oregano very finely, either by hand or with a food processor. If you use a food processor, you still may have to finish chopping by hand in order to get pieces that are fine enough to not clog the die.

3. Place the oregano and flour in the pasta machine. With the machine running, slowly add the liquid. Process until the dough reaches the consistency specified in the instruction booklet. If the dough is too dry or too wet, add more water or flour per the instruction booklet.

4. Extrude the pasta, following the directions in instruction booklet.

FOR HAND-CRANKED MACHINES:

1. Place the eggs in a large measuring cup, and beat lightly. Add the oil and tomato paste, and mix well. Add enough water to make 1 cup of liquid. Set aside.

2. Place the oregano in the food processor and pulse 3 to 5 times, or until the oregano is finely chopped.

3. Add the flour to the food processor, and pulse 3 times to mix. With the machine running, slowly add the liquid. Pulse until a ball begins to form, about 10 to 15 seconds.

4. If the dough is too dry when all the liquid has been added, add 1 teaspoon of water, and pulse until a ball begins to form. If the dough is too wet, add 1 tablespoon of flour, and pulse until a ball begins to form. Repeat either process as necessary.

5. Remove the dough from the food processor and place it on a lightly floured pastry board or work surface. Knead the dough, incorporating additional flour into the ball of dough until it becomes smooth and shiny. The dough should be kneaded for 2 minutes.

6. Cover the dough with plastic wrap and let it rest for 5 minutes on the counter, or refrigerate it for up to 2 days.

7. Cut or extrude the dough according to the instructions on pages 25 or 28.

COOKING INSTRUCTIONS:

At this point, you can cook the pasta immediately. However, we recommend drying it for 1 hour beforehand to improve both the taste and the texture. Cook the pasta in 4 to 5 quarts of vigorously boiling water. Add all of the pasta at once, covering the pot until the water returns to a rapid boil. After uncovering the pot, test the pasta for doneness by biting into a piece. It should be tender, yet firm. If the pasta's not done, test every 15 to 30 seconds thereafter. Total cooking time will depend on how fresh and how thick the pasta is—the drier and thicker it is, the longer it will take.

Take a Chance:

• Use ½ cup basil leaves or ¼ cup of the feathery leaves cut from fresh dill stalks instead of the oregano.

Suggested Sauces:

• Serve hot with the following sauces: Aglio e Olio (page 154), Quick Olive (page 156), Slow-Cooked Spaghetti With Chicken (page 162), Italian Cheese Medley (page 169), Feathery Light Alfredo (page 177), Garden Fresh Primavera (page 180), or Wild Mushroom (page 186).

• Serve cold with Pesto Sauce (page 159), Spicy Steamed Vegetable Sauce (page 178), or Green Yogurt Dressing (page 188).

Carrot Dill Pasta

Preparation Time: *Varies with the equipment used*
Yield: *1½ Pounds*

½ cup fresh carrot juice

½ cup water

¼ cup feathery leaves cut from fresh dill stalks

3½ cups unbleached white flour

The strong tastes of carrot and dill complement each other well, and make for a hearty pasta.

FOR ELECTRIC EXTRUSION MACHINES:

1. Place the juice and water in a measuring cup, and mix well. Set aside.

2. Chop the dill very finely, either by hand or with a food processor. If you use a food processor, you still may have to finish chopping by hand to get pieces that are fine enough to not clog the die.

3. Place the dill and flour in the pasta machine. With the machine running, slowly add the liquid. Process until the dough reaches the consistency specified in the instruction booklet. If the dough is too dry or too wet, add more water or flour per the instruction booklet.

4. Extrude the pasta, following the directions in instruction booklet.

FOR HAND-CRANKED MACHINES:

1. Place the juice and water in a measuring cup, and mix well. Set aside.

2. Place the dill in the food processor and pulse 3 to 5 times, or until the dill is finely chopped.

3. Add the flour to the food processor, and pulse 3 times to mix. With the machine running, slowly add the liquid. Pulse until a ball begins to form, about 10 to 15 seconds.

4. If the dough is too dry when all the liquid has been added, add 1 teaspoon of water, and pulse until a ball begins to form. If the dough is too wet, add 1 tablespoon of flour, and pulse until a ball begins to form. Repeat either process as necessary.

5. Remove the dough from the food processor and place it on a lightly floured pastry board or work surface. Knead the dough, incorporating additional flour into the ball of dough until it becomes smooth and shiny. The dough should be kneaded for 2 minutes.

6. Cover the dough with plastic wrap and let it rest for 5 minutes on the counter, or refrigerate it for up to 2 days.

7. Cut or extrude the dough according to the instructions on pages 25 or 28.

COOKING INSTRUCTIONS:

At this point, you can cook the pasta immediately. However, we recommend drying it for 1 hour beforehand to improve both the taste and the texture. Cook the pasta in 4 to 5 quarts of vigorously boiling water. Add all of the pasta at once, covering the pot until the water returns to a rapid boil. After uncovering the pot, test the pasta for doneness by biting into a piece. It should be tender, yet firm. If the pasta's not done, test every 15 to 30 seconds thereafter. Total cooking time will depend on how fresh and how thick the pasta is—the drier and thicker it is, the longer it will take.

Take a Chance:

• Decrease the unbleached white flour to 2 cups, and add 1½ cups whole wheat flour.

Suggested Sauces:

• Serve hot with the following sauces: Herbed Butter (page 166), Bolognese-Style (page 179), Garden Fresh Primavera (page 180), or Gingered Chickpeas With Garlic (page 191).

• Serve cold with Aglio e Olio (page 154), Sinless Summer Cheese Sauce (page 168), or Spicy Steamed Vegetable Sauce (page 178).

7

Flavors-You-Never-Thought-Of Pastas

There is nothing like an exotic spice to spark thoughts of romantic, faraway places. Spices also do a fine job of perking up a meal. The pastas in this chapter prove it! Remember, the fresher the spice, the cleaner and stronger the taste. So, don't use that dusty old tin of spice that you last used who knows when. If you haven't used it recently, discard it and buy fresh spice.

This chapter also contains directions for two Japanese noodles, udon and soba. Udon is made with whole wheat flour, while soba is made with buckwheat flour. Traditionally, they are both formed into what look like fat spaghetti, but if you're like us, you'll feel free to form them into whatever thick shape pleases your fancy (and can be produced by your machine).

Curry Pasta

Preparation Time: *Varies with the equipment used*
Yield: *1½ Pounds*

¼ teaspoon ground coriander

¼ teaspoon ground turmeric

⅛ teaspoon ground cumin

⅛ teaspoon cayenne pepper

⅛ teaspoon dry mustard

⅛ teaspoon freshly ground black pepper

4 large eggs

Water

3½ cups unbleached white flour

Commercial curry powder can be used, but we prefer to mix our own. Curry powder loses its taste when stored, so always mix it fresh.

FOR ELECTRIC EXTRUSION MACHINES:

1. Place all the spices in a small bowl, and mix. Set aside.

2. Place the eggs in a large measuring cup, and beat lightly. Add enough water to make 1 cup of liquid.

3. Place the spices and the flour in the pasta machine. With the machine running, slowly add the liquid. Process until the dough reaches the consistency specified in the instruction booklet. If the dough is too dry or too wet, add more water or flour per the instruction booklet.

4. Extrude the pasta, following the directions in instruction booklet.

FOR HAND-CRANKED MACHINES:

1. Place all the spices in a small bowl, and mix. Set aside.

2. Place the eggs in a large measuring cup, and beat lightly. Add enough water to make 1 cup of liquid.

3. Place the spices and the flour in the food processor, and pulse 3 times to mix. With the machine running, slowly add the liquid. Pulse until a ball begins to form, about 10 to 15 seconds.

4. If the dough is too dry when all the liquid has been added, add 1 teaspoon of water, and pulse until a ball begins to form. If the dough is too wet, add 1 tablespoon of flour, and pulse until a ball begins to form. Repeat either process as necessary.

5. Remove the dough from the food processor and place it on a lightly floured pastry board or work surface. Knead the dough, incorporating additional flour into the ball of dough until it becomes smooth and shiny. The dough should be kneaded for 2 minutes.

6. Cover the dough with plastic wrap and let it rest for 5 minutes on the counter, or refrigerate it for up to 2 days.

7. Cut or extrude the dough according to the instructions on pages 25 or 28.

COOKING INSTRUCTIONS:

At this point, you can cook the pasta immediately. However, we recommend drying it for 1 hour beforehand to improve both the taste and the texture. Cook the pasta in 4 to 5 quarts of vigorously boiling water. Add all of the pasta at once, covering the pot until the water returns to a rapid boil. After uncovering the pot, test the pasta for doneness by biting into a piece. It should be tender, yet firm. If the pasta's not done, test every 15 to 30 seconds thereafter. Total cooking time will depend on how fresh and how thick the pasta is—the drier and thicker it is, the longer it will take.

Take a Chance:

• Add ¼ teaspoon grated fresh ginger to the spices.

• Use different amounts and combinations of spices to satisfy your taste.

• Omit the first 6 ingredients, and use 1 teaspoon commercially prepared curry powder.

Suggested Sauces:

• Serve hot with the following sauces: Herbed Butter (page 166), Onion Raisin (page 173), Wild Mushroom (page 186), Spicy Ginger (page 189), or Gingered Chickpeas With Garlic (page 191).

• Serve cold with Aglio e Olio (page 154), Spicy Steamed Vegetable Sauce (page 178), or Green Yogurt Dressing (page 188).

Saffron Pasta

Preparation Time: *Varies with the equipment used*
Yield: *1½ Pounds*

4 large eggs

Water

½ teaspoon ground saffron

3½ cups unbleached white flour

Saffron, a spice harvested from the tip of a crocus flower, turns pasta a bright yellow-orange color and gives it a distinctive taste.

FOR ELECTRIC EXTRUSION MACHINES:

1. Place the eggs in a large measuring cup, and beat lightly. Add enough water to make 1 cup of liquid.

2. Place the saffron and flour in the pasta machine. With the machine running, slowly add the liquid. Process until the dough reaches the consistency specified in the instruction booklet. If the dough is too dry or too wet, add more water or flour per the instruction booklet.

3. Extrude the pasta, following the directions in instruction booklet.

FOR HAND-CRANKED MACHINES:

1. Place the eggs in a large measuring cup, and beat lightly. Add enough water to make 1 cup of liquid.

2. Place the saffron and flour in the food processor, and pulse 3 times to mix. With the machine running, slowly add the liquid. Pulse until a ball begins to form, about 10 to 15 seconds.

3. If the dough is too dry when all the liquid has been added, add 1 teaspoon of water, and pulse until a ball begins to form. If the dough is too wet, add 1 tablespoon of flour, and pulse until a ball begins to form. Repeat either process as necessary.

4. Remove the dough from the food processor and place it on a lightly floured pastry board or work surface. Knead the dough, incorporating additional flour into the ball of dough until it becomes smooth and shiny. The dough should be kneaded for 2 minutes.

5. Cover the dough with plastic wrap and let it rest for 5 minutes on the counter, or refrigerate it for up to 2 days.

6. Cut or extrude the dough according to the instructions on pages 25 or 28.

COOKING INSTRUCTIONS:

At this point, you can cook the pasta immediately. However, we recommend drying it for 1 hour beforehand to improve both the taste and the texture. Cook the pasta in 4 to 5 quarts of vigorously boiling water. Add all of the pasta at once, covering the pot until the water returns to a rapid boil. After uncovering the pot, test the pasta for doneness by biting into a piece. It should be tender, yet firm. If the pasta's not done, test every 15 to 30 seconds thereafter. Total cooking time will depend on how fresh and how thick the pasta is—the drier and thicker it is, the longer it will take.

Take a Chance:

• Decrease the unbleached white flour to 2 cups, and add 1½ cups whole wheat flour.

Suggested Sauces:

• Serve hot with the following sauces: Magnificent Mushroom (page 163), Herbed Butter (page 166), Spicy Steamed Vegetable (page 178), Amatriciana (page 174), Bolognese-Style (page 179), Confetti (page 187), or Verde (page 190).

• Serve cold with Sinless Summer Cheese Sauce (page 168), Uncooked Tomato Sauce (page 173), or Green Yogurt Dressing (page 188).

Sweet Paprika Pasta

Although the word "paprika" is practically synonymous with Hungary, the spice paprika was not invented until chili peppers had been brought back to Europe from the New World.

Preparation Time: *Varies with the equipment used*
Yield: *1½ Pounds*

4 large eggs

Water

2 teaspoons sweet paprika

3½ cups unbleached white flour

FOR ELECTRIC EXTRUSION MACHINES:

1. Place the eggs in a large measuring cup, and beat lightly. Add enough water to make 1 cup of liquid.

2. Place the paprika and flour in the pasta machine. With the machine running, slowly add the liquid. Process until the dough reaches the consistency specified in the instruction booklet. If the dough is too dry or too wet, add more water or flour per the instruction booklet.

3. Extrude the pasta, following the directions in the instruction booklet.

FOR HAND-CRANKED MACHINES:

1. Place the eggs in a large measuring cup, and beat lightly. Add enough water to make 1 cup of liquid.

2. Place the paprika and flour in the food processor, and pulse 3 times to mix. With the machine running, slowly add the liquid. Pulse until a ball begins to form, about 10 to 15 seconds.

3. If the dough is too dry when all the liquid has been added, add 1 teaspoon of water, and pulse until a ball begins to form. If the dough is too wet, add 1 tablespoon of flour, and pulse until a ball begins to form. Repeat either process as necessary.

4. Remove the dough from the food processor and place it on a lightly floured pastry board or work surface. Knead the dough, incorporating additional flour into the ball of dough until it becomes smooth and shiny. The dough should be kneaded for 2 minutes.

5. Cover the dough with plastic wrap and let it rest for 5 minutes on the counter, or refrigerate it for up to 2 days.

6. Cut or extrude dough according to instructions on pages 25 or 28.

COOKING INSTRUCTIONS:

At this point, you can cook the pasta immediately. However, we recommend drying it for 1 hour beforehand to improve both the taste and the texture. Cook the pasta in 4 to 5 quarts of vigorously boiling water. Add all of the pasta at once, covering the pot until the water returns to a rapid boil. After uncovering the pot, test the pasta for doneness by biting into a piece. It should be tender, yet firm. If the pasta's not done, test every 15 to 30 seconds thereafter. Total cooking time will depend on how fresh and how thick the pasta is—the drier and thicker it is, the longer it will take.

Take a Chance:

• Experiment with different types of paprika (available in gourmet shops).

Suggested Sauces:

• Serve hot with the following sauces: Smooth Tomato Marinara With Basil (page 160), Slow-Cooked Spaghetti With Chicken (page 162), Pescatore (page 167), Italian Cheese Medley (page 169), Herbed Butter (page 166), Onion Raisin (page 173), Hot Citrus (page 175), Bolognese-Style (page 179), Creamy Natural Tomato (page 176), Feathery Light Alfredo (page 177), or Garden Fresh Primavera (page 180).

• Serve warm with Fresh Lemongrass Sauce (page 185).

• Serve cold with Aglio e Olio (page 154), Sinless Summer Cheese Sauce (page 168), Spicy Ginger Sauce (page 189), or Cilantro Peanut Pesto (page 182).

Whole Wheat Lemon Pepper Pasta

There is something very satisfying about whole wheat and lemon. Add some spicy pepper, and you have a winning combination. Because of the lemon juice's stickiness and the whole wheat flour's high absorption rate, it may take more liquid than usual to get dough of the correct consistency. Use this pasta in Versatile Vegetable and Pasta Stew (page 204).

FOR ELECTRIC EXTRUSION MACHINES:

1. Place the juice and water in a large measuring cup, and mix well.

2. Place the pepper and the flours in the pasta machine. With the machine running, slowly add the liquid. Process until the dough reaches the consistency specified in the instruction booklet. If the dough is too dry or too wet, add more water or flour per the instruction booklet.

3. Extrude the pasta, following the directions in instruction booklet.

FOR HAND-CRANKED MACHINES:

1. Place the juice and water in a large measuring cup, and mix well.

2. Place the pepper and the flours in the food processor, and pulse 3 times to mix. With the machine running, slowly add the liquid. Pulse until a ball begins to form, about 10 to 15 seconds.

3. If the dough is too dry when all the liquid has been added, add 1 teaspoon of water, and pulse until a ball begins to form. If the dough is too wet, add 1 tablespoon of flour, and pulse until a ball begins to form. Repeat either process as necessary.

4. Remove the dough from the food processor and place it on a lightly floured pastry board or work surface. Knead the dough, incorporating additional flour into the ball of dough until it becomes smooth and shiny. The dough should be kneaded for 2 minutes.

5. Cover the dough with plastic wrap and let it rest for 5 minutes on the counter, or refrigerate it for up to 2 days.

6. Cut or extrude the dough according to the instructions on pages 25 or 28.

Preparation Time: *Varies with the equipment used*
Yield: *1 1/2 Pounds*

1/2 cup lemon juice, strained of pulp

1/2 cup water

2 teaspoons freshly ground black pepper

2 1/4 cups whole wheat flour

1 1/4 cups unbleached white flour

COOKING INSTRUCTIONS:

Because this pasta can be very sticky, we recommend drying it for 1 hour before cooking. This will not only improve both the taste and the texture, but will also reduce the tendency of the pasta to clump while cooking. Cook in 4 to 5 quarts of vigorously boiling water. Add all of the pasta at once, covering the pot until the water returns to a rapid boil. After uncovering the pot, test the pasta for doneness by biting into a piece. It should be tender, yet firm. If the pasta's not done, test every 15 to 30 seconds thereafter. Total cooking time will depend on how fresh and how thick the pasta is—the drier and thicker it is, the longer it will take.

Take a Chance:

• Make Whole Wheat Lemon Pasta by omitting the black pepper and making the pasta with 1 cup lemon juice, or a combination of lemon juice and eggs equal to 1 cup.

• Make Whole Wheat Black Pepper Pasta by omitting the lemon juice and making the pasta with 1 cup water, or 4 eggs.

• Use more pepper for a spicier taste.

Suggested Sauces:

• Serve hot with the following sauces: Chunky Marinara (page 158), Smooth Tomato Marinara With Basil (page 160), Slow-Cooked Spaghetti With Chicken (page 162), Puttanesca (page 157), White Clam (page 164), Herbed Butter (page 166), Onion Raisin (page 173), Hot Citrus (page 175), Amatriciana (page 174), Creamy Natural Tomato (page 176), Feathery Light Alfredo (page 177), Garden Fresh Primavera (page 180), Gingered Chickpeas With Garlic (page 191), or Curry With Chicken (page 184).

• Serve hot or cold with Pesto Sauce (page 159).

• Serve cold with Quick Olive Sauce (page 156), Sinless Summer Cheese Sauce (page 168), Lavender-Scented Roasted Garlic Sauce (page 172), or Uncooked Tomato Sauce (page 173).

Chili Powder Pasta

Not all chili powders are created the same. Regular chili powder contains chili pepper, cumin, oregano, salt, and garlic. Texas-style chili powder contains chili pepper, cumin, oregano, black pepper, and garlic. But no matter how you like it, chili powder certainly spices up pasta. Use this pasta in Spinach Lasagna Noodle Soup (page 202) or Versatile Vegetable and Pasta Stew (page 204).

Preparation Time: *Varies with the equipment used*
Yield: *1½ Pounds*

4 large eggs

Water

1 tablespoon chili powder

3½ cups unbleached white flour

FOR ELECTRIC EXTRUSION MACHINES:

1. Place the eggs in a large measuring cup, and beat lightly. Add enough water to make 1 cup of liquid.

2. Place the chili powder and flour in the pasta machine. With the machine running, slowly add the liquid. Process until the dough reaches the consistency specified in the instruction booklet. If the dough is too dry or too wet, add more water or flour per the instruction booklet.

3. Extrude the pasta, following the directions in instruction booklet.

FOR HAND-CRANKED MACHINES:

1. Place the eggs in a large measuring cup, and beat lightly. Add enough water to make 1 cup of liquid.

2. Place the chili powder and flour in the food processor, and pulse 3 times to mix. With the machine running, slowly add the liquid. Pulse until a ball begins to form, about 10 to 15 seconds.

3. If the dough is too dry when all the liquid has been added, add 1 teaspoon of water, and pulse until a ball begins to form. If the dough is too wet, add 1 tablespoon of flour, and pulse until a ball begins to form. Repeat either process as necessary.

4. Remove the dough from the food processor and place it on a lightly floured pastry board or work surface. Knead the dough, incorporating additional flour into the ball of dough until it becomes smooth and shiny. The dough should be kneaded for 2 minutes.

5. Cover the dough with plastic wrap and let it rest for 5 minutes on the counter, or refrigerate it for up to 2 days.

6. Cut or extrude the dough according to the instructions on pages 25 or 28.

COOKING INSTRUCTIONS:

At this point, you can cook the pasta immediately. However, we recommend drying it for 1 hour beforehand to improve both the taste and the texture. Cook the pasta in 4 to 5 quarts of vigorously boiling water. Add all of the pasta at once, covering the pot until the water returns to a rapid boil. After uncovering the pot, test the pasta for doneness by biting into a piece. It should be tender, yet firm. If the pasta's not done, test every 15 to 30 seconds thereafter. Total cooking time will depend on how fresh and how thick the pasta is—the drier and thicker it is, the longer it will take.

Take a Chance:

• Decrease the chili powder to 1½ teaspoons, and add 1½ teaspoons cayenne pepper.

• For a spicier taste, use Mexican chili powder instead of regular chili powder.

Suggested Sauces:

• Serve hot with the following sauces: Smooth Tomato Marinara With Basil (page 160), Slow-Cooked Spaghetti With Chicken (page 162), Pescatore (page 167), Italian Cheese Medley (page 169), Herbed Butter (page 166), Onion Raisin (page 173), Hot Citrus (page 175), Bolognese-Style (page 179), Creamy Natural Tomato (page 176), Feathery Light Alfredo (page 177), or Garden Fresh Primavera (page 180).

• Serve warm with Fresh Lemongrass Sauce (page 185).

• Serve cold with Aglio e Olio (page 154), Sinless Summer Cheese Sauce (page 168), Spicy Ginger Sauce (page 189), or Cilantro Peanut Pesto (page 182).

Left: Pretzels (page 140)
Center: Cottage Cheese Pesto Dip (page 145)
Right: Whole Wheat Pasta Chips (page 142)

Top: Spinach Pasta (page 66)
    with Pesto Sauce (page 159)
Bottom: Saffron Pasta (page 104)
    with Green Yogurt Dressing (page 188)

Red Wine Pasta

This is a unique concept in pasta. Most of the alcohol is lost during the cooking process. Use this pasta in Traditional Lasagna (page 206) or Lasagna Roll-Ups With Chunky Marinara Sauce (page 213).

Preparation Time: *Varies with the equipment used*
Yield: *1½ Pounds*

3½ cups unbleached white flour

1 cup dry red wine

FOR ELECTRIC EXTRUSION MACHINES:

1. Place the flour in the pasta machine. With the machine running, slowly add the wine. Process until the dough reaches the consistency specified in the instruction booklet. If the dough is too dry or too wet, add more wine or flour per the instruction booklet.

2. Extrude the pasta, following the directions in the instruction booklet.

FOR HAND-CRANKED MACHINES:

1. Place the flour in the food processor. With the machine running, slowly add the wine. Pulse until a ball begins to form, about 10 to 15 seconds.

2. If the dough is too dry when all the wine has been added, add 1 teaspoon of wine, and pulse until a ball begins to form. If the dough is too wet, add 1 tablespoon of flour, and pulse until a ball begins to form. Repeat either process as necessary.

3. Remove the dough from the food processor and place it on a lightly floured pastry board or work surface. Knead the dough, incorporating additional flour into the ball of dough until it becomes smooth and shiny. The dough should be kneaded for 2 minutes.

4. Cover the dough with plastic wrap and let it rest for 5 minutes on the counter, or refrigerate it for up to 2 days.

5. Cut or extrude the dough according to the instructions on pages 25 or 28.

COOKING INSTRUCTIONS:

At this point, you can cook the pasta immediately. However, we recommend drying it for 1 hour beforehand to improve both the taste and the texture. Cook the pasta in 4 to 5 quarts of vigorously boiling water. Add all of the pasta at once, covering the pot until the water returns to a rapid boil. After uncovering the pot, test the pasta for doneness by biting into a piece. It should be tender, yet firm. If the pasta's not done, test every 15 to 30 seconds thereafter. Total cooking time will depend on how fresh and how thick the pasta is—the drier and thicker it is, the longer it will take.

Take a Chance:

- Make White Wine Pasta by omitting the red wine and using white wine.

Suggested Sauces:

- Serve hot with the following sauces: Chunky Marinara (page 158), Smooth Tomato Marinara With Basil (page 160), Slow-Cooked Spaghetti With Chicken (page 162), Puttanesca (page 157), Magnificent Mushroom (page 163), Pescatore (page 167), Creamy Natural Tomato (page 176), or Greek Tomato (page 183).

- Serve cold with the following sauces: Pesto (page 159), Lavender-Scented Roasted Garlic (page 172), Spicy Steamed Vegetable (page 178), Truffles (page 182), or Confetti (page 187).

Tomato Chili Pasta

Preparation Time: *Varies with the equipment used*
Yield: *1½ Pounds*

2 large eggs

1 tablespoon olive oil

4 tablespoons tomato paste

Water

2 tablespoons ground chili powder

3½ cups unbleached white flour

This mixture of flavors is a natural for pasta.

FOR ELECTRIC EXTRUSION MACHINES:

1. Place the eggs in a large measuring cup, and beat lightly. Add the oil and tomato paste, and mix well. Add enough water to make 1 cup of liquid.

2. Place the chili powder and flour in the pasta machine. With the machine running, slowly add the liquid. Process until the dough reaches the consistency specified in the instruction booklet. If the dough is too dry or too wet, add more water or flour per the instruction booklet.

3. Extrude the pasta, following the directions in instruction booklet.

FOR HAND-CRANKED MACHINES:

1. Place the eggs in a large measuring cup, and beat lightly. Add the oil and tomato paste, and mix well. Add enough water to make 1 cup of liquid.

2. Place the chili powder and flour in the food processor, and pulse 3 times to mix. With the machine running, slowly add the liquid. Pulse until a ball begins to form, about 10 to 15 seconds.

3. If the dough is too dry when all the liquid has been added, add 1 teaspoon of water, and pulse until a ball begins to form. If the dough is too wet, add 1 tablespoon of flour, and pulse until a ball begins to form. Repeat either process as necessary.

4. Remove the dough from the food processor and place it on a lightly floured pastry board or work surface. Knead the dough, incorporating additional flour into the ball of dough until it becomes smooth and shiny. The dough should be kneaded for 2 minutes.

5. Cover the dough with plastic wrap and let it rest for 5 minutes on the counter, or refrigerate it for up to 2 days.

6. Cut or extrude the dough according to the instructions on pages 25 or 28.

COOKING INSTRUCTIONS:

At this point, you can cook the pasta immediately. However, we recommend drying it for 1 hour beforehand to improve both the taste and the texture. Cook the pasta in 4 to 5 quarts of vigorously boiling water. Add all of the pasta at once, covering the pot until the water returns to a rapid boil. After uncovering the pot, test the pasta for doneness by biting into a piece. It should be tender, yet firm. If the pasta's not done, test every 15 to 30 seconds thereafter. Total cooking time will depend on how fresh and how thick the pasta is—the drier and thicker it is, the longer it will take.

Take a Chance:

• Grind your own chili powder by placing seeded, dried red chili peppers in a blender or food processor, and pulsing until the peppers turn into a fine powder.

• Make into any small shape and create a tri-colored dish along with egg pasta and Spinach Pasta (page 66).

Suggested Sauces:

• Serve hot with the following sauces: Slow-Cooked Spaghetti With Chicken (page 162), Italian Cheese Medley (page 169), Herbed Butter (page 166), Spicy Steamed Vegetable (page 178), Wild Mushroom (page 186), or Confetti (page 187).

• Serve cold with Pesto Sauce (page 159).

Curry Spinach Pasta

Preparation Time: *Varies with the equipment used*
Yield: *1½ Pounds*

¼ teaspoon ground coriander

¼ teaspoon ground turmeric

⅛ teaspoon ground cumin

⅛ teaspoon cayenne pepper

⅛ teaspoon dry mustard

⅛ teaspoon freshly ground black pepper

3 large eggs

¼ cup cooked and finely chopped spinach (reserve cooking water)

3½ cups unbleached white flour

You can use commercially mixed curry powder, but we much prefer to mix our own. It's fresher that way.

FOR ELECTRIC EXTRUSION MACHINES:

1. Place all the spices together in a small bowl, and mix. Set aside.

2. Place the eggs in a large measuring cup, and beat lightly. Add enough reserved cooking water to make 1 cup of liquid.

3. Place the spices, spinach, and flour in the pasta machine. With the machine running, slowly add the liquid. Process until the dough reaches the consistency specified in the instruction booklet. If the dough is too dry or too wet, add more water or flour per the instruction booklet.

4. Extrude the pasta, following the directions in instruction booklet.

FOR HAND-CRANKED MACHINES:

1. Place all the spices together in a small bowl, and mix. Set aside.

2. Place the eggs in a large measuring cup, and beat lightly. Add enough reserved cooking water to make 1 cup of liquid.

3. Place the spices, spinach, and flour in the food processor, and pulse 3 times to mix. With the machine running, slowly add the liquid. Pulse until a ball begins to form, about 10 to 15 seconds.

4. If the dough is too dry when all the liquid has been added, add 1 teaspoon of water, and pulse until a ball begins to form. If the dough is too wet, add 1 tablespoon of flour, and pulse until a ball begins to form. Repeat either process as necessary.

5. Remove the dough from the food processor and place it on a lightly floured pastry board or work surface. Knead the dough, incorporating additional flour into the ball of dough until it becomes smooth and shiny. The dough should be kneaded for 2 minutes.

6. Cover the dough with plastic wrap and let it rest for 5 minutes on the counter, or refrigerate it for up to 2 days.

7. Cut or extrude the dough according to the instructions on pages 25 or 28.

COOKING INSTRUCTIONS:

At this point, you can cook the pasta immediately. However, we recommend drying it for 1 hour beforehand to improve both the taste and the texture. Cook the pasta in 4 to 5 quarts of vigorously boiling water. Add all of the pasta at once, covering the pot until the water returns to a rapid boil. After uncovering the pot, test the pasta for doneness by biting into a piece. It should be tender, yet firm. If the pasta's not done, test every 15 to 30 seconds thereafter. Total cooking time will depend on how fresh and how thick the pasta is—the drier and thicker it is, the longer it will take.

Take a Chance:

- Omit the reserved cooking water, and make the dough with 4 eggs.

- Omit the eggs, and use only the reserved cooking water as the liquid.

- Omit the first 6 ingredients, and use a commercially prepared curry powder.

Suggested Sauces:

- Serve hot with the following sauces: Sautéed Garlic and Bread Crumbs (page 155), Slow-Cooked Spaghetti With Chicken (page 162), Creamy Natural Tomato (page 176), Garden Fresh Primavera (page 180), Wild Mushroom (page 186), or Gingered Chickpeas With Garlic (page 191).

- Serve cold with Pesto Sauce (page 159), Uncooked Tomato Sauce (page 173), or Spicy Ginger Sauce (page 189).

Cheesy Parmesan Noodles

Preparation Time: *Varies with the equipment used*
Yield: *1½ Pounds*

4 large eggs

Water

½ cup finely grated fresh Parmesan cheese

3 cups unbleached white flour

It is much easier to mix cheese with cooked noodles than to mix it into the noodles themselves. Soft cheeses tend to melt and become very sticky in the heat of an electric extrusion machine. The pasta can also become very sticky in the cooking water. However, we were able to create a delicious pasta using Parmesan cheese. Grate the cheese on the smallest holes of the grater. This pasta goes especially well with Spinach Lasagna Noodle Soup (page 202), Minestrone Soup (page 201), Baked Ziti (page 205), or Traditional Lasagna (page 206).

FOR ELECTRIC EXTRUSION MACHINES:

1. Place the eggs in a large measuring cup, and beat lightly. Add enough water to make 1 cup of liquid.

2. Place the cheese and flour in the pasta machine. With the machine running, slowly add the liquid. Process until the dough reaches the consistency specified in the instruction booklet. If the dough is too dry or too wet, add more water or flour per the instruction booklet.

3. Extrude the pasta, following the directions in instruction booklet.

FOR HAND-CRANKED MACHINES:

1. Place the eggs in a large measuring cup, and beat lightly. Add enough water to make 1 cup of liquid.

2. Place the cheese and flour in the food processor, and pulse 3 times to mix. With the machine running, slowly add the liquid. Pulse until a ball begins to form, about 10 to 15 seconds.

3. If the dough is too dry when all the liquid has been added, add 1 teaspoon of water, and pulse until a ball begins to form. If the dough is too wet, add 1 tablespoon of flour, and pulse until a ball begins to form. Repeat either process as necessary.

4. Remove the dough from the food processor and place it on a lightly floured pastry board or work surface. Knead the dough, incorporating additional flour into the ball of dough until it becomes smooth and shiny. The dough should be kneaded for 2 minutes.

5. Cover the dough with plastic wrap and let it rest for 5 minutes on the counter, or refrigerate it for up to 2 days.

6. Cut or extrude the dough according to the instructions on pages 25 or 28.

COOKING INSTRUCTIONS:

At this point, you can cook the pasta immediately. However, we recommend drying it for 1 hour beforehand to improve both the taste and the texture. Cook the pasta in 4 to 5 quarts of vigorously boiling water. Add all of the pasta at once, covering the pot until the water returns to a rapid boil. After uncovering the pot, test the pasta for doneness by biting into a piece. It should be tender, yet firm. If the pasta's not done, test every 15 to 30 seconds thereafter. Total cooking time will depend on how fresh and how thick the pasta is—the drier and thicker it is, the longer it will take.

Take a Chance:

• Make Cheesy Romano Noodles by omitting the Parmesan cheese and using Romano cheese.

Suggested Sauces:

• Serve hot with the following sauces: Aglio e Olio (page 154), Sautéed Garlic and Bread Crumbs (page 155), Chunky Marinara (page 158), Smooth Tomato Marinara With Basil (page 160), Slow-Cooked Spaghetti With Chicken (page 162), Arrabbiata (page 161), Puttanesca (page 157), Magnificent Mushroom (page 163), Herbed Butter (page 166), Italian Cheese Medley (page 169), Onion Raisin (page 173), Hot Citrus (page 175), Amatriciana (page 174), Carbonara (page 176), Creamy Natural Tomato (page 176), Feathery Light Alfredo (page 177), Bolognese-Style (page 179), Garden Fresh Primavera (page 180), Wild Mushroom (page 186), Greek Tomato (page 183), Verde (page 190), Gingered Chickpeas With Garlic (page 191), or Curry With Chicken (page 184).

• Serve warm with Fresh Lemongrass Sauce (page 185).

• Serve hot or cold with the following sauces: Pesto (page 159), Quick Olive (page 156), Lavender-Scented Roasted Garlic (page 172), Spicy Steamed Vegetable (page 178), Truffles (page 182), Confetti (page 187), Spicy Ginger (page 189), or Cilantro Peanut Pesto (page 182).

• Serve cold with Sinless Summer Cheese Sauce (page 168), Uncooked Tomato Sauce (page 173), or Green Yogurt Dressing (page 188).

Udon Noodles

Preparation Time: *Varies with the equipment used*
Yield: *1½ Pounds*

2 large eggs

1 tablespoon canola oil

Water

2½ cups whole wheat flour

1 cup unbleached white flour

Udon noodles are thick whole wheat flour noodles from Japan. Use a thicker spaghetti die, or one for linguine, fettuccine, or lasagna noodles. If you want to turn out shaped udon, try penne, ziti, or rigatoni.

Udon Noodles can be used in Chicken Soup With Noodles (page 202), Minestrone Soup (page 201), or Versatile Vegetable and Pasta Stew (page 204), or added to Vegetable Broth (page 200).

FOR ELECTRIC EXTRUSION MACHINES:

1. Place the eggs in a large measuring cup, and beat lightly. Add the oil, and mix well. Add enough water to make 1 cup of liquid.

2. Place the flours in the pasta machine. With the machine running, slowly add the liquid. Process until the dough reaches the consistency specified in the instruction booklet. If the dough is too dry or too wet, add more water or flour per the instruction booklet.

3. Extrude the pasta, following the directions in instruction booklet.

FOR HAND-CRANKED MACHINES:

1. Place the eggs in a large measuring cup, and beat lightly. Add the oil, and mix well. Add enough water to make 1 cup of liquid.

2. Place the flours in the food processor, and pulse 3 times to mix. With the machine running, slowly add the liquid. Pulse until a ball begins to form, about 10 to 15 seconds.

3. If the dough is too dry when all the liquid has been added, add 1 teaspoon of water, and pulse until a ball begins to form. If the dough is too wet, add 1 tablespoon of flour, and pulse until a ball begins to form. Repeat either process as necessary.

4. Remove the dough from the food processor and place it on a lightly floured pastry board or work surface. Knead the dough, incorporating additional flour into the ball of dough until it becomes smooth and shiny. The dough should be kneaded for 2 minutes.

5. Cover the dough with plastic wrap and let it rest for 5 minutes on the counter, or refrigerate it for up to 2 days.

6. Cut or extrude the dough according to the instructions on pages 25 or 28. If using a roller machine, roll the dough to the number 4 or 5 setting before cutting.

COOKING INSTRUCTIONS:

At this point, you can cook the pasta immediately. However, we recommend drying it for 1 hour beforehand to improve both the taste and the texture. Cook the pasta in 4 to 5 quarts of vigorously boiling water. Add all of the pasta at once, covering the pot until the water returns to a rapid boil. After uncovering the pot, test the pasta for doneness by biting into a piece. It should be tender, yet firm. If the pasta's not done, test every 15 to 30 seconds thereafter. Total cooking time will depend on how fresh and how thick the pasta is—the drier and thicker it is, the longer it will take.

Take a Chance:

• Omit the eggs and oil, and use plain water.

Suggested Sauces:

• Serve hot with the following sauces: Slow-Cooked Spaghetti With Chicken (page 162), Arrabbiata (page 161), Magnificent Mushroom (page 163), Herbed Butter (page 166), Onion Raisin (page 173), Hot Citrus (page 175), Creamy Natural Tomato (page 176), Gingered Chickpeas With Garlic (page 191), or Curry With Chicken (page 184).

• Serve warm with Fresh Lemongrass Sauce (page 185).

• Serve cold with Pesto Sauce (page 159), Uncooked Tomato Sauce (page 173), Spicy Ginger Sauce (page 189), or Cilantro Peanut Pesto (page 182).

Soba Noodles

Preparation Time: *Varies with the equipment used*
Yield: *1¹/2 Pounds*

3 large egg yolks

1 tablespoon canola oil

Water

2¹/2 cups buckwheat flour

1 cup unbleached white flour

This Japanese noodle has a very pronounced buckwheat flavor. The flour ratio is different compared to the buckwheat pasta directions on page 54. Thus, more liquid may need to be added to reach the consistency needed to process the dough. Remember, buckwheat dough tends to thin out quickly. Use a thicker spaghetti die, or one for linguine, fettuccine, or lasagna noodles. If you want to turn out shaped soba, try penne, ziti, or rigatoni.

Like Udon Noodles, Soba Noodles can be used in Chicken Soup With Noodles (page 202), Minestrone Soup (page 201), or Versatile Vegetable and Pasta Stew (page 204), or added to Vegetable Broth (page 200).

FOR ELECTRIC EXTRUSION MACHINES:

1. Place the egg yolks in a large measuring cup, and beat lightly. Add the oil, and mix well. Add enough water to make 1 cup of liquid.

2. Place the flours in the pasta machine. With the machine running, slowly add the liquid. Process until the dough reaches the consistency specified in the instruction booklet. If the dough is too dry or too wet, add more water or flour per the instruction booklet.

3. Extrude the pasta, following the directions in instruction booklet.

FOR HAND-CRANKED MACHINES:

1. Place the egg yolks in a large measuring cup, and beat lightly. Add the oil, and mix well. Add enough water to make 1 cup of liquid.

2. Place the flours in the food processor, and pulse 3 times to mix. With the machine running, slowly add the liquid. Pulse until a ball begins to form, about 10 to 15 seconds.

3. If the dough is too dry when all the liquid has been added, add 1 teaspoon of water, and pulse until a ball begins to form. If the dough is too wet, add 1 tablespoon of flour, and pulse until a ball begins to form. Repeat either process as necessary.

4. Remove the dough from the food processor and place it on a lightly floured pastry board or work surface. Knead the dough, incorporating additional flour into the ball of dough until it becomes smooth and shiny. The dough should be kneaded for 2 minutes.

5. Cover the dough with plastic wrap and let it rest for 5 minutes on the counter, or refrigerate it for up to 2 days.

6. Cut or extrude the dough according to the instructions on pages 25 or 28. If using a roller machine, roll the dough to the number 4 or 5 setting before cutting.

COOKING INSTRUCTIONS:

At this point, you can cook the pasta immediately. However, we recommend drying it for 1 hour beforehand to improve both the taste and the texture. Cook the pasta in 4 to 5 quarts of vigorously boiling water. Add all of the pasta at once, covering the pot until the water returns to a rapid boil. After uncovering the pot, test the pasta for doneness by biting into a piece. It should be tender, yet firm. If the pasta's not done, test every 15 to 30 seconds thereafter. Total cooking time will depend on how fresh and how thick the pasta is—the drier and thicker it is, the longer it will take.

Take a Chance:

• Omit the eggs and oil, and use plain water.

Suggested Sauces:

• Serve hot with the following sauces: Slow-Cooked Spaghetti With Chicken (page 162), Arrabbiata (page 161), Magnificent Mushroom (page 163), Herbed Butter (page 166), Onion Raisin (page 173), Hot Citrus (page 175), Creamy Natural Tomato (page 176), Gingered Chickpeas With Garlic (page 191), or Curry With Chicken (page 184).

• Serve warm with Fresh Lemongrass Sauce (page 185).

• Serve cold with Pesto Sauce (page 159), Uncooked Tomato Sauce (page 175), Spicy Ginger Sauce (page 189), or Cilantro Peanut Pesto (page 182).

8

Fruit and Dessert Pastas

Pasta for dessert—why not? It may seem indulgent, but pasta is the fitting end to a perfect meal. As usual, if you have an extrusion machine, you should adjust the liquid-to-flour ratios according to the instructions in the manual. These pastas can be made into any shape, but work best when cut into linguine, fettuccine, or lasagna noodles. Shapes such as fusilli and shells are also fun.

Fruit pastas are a bit tricky to make. Fruit and fruit juices are very sticky. It is possible to get the dough to extrude or cut correctly, but when the pasta is cooked, it tends to get very sticky. It will still taste good, but it can look less than appetizing. For this reason, we use water with our fruit juices or concentrates as the liquid in several of these directions. This helps reduce the tendency of the pasta to clump while cooking.

Carob Pasta

Preparation Time: *Varies with the equipment used*
Yield: *1¹/₂ Pounds*

2 teaspoons barley malt syrup (see page 194)

2 tablespoons canola oil

Water

¹/₂ cup carob powder

3 cups unbleached white flour

Rich, chocolately carob makes a naturally sweet pasta.

FOR ELECTRIC EXTRUSION MACHINES:

1. Place the malt syrup and oil in a large measuring cup, and mix well. Add enough water to make 1 cup of liquid.

2. Place the carob powder and flour in the pasta machine. With the machine running, slowly add the liquid. Process until the dough reaches the consistency specified in the instruction booklet. If the dough is too dry or too wet, add more water or flour per the instruction booklet.

3. Extrude the pasta, following the directions in instruction booklet.

FOR HAND-CRANKED MACHINES:

1. Place the malt syrup and oil in a large measuring cup, and mix well. Add enough water to make 1 cup of liquid.

2. Place the carob powder and flour in the food processor, and pulse 3 times to mix. With the machine running, slowly add the liquid. Pulse until a ball of dough begins to form, about 10 to 15 seconds.

3. If the dough is too dry when all the liquid has been added, add 1 teaspoon of water, and pulse until a ball begins to form. If the dough is too wet, add 1 tablespoon of flour, and pulse until a ball begins to form. Repeat either process as necessary.

4. Remove the dough from the food processor and place it on a lightly floured pastry board or work surface. Knead the dough, incorporating additional flour into the ball of dough until it becomes smooth and shiny. The dough should be kneaded for 2 minutes.

5. Cover the dough with plastic wrap and let it rest for 5 minutes on the counter, or refrigerate it for up to 2 days.

6. Cut or extrude the dough according to the instructions on pages 25 or 28.

COOKING INSTRUCTIONS:

At this point, you can cook the pasta immediately. However, we recommend drying it for 1 hour beforehand to improve both the taste and the texture. Cook the pasta in 4 to 5 quarts of vigorously boiling water. Add all of the pasta at once, covering the pot until the water returns to a rapid boil. After uncovering the pot, test the pasta for doneness by biting into a piece. It should be tender, yet firm. If the

pasta's not done, test every 15 to 30 seconds thereafter. Total cooking time will depend on how fresh and how thick the pasta is—the drier and thicker it is, the longer it will take.

Take a Chance:

• Omit the carob powder. Add ¼ cup of carob syrup to the oil, and mix well. Add enough water to make 1 cup of liquid.

• Add ½ teaspoon mint flavoring with the liquid.

• Make Carob Chocolate Nests by cutting the dough into fettuccine noodles and piling them into nests (page 47). Heat 2 quarts of canola oil in a deep fryer until the oil just begins to smoke. Put the nests into a wire mesh basket and deep fry for 2 minutes, or until the pasta begins to brown.

Suggested Sauces:

• Serve hot with Tart Cherry Sauce (page 195).

• Serve cold with Sticky Sweet Honey Yogurt Sauce (page 196) or Ricotta Cheese Dessert Topping (page 195).

Cinnamon Pasta

We wondered where to include this pasta, since cinnamon is a spice, but this is definitely a dessert dish. So here it is. Dessert always wins any argument.

Preparation Time: *Varies with the equipment used*
Yield: *1½ Pounds*

4 large eggs

Water

1 tablespoon ground cinnamon

3½ cups unbleached white flour

FOR ELECTRIC EXTRUSION MACHINES:

1. Place the eggs in a large measuring cup, and beat lightly. Add enough water to make 1 cup of liquid.

2. Place the cinnamon and flour in the pasta machine. With the machine running, slowly add the liquid. Process until the dough reaches the consistency specified in the instruction booklet. If the dough is too dry or too wet, add more water or flour per the instruction booklet.

3. Extrude the pasta, following the directions in instruction booklet.

FOR HAND-CRANKED MACHINES:

1. Place the eggs in a large measuring cup, and beat lightly. Add enough water to make 1 cup of liquid.

2. Place the cinnamon and flour in the food processor, and pulse 3 times to mix. With the machine running, slowly add the liquid. Pulse until a ball of dough begins to form, about 10 to 15 seconds.

3. If the dough is too dry when all the liquid has been added, add 1 teaspoon of water, and pulse until a ball begins to form. If the dough is too wet, add 1 tablespoon of flour, and pulse until a ball begins to form. Repeat either process as necessary.

4. Remove the dough from the food processor and place it on a lightly floured pastry board or work surface. Knead the dough, incorporating additional flour into the ball of dough until it becomes smooth and shiny. The dough should be kneaded for 2 minutes.

5. Cover the dough with plastic wrap and let it rest for 5 minutes on the counter, or refrigerate it for up to 2 days.

6. Cut or extrude dough according to instructions on pages 25 or 28.

COOKING INSTRUCTIONS:

At this point, you can cook the pasta immediately. However, we recommend drying it for 1 hour beforehand to improve both the taste and the texture. Cook the pasta in 4 to 5 quarts of vigorously boiling water. Add all of the pasta at once, covering the pot until the water returns to a rapid boil. After uncovering the pot, test the pasta for doneness by biting into a piece. It should be tender, yet firm. If the pasta's not done, test every 15 to 30 seconds thereafter. Total cooking time will depend on how fresh and how thick the pasta is—the drier and thicker it is, the longer it will take.

Take a Chance:

• Use a cinnamon stick and grate your own cinnamon.

Suggested Sauces:

• Serve hot with Raisin Nut Sauce (page 194).

• Serve warm with Apple Pear Compote (page 198).

• Serve hot or cold with Cinnamon Orange Cranberry Topping (page 197).

• Serve cold with Sticky Sweet Honey Yogurt Sauce (page 196), Ricotta Cheese Dessert Topping (page 195), or Fresh Berry Medley (page 198).

Oatmeal Cookie Pasta

It's not quite oatmeal cookies, but it's very close.

Preparation Time: *Varies with the equipment used*
Yield: *1½ Pounds*

2 large eggs

Water

1 teaspoon ground cinnamon

½ teaspoon ground nutmeg

½ teaspoon ground cloves

2 cups oat flour

1½ cups unbleached white flour

FOR ELECTRIC EXTRUSION MACHINES:

1. Place the eggs in a large measuring cup, and beat lightly. Add enough water to make 1 cup of liquid.

2. Place the spices and flours in the pasta machine. With the machine running, slowly add the liquid. Process until the dough reaches the consistency specified in the instruction booklet. If the dough is too dry or too wet, add more water or flour per the instruction booklet.

3. Extrude the pasta, following the directions in the instruction booklet.

FOR HAND-CRANKED MACHINES:

1. Place the eggs in a large measuring cup, and beat lightly. Add enough water to make 1 cup of liquid.

2. Place the spices and flours in the food processor, and pulse 3 times to mix. With the machine running, slowly add the liquid. Pulse until a ball begins to form, about 10 to 15 seconds.

3. If the dough is too dry when all the liquid has been added, add 1 teaspoon of water, and pulse until a ball begins to form. If the dough is too wet, add 1 tablespoon of flour, and pulse until a ball begins to form. Repeat either process as necessary.

4. Remove the dough from the food processor and place it on a lightly floured pastry board or work surface. Knead the dough, incorporating additional flour into the ball of dough until it becomes smooth and shiny. The dough should be kneaded for 2 minutes.

5. Cover the dough with plastic wrap and let it rest for 5 minutes on the counter, or refrigerate it for up to 2 days.

6. Cut or extrude dough according to instructions on pages 25 or 28.

COOKING INSTRUCTIONS:

At this point, you can cook the pasta immediately. However, we recommend drying it for 1 hour beforehand to improve both the taste and the texture. Cook the pasta in 4 to 5 quarts of vigorously boiling water. Add all of the pasta at once, covering the pot until the water returns to a rapid boil. After uncovering the pot, test the pasta for doneness by biting into a piece. It should be tender, yet firm. If the pasta's not done, test every 15 to 30 seconds thereafter. Total cooking time will depend on how fresh and how thick the pasta is—the drier and thicker it is, the longer it will take.

Take a Chance:

- Reduce the cinnamon to $\frac{1}{2}$ teaspoon, and add $\frac{1}{2}$ teaspoon of ginger.
- Omit the nutmeg and cloves, and increase the cinnamon to $1\frac{1}{2}$ teaspoons.

Suggested Sauces:

- Serve hot with Raisin Nut Sauce (page 194) or Tart Cherry Sauce (page 195).
- Serve warm with Apple Pear Compote (page 198).
- Serve hot or cold with Cinnamon Orange Cranberry Topping (page 197).
- Serve cold with Sticky Sweet Honey Yogurt Sauce (page 196) or Ricotta Cheese Dessert Topping (page 195).

Apple Pie Pasta

Preparation Time: *Varies with the equipment used*
Yield: *1½ Pounds*

$\frac{1}{2}$ cup apple juice concentrate

$\frac{1}{2}$ cup water

1 teaspoon ground cinnamon

1 teaspoon ground nutmeg

$3\frac{1}{2}$ cups unbleached white flour

Everyone thought we had made an apple pie when we were supposed to be creating pasta. They were delighted and surprised, and so were we!

FOR ELECTRIC EXTRUSION MACHINES:

1. Place concentrate and water in a large measuring cup, and mix well.

2. Place the spices and the flour in the pasta machine. With the machine running, slowly add the liquid. Process until the dough reaches the consistency specified in the instruction booklet. If the dough is too dry or too wet, add more water or flour per the instruction booklet.

3. Extrude the pasta, following the directions in instruction booklet.

FOR HAND-CRANKED MACHINES:

1. Place concentrate and water in a large measuring cup, and mix well.

2. Place the spices and the flour in the food processor, and pulse 3 times to mix. With the machine running, slowly add the liquid. Pulse until a ball begins to form, about 10 to 15 seconds.

3. If the dough is too dry when all the liquid has been added, add 1 teaspoon of water, and pulse until a ball begins to form. If the dough is too wet, add 1 tablespoon of flour, and pulse until a ball begins to form. Repeat either process as necessary.

4. Remove the dough from the food processor and place it on a lightly floured pastry board or work surface. Knead the dough, incorporating additional flour into the ball of dough until it becomes smooth and shiny. The dough should be kneaded for 2 minutes.

5. Cover the dough with plastic wrap and let it rest for 5 minutes on the counter, or refrigerate it for up to 2 days.

6. Cut or extrude the dough according to the instructions on pages 25 or 28.

COOKING INSTRUCTIONS:

At this point, you can cook the pasta immediately. However, we recommend drying it for 1 hour beforehand to improve both the taste and the texture. Cook the pasta in 4 to 5 quarts of vigorously boiling water. Add all of the pasta at once, covering the pot until the water returns to a rapid boil. After uncovering the pot, test the pasta for doneness by biting into a piece. It should be tender, yet firm. If the pasta's not done, test every 15 to 30 seconds thereafter. Total cooking time will depend on how fresh and how thick the pasta is—the drier and thicker it is, the longer it will take.

Take a Chance:

• Decrease the unbleached flour to 2 cups, and add 1½ cups finely ground whole wheat flour (also called pastry flour).

Suggested Sauces:

• Make Apple Pie à la Mode by serving this pasta cold topped with ice cream and Sticky Sweet Honey Yogurt Sauce (page 196).

• Serve hot with Raisin Nut Sauce (page 194) or Tart Cherry Sauce (page 195).

• Serve warm with Apple Pear Compote (page 198).

• Serve hot or cold with Cinnamon Orange Cranberry Topping (page 197).

Lemon Pasta

Preparation Time: *Varies with the equipment used*
Yield: *1½ Pounds*

½ cup lemon juice, strained of pulp

½ cup water

1 tablespoon finely grated lemon zest (see page 175)

3½ cups unbleached white flour

Sunny, bright lemon adds just the right note to the end of a meal.

FOR ELECTRIC EXTRUSION MACHINES:

1. Place the juice and water in a large measuring cup, and mix well.

2. Place the zest and flour in the pasta machine. With the machine running, slowly add the liquid. Process until the dough reaches the consistency specified in the instruction booklet. If the dough is too dry or too wet, add more water or flour per the instruction booklet.

3. Extrude the pasta, following the directions in the instruction booklet.

FOR HAND-CRANKED MACHINES:

1. Place the juice and water in a large measuring cup, and mix well.

2. Place the zest and flour in the food processor, and pulse 3 times to mix. With the machine running, slowly add the liquid. Pulse until a ball begins to form, about 10 to 15 seconds.

3. If the dough is too dry when all the liquid has been added, add 1 teaspoon of water, and pulse until a ball begins to form. If the dough is too wet, add 1 tablespoon of flour, and pulse until a ball begins to form. Repeat either process as necessary.

4. Remove the dough from the food processor and place it on a lightly floured pastry board or work surface. Knead the dough, incorporating additional flour into the ball of dough until it becomes smooth and shiny. The dough should be kneaded for 2 minutes.

5. Cover the dough with plastic wrap and let it rest for 5 minutes on the counter, or refrigerate it for up to 2 days.

6. Cut or extrude the dough according to the instructions on pages 25 or 28.

COOKING INSTRUCTIONS:

Because this pasta can be very sticky, we recommend drying it for 1 hour before cooking. This will not only improve both the taste and the texture, but will also reduce the tendency of the pasta to clump while cooking. Cook in 4 to 5 quarts of vigorously boiling water. Add all of the pasta at once, covering the pot until the water returns to a rapid boil. After uncovering the pot, test the pasta for doneness by biting into a piece. It should be tender, yet firm. If the pasta's not done, test every 15 to 30 seconds thereafter. Total cooking time will depend on how fresh and how thick the pasta is—the drier and thicker it is, the longer it will take.

Take a Chance:

• Make Orange Pasta by omitting the lemon juice and zest, and using orange juice and zest.

• Make Citrus Pasta by reducing the lemon juice to ¼ cup, and adding ¼ cup of orange juice. Add 1 tablespoon finely grated orange zest to the food processor with the lemon zest.

• Make Pineapple Pasta by omitting the lemon juice and zest, and using pineapple juice.

Suggested Sauces:

• Serve with any of the dessert sauces or toppings in Chapter 13.

Whole Wheat Almond Pasta

To make this pasta in an extrusion machine, you must grind the almonds very fine, or else they will clog the die. Both the whole wheat and the ground almonds will absorb additional liquid.

Preparation Time: *Varies with the equipment used*
Yield: *1½ Pounds*

2 large eggs

Water

½ cup finely ground almonds

2 cups whole wheat flour

1 cup unbleached white flour

FOR ELECTRIC EXTRUSION MACHINES:

1. Place the eggs in a large measuring cup, and beat lightly. Add enough water to make 1 cup of liquid.

2. Place the almonds and the flours in the pasta machine. With the machine running, slowly add the liquid. Process until the dough reaches the consistency specified in the instruction booklet. If the dough is too dry or too wet, add more water or flour per the instruction booklet.

3. Extrude the pasta, following the directions in instruction booklet.

FOR HAND-CRANKED MACHINES:

1. Place the eggs in a large measuring cup, and beat lightly. Add enough water to make 1 cup of liquid.

2. Place the almonds and the flours in the food processor, and pulse 3 times to mix. With the machine running, slowly add the liquid. Pulse until a ball begins to form, about 10 to 15 seconds.

3. If the dough is too dry when all the liquid has been added, add 1 teaspoon of water, and pulse until a ball begins to form. If the dough is too wet, add 1 tablespoon of flour, and pulse until a ball begins to form. Repeat either process as necessary.

4. Remove the dough from the food processor and place it on a lightly floured pastry board or work surface. Knead the dough, incorporating additional flour into the ball of dough until it becomes smooth and shiny. The dough should be kneaded for 2 minutes.

5. Cover the dough with plastic wrap and let it rest for 5 minutes on the counter, or refrigerate it for up to 2 days.

6. Cut or extrude the dough according to the instructions on pages 25 or 28.

COOKING INSTRUCTIONS:

At this point, you can cook the pasta immediately. However, we recommend drying it for 1 hour beforehand to improve both the taste and the texture. Cook the pasta in 4 to 5 quarts of vigorously boiling water. Add all of the pasta at once, covering the pot until the water returns to a rapid boil. After uncovering the pot, test the pasta for doneness by biting into a piece. It should be tender, yet firm. If the pasta's not done, test every 15 to 30 seconds thereafter. Total cooking time will depend on how fresh and how thick the pasta is—the drier and thicker it is, the longer it will take.

Take a Chance:

• Make Whole Wheat Walnut Pasta by omitting the almonds, and using finely ground walnuts.

Suggested Sauces:

• Serve hot with Raisin Nut Sauce (page 194) or Tart Cherry Sauce (page 195).

• Serve cold with Lucious Lemon Sauce (page 196), Ricotta Cheese Dessert Topping (page 195), or Fresh Berry Medley (page 198).

Strawberry Pasta

Fresh, sweet strawberries never tasted so good.

Preparation Time: *Varies with the equipment used*
Yield: *1½ Pounds*

1 cup trimmed and halved fresh strawberries

Water

3½ cups unbleached white flour

FOR ELECTRIC EXTRUSION MACHINES:

1. Place the strawberries in a small saucepan over medium heat. Simmer for 20 minutes or until the strawberries are very soft, stirring occasionally.

2. Place a fine mesh strainer over a bowl. Pour the strawberries and their juices into the strainer. Using the back of a spoon, press the strawberries into the strainer, removing as much juice as possible from the fruit without crushing the berries through the strainer. The fruit pulp can be saved for another use, such as a spread for toast.

3. Place the strained strawberry juice in a large measuring cup. Add enough water to make 1 cup of liquid.

4. Place the flour in the pasta machine. With the machine running, slowly add the liquid. Process until the dough reaches the consistency specified in the instruction booklet. If the dough is too dry or too wet, add more water or flour per the instruction booklet.

5. Extrude the pasta, following the directions in instruction booklet.

FOR HAND-CRANKED MACHINES:

1. Place the strawberries in a small saucepan over medium heat. Simmer for 20 minutes or until the strawberries are very soft, stirring occasionally.

2. Place a fine mesh strainer over a bowl. Pour the strawberries and their juices into the strainer. Using the back of a spoon, press the strawberries into the strainer, removing as much juice as possible from the fruit without crushing the berries through the strainer. The fruit pulp can be saved for another use, such as a spread for toast.

3. Place the strained strawberry juice in a large measuring cup. Add enough water to make 1 cup of liquid.

4. Place the flour in the food processor. With the machine running, slowly add the liquid. Pulse until a ball begins to form, about 10 to 15 seconds.

5. If the dough is too dry when all the liquid has been added, add 1 teaspoon of water, and pulse until a ball begins to form. If the dough is too wet, add 1 tablespoon of flour, and pulse until a ball begins to form. Repeat either process as necessary.

6. Remove the dough from the food processor and place it on a lightly floured pastry board or work surface. Knead the dough, incorporating additional flour into the ball of dough until it becomes smooth and shiny. The dough should be kneaded for 2 minutes.

7. Cover the dough with plastic wrap and let it rest for 5 minutes on the counter, or refrigerate it for up to 2 days.

8. Cut or extrude the dough according to the instructions on pages 25 or 28.

COOKING INSTRUCTIONS:

At this point, you can cook the pasta immediately. However, we recommend drying it for 1 hour beforehand to improve both the taste and the texture. Cook the pasta in 4 to 5 quarts of vigorously boiling water. Add all of the pasta at once, covering the pot until the water returns to a rapid boil. After uncovering the pot, test the pasta for doneness by biting into a piece. It should be tender, yet firm. If the pasta's not done, test every 15 to 30 seconds thereafter. Total cooking time will depend on how fresh and how thick the pasta is—the drier and thicker it is, the longer it will take.

Take a Chance:

• Use frozen strawberries instead of fresh.

• Omit the strawberries, and use 1 cup blueberries.

Suggested Sauces:

• Serve warm with Apple Pear Compote (page 198).

• Serve cold with Lucious Lemon Sauce (page 196), Ricotta Cheese Dessert Topping (page 195), or Fresh Berry Medley (page 198).

Top: Corn Tortilla Chips (page 143)
with Salsa Serrano (page 145)
Bottom: Jalapeño Pepper Pasta (page 75)
with Verde Sauce (page 190)

Top: Baked Ziti (page 205)
with Chunky Marinara Sauce (page 158)
Center: Festive Macaroni and Cheese (page 207)
Bottom: Shrimp Egg Rolls (page 148)

Apricot-Peach Pasta

This is a wonderful mixture of sweet summer fruits to tempt your pasta palate.

Preparation Time: *Varies with the equipment used*
Yield: *1½ Pounds*

2 fresh apricots, peeled, pitted, and sliced

1 large fresh peach, peeled, pitted, and sliced

Water

3½ cups unbleached white flour

FOR ELECTRIC EXTRUSION MACHINES:

1. Place the fruit in a small saucepan over medium heat. Simmer for 20 minutes, or until the fruit is very soft, stirring occasionally.

2. Place a fine mesh strainer over a bowl. Pour the fruit and its juices into the strainer. Using the back of a spoon, press the fruit into the strainer, removing as much juice as possible without crushing the fruit through the strainer. The fruit pulp can be saved for another use, such as a spread for toast.

3. Place the strained fruit juice in a large measuring cup. Add enough water to make 1 cup of liquid.

4. Place the flour in the pasta machine. With the machine running, slowly add the liquid. Process until the dough reaches the consistency specified in the instruction booklet. If the dough is too dry or too wet, add more water or flour per the instruction booklet.

5. Extrude the pasta, following the directions in instruction booklet.

FOR HAND-CRANKED MACHINES:

1. Place the fruit in a small saucepan over medium heat. Simmer for 20 minutes, or until the fruit is very soft, stirring occasionally.

2. Place a fine mesh strainer over a bowl. Pour the fruit and its juices into the strainer. Using the back of a spoon, press the fruit into the strainer, removing as much juice as possible without crushing the fruit through the strainer. The fruit pulp can be saved for another use, such as a spread for toast.

3. Place the strained fruit juice in a large measuring cup. Add enough water to make 1 cup of liquid.

4. Place the flour in the food processor. With the machine running, slowly add the liquid. Pulse until a ball begins to form, about 10 to 15 seconds.

5. If the dough is too dry when all the liquid has been added, add 1 teaspoon of water, and pulse until a ball begins to form. If the dough is too wet, add 1 tablespoon of flour, and pulse until a ball begins to form. Repeat either process as necessary.

6. Remove the dough from the food processor and place it on a lightly floured pastry board or work surface. Knead the dough, incorporating additional flour into the ball of dough until it becomes smooth and shiny. The dough should be kneaded for 2 minutes.

7. Cover the dough with plastic wrap and let it rest for 5 minutes on the counter, or refrigerate it for up to 2 days.

8. Cut or extrude the dough according to the instructions on pages 25 or 28.

COOKING INSTRUCTIONS:

At this point, you can cook the pasta immediately. However, we recommend drying it for 1 hour beforehand to improve both the taste and the texture. Cook the pasta in 4 to 5 quarts of vigorously boiling water. Add all of the pasta at once, covering the pot until the water returns to a rapid boil. After uncovering the pot, test the pasta for doneness by biting into a piece. It should be tender, yet firm. If the pasta's not done, test every 15 to 30 seconds thereafter. Total cooking time will depend on how fresh and how thick the pasta is—the drier and thicker it is, the longer it will take.

Take a Chance:

• Decrease the unbleached white flour to 2 cups, and add 1½ cups finely ground whole wheat flour (also called pastry flour).

Suggested Sauces:

• Serve cold with Sticky Sweet Honey Yogurt Sauce (page 196), Ricotta Cheese Dessert Topping (page 195), or Fresh Berry Medley (page 198).

9

Munchies

This chapter covers some other goodies you can make with your pasta machine, or by hand, if you wish. Homemade breadsticks are the perfect complement to your homemade pasta. Try the chips and dips at your next party, and see if your friends aren't impressed. And the won tons and egg rolls are perfect for buffets, or as delicious snacks or appetizers–
make a bunch and freeze the leftovers.

If you use an electric extrusion machine, you may need to experiment with the liquid in these recipes to establish the correct liquid-to-flour ratio.
If you use a hand-cranked machine, you should note that these recipes require a roller machine, not an extrusion machine.

Whole Wheat Breadsticks

Preparation Time: *Varies with the equipment used*
Yield: *Approximately 2½ Dozen*

1 package active dry yeast (¼ ounce)

1 teaspoon Sucanat (see page 194)

Water

1 large egg

1 tablespoon oil

2½ cups whole wheat flour

1 cup unbleached white flour

1 large egg yolk

These breadsticks are great with meals, or as a snack. There is no cutting attachment on a hand-cranked machine for breadsticks, so it's a good thing that this recipe can be made easily by hand. If you use an extrusion machine, use the breadstick die.

FOR ELECTRIC EXTRUSION MACHINES:

1. Place the yeast and Sucanat in a large measuring cup. Add water to make ½ cup of liquid, and stir well. Set aside for 10 minutes.

2. Add the egg and the oil to the yeast mixture, and beat well. Add more water to make 1 cup of liquid.

3. Place the flours in the pasta machine. With the machine running, slowly add the liquid. Process until the dough reaches the consistency specified in the instruction booklet. If the dough is too dry or too wet, add more water or flour per the instruction booklet.

4. Extrude the breadsticks, following the directions in the instruction booklet.

FOR HAND CUTTING:

1. Place the yeast and Sucanat in a large measuring cup. Add water to make ½ cup of liquid, and stir well. Set aside for 10 minutes.

2. Add the egg and the oil to the yeast mixture, and beat well. Add more water to make 1 cup of liquid.

3. Place the flours in the food processor, and pulse 3 times to mix. With the machine running, slowly add the liquid. Pulse until a ball begins to form, about 10 to 15 seconds.

4. If the dough is too dry when all the liquid has been added, add 1 teaspoon of water, and pulse until a ball begins to form. If the dough is too wet, add 1 tablespoon of flour, and pulse until a ball begins to form. Repeat either process as necessary.

5. Remove the dough from the food processor and place it on a lightly floured pastry board or work surface. Knead the dough, incorporating additional flour into the ball of dough until it becomes smooth and shiny. The dough should be kneaded for 20 minutes.

6. Cover the dough with plastic wrap and let it rest for 20 minutes on the counter, or refrigerate it for up to 2 days.

7. Pinch off a piece of dough about the size of a walnut. Then roll the dough in your hands or on the work surface until a rope is formed, about $\frac{1}{4}$-inch thick. Repeat this step until all the dough is used.

BAKING INSTRUCTIONS:

1. Place the breadsticks on an uncoated baking sheet. They do not have to be of a uniform length, but should be of a fairly uniform width to facilitate even cooking.

2. Cover the breadsticks with a kitchen towel, and let the dough rise for 1 hour.

3. Place the egg yolk in a small bowl, and beat lightly. Using a brush or the back of a spoon, coat the top of the breadsticks with the egg.

4. Bake the breadsticks at 350°F for 10 to 12 minutes, or until they are lightly browned.

Take a Chance:

• Make Whole Wheat Poppy Seed Breadsticks by sprinkling the breadsticks with 3 tablespoons of poppy seeds after coating them with the egg. Or make Poppy Seed Breadsticks by omitting the whole wheat flour and using all unbleached white flour.

• Make Garlic Breadsticks by adding 4 crushed garlic cloves to the measuring cup with the oil.

• Make Herbed Breadsticks by adding $\frac{1}{4}$ cup basil, oregano, or other finely ground dried herb to the flour.

Pretzels

Preparation Time: *Varies with the equipment used*
Yield: *Approximately 2½ Dozen*

1 package active dry yeast (¼ ounce)

1 teaspoon Sucanat (see page 194)

Water

1 large egg

1 tablespoon oil

2 cups whole wheat flour

1½ cups unbleached white flour

1 large egg yolk

2 tablespoons sea salt

Pretzels are based on the same principle as breadsticks, but are topped with sea salt before baking. They can be left long, or formed into the familiar pretzel shape.

FOR ELECTRIC EXTRUSION MACHINES:

1. Place the yeast and Sucanat in a large measuring cup. Add water to make ½ cup of liquid, and stir well. Set aside for 10 minutes.

2. Add the egg and the oil to the yeast mixture, and beat well. Add more water to make 1 cup of liquid.

3. Place the flours in the pasta machine. With the machine running, slowly add the liquid. Process until the dough reaches the consistency specified in the instruction booklet. If the dough is too dry or too wet, add more water or flour per the instruction booklet.

4. Using the breadstick die, extrude the pretzels, following the directions in the instruction booklet.

5. Take each rope of dough and fold it evenly in half. Make a knot by crossing the halves twice about 1 inch from the ends. To make a pretzel shape, bring the circle of dough over the knot, and press it down into the two ends. The dough can also be left long, like a breadstick, instead of being folded.

FOR HAND CUTTING:

1. Place the yeast and Sucanat in a large measuring cup. Add water to make ½ cup of liquid, and stir well. Set aside for 10 minutes.

2. Add the egg and the oil to the yeast mixture, and beat well. Add more water to make 1 cup of liquid.

3. Place the flours in the food processor, and pulse 3 times to mix. With the machine running, slowly add the liquid. Pulse until a ball begins to form, about 10 to 15 seconds.

4. If the dough is too dry when all the liquid has been added, add 1 teaspoon of water, and pulse until a ball begins to form. If the dough is too wet, add 1 tablespoon of flour, and pulse until a ball begins to form. Repeat either process as necessary.

5. Remove the dough from the food processor and place it on a lightly floured pastry board or work surface. Knead the dough, incorporating additional flour into the ball of dough until it becomes smooth and shiny. The dough should be kneaded for 20 minutes.

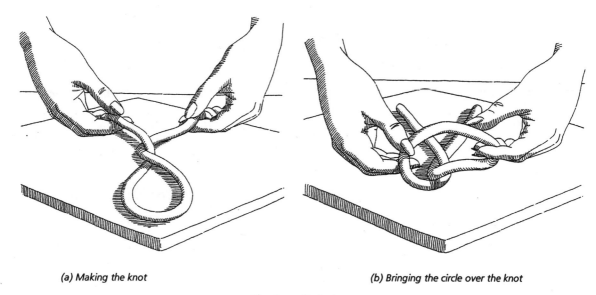

(a) Making the knot   (b) Bringing the circle over the knot

Shaping a Pretzel

6. Cover the dough with plastic wrap and let it rest for 20 minutes on the counter, or refrigerate it for up to 2 days.

7. Pinch off a piece of dough about the size of a walnut. Then roll the dough in your hands or on the work surface until a rope is formed, about ¼-inch thick and 12 inches long. Repeat this step until all the dough is used.

8. Take each rope of dough and fold it evenly in half. Make a knot by crossing the halves twice about 1 inch from the ends. To make a pretzel shape, bring the circle of dough over the knot, and press it down into the two ends. The dough can also be left long, like a breadstick, instead of being folded.

BAKING INSTRUCTIONS:

1. Place the pretzels on an uncoated baking sheet. Cover with a kitchen towel, and let the dough rise for 1 hour.

2. Place the egg yolk in a small bowl, and beat lightly. Using a brush or the back of a spoon, coat the top of the pretzels with the egg. Sprinkle with the sea salt.

3. Bake at 350°F for 10 to 12 minutes, or until lightly browned.

Take a Chance:

- Make Pretzel Nuggets by cutting the rolled dough into 1-inch lengths.

Whole Wheat Pasta Chips

Preparation Time: *Varies with the equipment used*
Yield: *1½ Pounds*

4 large eggs

Water

2½ cups whole wheat flour

1 cup unbleached white flour

¼ cup olive oil, divided

¾ cup freshly grated Parmesan cheese

The instruction booklet for the Waring Primo Pasta machine includes a recipe for pasta chips that can be adapted to almost any electric pasta machine or to a hand-cranked roller machine. Although this recipe is made with whole wheat and eggs, the chips can be made using any of the basic pasta recipes in Chapter 5.

FOR ELECTRIC EXTRUSION MACHINES:

1. Place the eggs in a large measuring cup, and beat lightly. Add enough water to make 1 cup of liquid.

2. Place the flours in the pasta machine. With the machine running, slowly add the liquid. Process until the dough reaches the consistency specified in the instruction booklet. If the dough is too dry or too wet, add more water or flour per the instruction booklet.

3. Extrude the pasta, following the directions in the instruction booklet. Use a die for a wide, flat noodle, such as lasagna.

FOR HAND-CRANKED MACHINES OR FOR HAND CUTTING:

1. Place the eggs in a large measuring cup, and beat lightly. Add enough water to make 1 cup of liquid.

2. Place the flours in the food processor, and pulse 3 times to mix. With the machine running, slowly add the liquid. Pulse until a ball begins to form, about 10 to 15 seconds.

3. If the dough is too dry when all the liquid has been added, add 1 teaspoon of water, and pulse until a ball begins to form. If the dough is too wet, add 1 tablespoon of flour, and pulse until a ball begins to form. Repeat either process as necessary.

4. Remove the dough from the food processor and place it on a lightly floured pastry board or work surface. Knead the dough, incorporating additional flour into the ball of dough until it becomes smooth and shiny. The dough should be kneaded for 2 minutes if it is being cut on a machine, or 20 minutes if it is being cut entirely by hand.

5. Cover the dough with plastic wrap and let it rest for 5 minutes on the counter, or refrigerate it for up to 2 days.

6. If using a hand-cranked cutting machine, use a cutting attachment for a wide, flat noodle, such as lasagna or ravioli, and see page 25. If cutting by hand, follow the instructions on page 28.

BAKING INSTRUCTIONS:

1. After the dough is shaped, cut it with a sharp knife into 2-inch squares.

2. Cook the pasta according to the instructions on page 12. Drain the pasta, and mix it with 1 tablespoon of the olive oil to prevent sticking. Cool to room temperature.

3. Toss the cooled pasta with the remaining oil and the Parmesan cheese, and place on a baking sheet. Bake the chips at 350°F for 15 minutes, or until brown and crisp.

Take a Chance:

• Make Herbed Pasta Chips by adding 1 tablespoon of dried herbs, such as oregano, basil, or thyme, to the flour.

• Make Garlic Pasta Chips by adding 6 crushed garlic cloves to the flour.

Corn Tortilla Chips

Simac has provided directions for tortilla chips using masa harina, which is a flour used in making corn tortillas. It is available in gourmet shops and stores that specialize in Mexican foodstuffs, as well as in well-stocked supermarkets.

Preparation Time: *Varies with the equipment used*
Yield: *1½ Pounds*

2 eggs

Water

3½ cups masa harina

2 cups canola oil

3 tablespoons sea salt

FOR ELECTRIC EXTRUSION MACHINES:

1. Place the eggs in a large measuring cup, and beat lightly. Add enough water to make 1 cup of liquid.

2. Place the masa harina in the pasta machine. With the machine running, slowly add the liquid. Process until the dough reaches the consistency specified in the instruction booklet. If the dough is too dry or too wet, add more water or masa harina per the instruction booklet.

3. Extrude the chips, following the directions in the instruction booklet. Use a die for a wide, flat noodle, such as lasagna.

FOR HAND-CRANKED MACHINES OR FOR HAND CUTTING:

1. Place the eggs in a measuring cup, and beat lightly. Add enough water to make 1 cup of liquid.

2. Place the masa harina in the food processor. With the machine running, slowly add the liquid. Pulse until a ball begins to form, about 10 to 15 seconds.

3. If the dough is too dry when all the liquid has been added, add 1 teaspoon of water, and pulse until a ball begins to form. If the dough is too wet, add 1 tablespoon of masa, and pulse until a ball begins to form. Repeat either process as necessary.

4. Remove the dough from the food processor and place it on a pastry board or work surface coated with a light dusting of masa harina. Knead the dough, incorporating additional masa into the ball of dough until it becomes smooth and shiny. The dough should be kneaded for 2 minutes if it is being cut on a machine, or 20 minutes if it is being cut entirely by hand.

5. Cover the dough with plastic wrap and let it rest for 5 minutes on the counter, or refrigerate it for up to 2 days.

6. If using a hand-cranked cutting machine, use a cutting attachment for a wide, flat noodle, such as lasagna or ravioli, and see page 25. If cutting by hand, follow the instructions on page 28.

COOKING INSTRUCTIONS:

1. After the dough is shaped, cut it with a sharp knife into $1\frac{1}{2}$-inch lengths.

2. In a medium-sized skillet, heat the oil until it just begins to smoke. Add the chips a few at a time to the hot oil and deep fry for 1 minute, or until they are golden brown.

3. Drain the chips on paper toweling, and sprinkle with the salt.

4. Serve the chips warm or at room temperature.

Take a Chance:

• Make Blue Corn Tortilla Chips by decreasing the masa harina to 2 cups and adding 1 cup blue corn meal.

• Make Black Bean Tortilla Chips by adding $\frac{1}{4}$ cup puréed black beans to the beaten egg. Add enough water to make 1 cup of liquid.

Dips for Chips

Why make fresh, homemade chips if you're not going to make fresh, homemade dips to go with them? You could use the Sinless Summer Cheese Sauce on page 168 or the Verde Sauce on page 190, or the cheese sauce from Festive Macaroni and Cheese on page 207. Or try one of these tasty dips.

Cottage Cheese Pesto Dip

We love the chips with this dip. You can mix it by hand, instead of using the food processor, as long as you make sure that the cheese is smooth and that all the ingredients are thoroughly mixed.

1. Place the cottage cheese and the milk in a food processor and pulse 4 times, or until the cheese is smooth.

2. Add the Pesto Sauce and the pepper, and pulse 3 times.

3. Serve cold.

Preparation Time: *5 Minutes*
Yield: *2 Cups*

2 cups low-fat cottage cheese

2 tablespoons soy milk

¼ cup Pesto Sauce (page 159)

¼ teaspoon freshly ground black pepper

Salsa Serrano

Want a salsa with some bite? Try this!

1. Mix all the ingredients in a glass bowl or jar. Cover, and refrigerate 1 hour before serving.

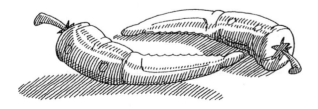

Preparation Time: *1¼ Hours*
Yield: *Approximately 1¼ Cups*

10 serrano peppers (jalapeños may be used), seeded and coarsely chopped

3 tablespoons finely chopped onion

2 garlic cloves, coarsely chopped

4 plum tomatoes, coarsely chopped

¼ cup finely chopped fresh cilantro

Chicken Won Tons

Preparation Time: *Varies with the equipment used*
Yield: *Approximately 3 Dozen*

WON TON SKINS

1 teaspoon baking powder

3½ cups unbleached white flour

1 cup water

FILLING

1 teaspoon arrowroot

4 teaspoons water

1 teaspoon rice wine

1 teaspoon sesame oil

¼ cup ground cooked chicken

2 teaspoons shoyu or tamari sauce

1 teaspoon finely chopped green onions

½ teaspoon grated fresh ginger

½ teaspoon freshly ground black pepper

Don't lose that lasagna die! Simac has figured out an easy way to make won ton skins with a pasta machine. The dough is just a tiny bit thicker than traditional skins, but very tasty. You can use wontons in Chicken Soup With Noodles (page 202) or Spinach Lasagna Noodle Soup (page 202).

FOR ELECTRIC EXTRUSION MACHINES:

1. To make the won ton skins, place the baking powder and flour in the pasta machine. With the machine running, slowly add the water. Process until the dough reaches the consistency specified in the instruction booklet. If the dough is too dry or too wet, add more water or flour per the instruction booklet.

2. Extrude the pasta, following the directions in the instruction booklet. Use a die for a wide, flat noodle, such as lasagna.

FOR HAND-CRANKED MACHINES
OR FOR HAND CUTTING:

1. To make the won ton skins, place the baking powder and flour in the food processor, and pulse 3 times to mix. With the machine running, slowly add the water. Pulse until a ball begins to form, about 10 to 15 seconds.

2. If the dough is too dry when all the water has been added, add 1 teaspoon of water, and pulse until a ball begins to form. If the dough is too wet, add 1 tablespoon of flour, and pulse until a ball begins to form. Repeat either process as necessary.

3. Remove the dough from the food processor and place it on a lightly floured pastry board or work surface. Knead the dough, incorporating additional flour into the ball of dough until it becomes smooth and shiny. The dough should be kneaded for 2 minutes if it is being cut on a machine, or 20 minutes if it is being cut entirely by hand.

4. Cover the dough with plastic wrap and let it rest for 5 minutes on the counter, or refrigerate it for up to 2 days.

5. If using a hand-cranked cutting machine, cut the dough according to the instructions on page 25. Roll the dough thin, finishing with a setting of 5 or 6. If cutting by hand, follow the instructions on page 28.

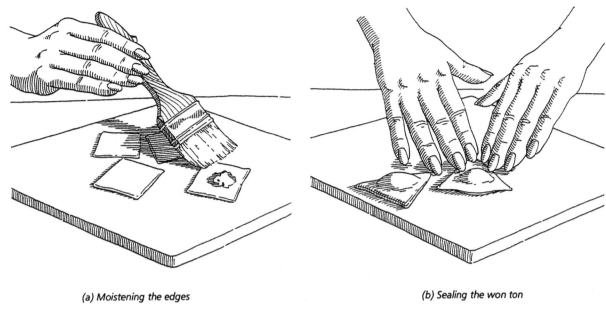

(a) Moistening the edges   (b) Sealing the won ton

Forming a Won Ton

ASSEMBLING AND COOKING INSTRUCTIONS:

1. After the dough has been formed, cut the pieces into 2-inch squares.

2. To make the filling, dissolve the arrowroot in the water in a small bowl. Add the remaining ingredients, and mix well.

3. To assemble the won tons, place less than ¼ teaspoon of the filling in the center of each square.

4. Using your fingers or a brush, moisten the edges of the dough with water. Fold the dough diagonally over the filling to form a triangle. Press the edges of the dough, and seal well.

5. Place the completed won tons on a flat plate. Do not let them touch, or they will stick together. Repeat this step until all the ingredients are used.

6. To cook, bring 6 quarts of water to a full boil. Add the won tons and cook for 5 to 6 minutes, or until done.

Take a Chance:

• Deep fry the won tons. Place 2 cups of canola oil in a medium-sized skillet, and heat until it just begins to smoke. Add a few won tons to the skillet and cook for 3 to 4 minutes, or until they turn a golden brown. Remove with a slotted spoon, and drain on paper toweling.

Shrimp Egg Rolls

Preparation Time: *Varies with the equipment used*
Yield: *6 Egg Rolls*

EGG ROLL SKINS

2 eggs

Water

3$\frac{1}{2}$ cups unbleached white flour

FILLING

2 dried Chinese black mushrooms, soaked in warm water for 30 minutes

1 teaspoon canola oil

1 teaspoon shoyu or tamari sauce

1 teaspoon rice wine

$\frac{1}{2}$ teaspoon grated fresh ginger

2 green onions, finely chopped

2 ounces shrimp, deveined and shells removed, finely chopped

$\frac{1}{4}$ cup finely chopped bean sprouts

1 tablespoon arrowroot

4 tablespoons water

2 cups canola oil

Because strips made for lasagna are not wide enough for egg rolls, these rolls do look somewhat funny. Maybe we should call them "Mummy Rolls"? If you can't find some of the ingredients for the filling in the supermarket, try an Asian food store or a gourmet shop.

FOR ELECTRIC EXTRUSION MACHINES:

1. To make the egg roll skins, place the eggs in a large measuring cup, and beat lightly. Add enough water to make 1 cup of liquid.

2. Place the flour in the pasta machine. With the machine running, slowly add the liquid. Process until the dough reaches the consistency specified in the instruction booklet. If the dough is too dry or too wet, add more water or flour per the instruction booklet.

3. Extrude the pasta, following the directions in the instruction booklet. Use a die for a wide, flat noodle, such as lasagna.

FOR HAND-CRANKED MACHINES OR FOR HAND CUTTING:

1. To make the egg roll skins, place the eggs in a large measuring cup, and beat lightly. Add enough water to make 1 cup of liquid.

2. Place the flour in the food processor. With the machine running, slowly add the liquid. Pulse until a ball begins to form, about 10 to 15 seconds.

3. If the dough is too dry when all the liquid has been added, add 1 teaspoon of water, and pulse until a ball begins to form. If the dough is too wet, add 1 tablespoon of flour, and pulse until a ball begins to form. Repeat either process as necessary.

4. Remove the dough from the food processor and place it on a lightly floured pastry board or work surface. Knead the dough, incorporating additional flour into the ball of dough until it becomes smooth and shiny. The dough should be kneaded for 2 minutes if it is being cut on a machine, or 20 minutes if it is being cut entirely by hand.

5. Cover the dough with plastic wrap and let it rest for 5 minutes on the counter, or refrigerate it for up to 2 days.

6. If using a hand-cranked cutting machine, cut the dough according to the instructions on page 25. If cutting by hand, follow the instructions on page 28.

ASSEMBLING AND COOKING INSTRUCTIONS:

1. After the dough is shaped, cut it with a sharp knife into 9-inch lengths.

2. To make the filling, remove the black mushrooms from the water, and squeeze dry. Using a sharp knife, chop them finely, removing any stems or hard pieces. Set aside.

3. Place the oil in a medium-sized skillet over medium-high heat. Add the shoyu, rice wine, ginger, and green onions. Sauté for 1 minute.

4. Add the shrimp and the mushrooms, and cook until the shrimp just begins to turn pink. Using a slotted spoon, remove the shrimp to a small bowl.

5. Add the bean sprouts to the skillet, and cook for 1 minute.

6. Place the arrowroot and water in a small bowl, and mix until the arrowroot dissolves. Add the mixture to the skillet. Turn the heat to medium-high, and cook until the liquid begins to thicken.

7. Remove the pan from the heat, and transfer the contents of the skillet to the bowl containing the shrimp. Cool the mixture thoroughly.

8. To assemble the egg rolls, lay the strips of dough on a work surface. Place 1½ tablespoons of the filling on each strip, leaving ½ inch of dough at each end.

9. With your fingers or a brush, moisten the ends of the dough with water.

10. Fold the ends of the dough toward the center of the filling until they meet.

Folding the Ends Toward the Center

11. Take another strip of dough and moisten the edges with water. Starting at one end, wrap the strip of dough around the filled dough in a spiral.

Wrapping With the Second Strip of Dough

12. Press the edges of the dough all around the egg roll to seal.

13. Place the 2 cups of oil in a medium-sized pot and heat until it just begins to smoke. Add the egg rolls, two at a time, to the pot and cook for 4 to 5 minutes, or until they turn a golden brown. Remove with a slotted spoon, and drain on paper toweling.

Take a Chance:

• Omit the shrimp, and use 2 ounces finely chopped cooked chicken. Cook the mushrooms by themselves for 1 minute.

PART FOUR

Pasta Sauces and Dishes

Sauces complement the taste of pasta and allow any one type of pasta to fill many culinary roles, from piquant appetizer to hearty dinner entrée to chilled salad. And while there are good sauces to be found at the supermarket, nothing compares to the taste of your own homemade sauce.

The recipes given in Chapters 10 through 13 will let you whip up everything from a fast weeknight dinner to a sumptuous weekend feast. And while making your own sauce does not have to be a time-consuming process, it can be a lovely way to spend a long, rainy weekend afternoon. It can also be a good meal-planning device, since many sauces–especially tomato-based ones– benefit from being made ahead of time, even up to a day or two beforehand. This lets you create a batch on Sunday for use during the week, while giving the flavors a chance to blend together. You can also freeze many sauces, especially pesto and tomato-based sauces. We also provide recipes for sweet toppings that transform main-dish pasta into a delightful dessert.

Obviously, all these sauces go well with basic pasta–pasta made from varying combinations of flour, water, and eggs. (See Chapter 5.) But the flavor possibilities multiply when you combine various sauces with various flavored pastas. In each recipe, the Suggested Pastas section will give you an idea which of the flavored pastas in Part Three that sauce would go best with. The list is by no means cast in stone, nor is it complete. It is meant to spark your imagination.

A note on sauce amounts: While we provide yields for all our recipes, including our sauces, it is difficult to say how much sauce is required to cover a given amount of pasta. It depends on the sauce, the flavor and shape of the pasta, and your prefer- ence–some people like a little, some like a lot. As you become familiar with the recipes, you'll be able to adjust amounts as needed.

Chapter 14 contains recipes for pasta main dishes. Soups, traditional lasagna, ravioli, even maca- roni and cheese–you can find them all here. We also give you recipes with a different twist, such as lasagna roll-ups. Each of these recipes contains either a Suggested Pastas section or a Suggested Sauces section, depending on the nature of the dish.

Each recipe in all five chapters contains a Take a Chance section. This section gives you some tips on how to creatively manipulate each recipe to create new tastes and textures.

10

Traditional Sauces

The sauces presented in this chapter are the oldies-but-goodies that pasta lovers have enjoyed for years. Most of them originated in Italy. Not surprisingly, they feature the staples of southern Italian cooking: tomatoes, olives and olive oil, garlic, basil, oregano, and parsley. (See page 63 for tips on using garlic and page 83 for information on storing basil.) Some recipes, such as our Sinless Summer Cheese Sauce, use these ingredients in new, tasty ways.

For many of us, these recipes bring back memories of families around a table laden with pasta topped with tomato sauce and fragrant Parmesan cheese. Who says you can't go home again? Get the pasta water boiling and, as Grandma would say, "*Mangia!*"

Aglio e Olio

Preparation Time: *10 Minutes*
Yield: *¾ Cup*

¼ cup Chicken Broth (page 200)

½ cup extra virgin olive oil

3 large garlic cloves, minced

¼ teaspoon freshly ground black
   pepper

¼ cup chopped fresh Italian
   parsley

Cloves of fresh garlic and the best grade of olive oil combine to make this classic dressing for pasta. We have reduced the amount of oil used by adding chicken broth. Serve over Tortellini With Fresh Spinach Filling (page 217).

1. Place the chicken broth and the oil in a small saucepan over medium heat. Reduce the heat to medium-low, add the garlic and black pepper, and sauté for 1 to 2 minutes. Do not let the garlic turn brown or it will taste bitter.

2. Spoon over the pasta and garnish with the parsley. Serve hot or cold. If serving cold, cool the pasta and the sauce together.

Take a Chance:

- Add ½ teaspoon crushed red pepper with the garlic.
- Use fresh basil leaves as a garnish instead of the parsley.
- Mix with vegetables and serve hot over spaghetti, linguine, or fettuccine.
- Mix with vegetables and either shells, fusilli, or rigatoni, and serve as a cold salad.

Suggested Pastas:

- Serve hot over the following pastas or noodles: Tomato (page 77), Corn (page 79), Blue Corn (page 80), Basil (page 82), Whole Wheat Basil (page 84), Lemon Basil (page 86), Tomato Oregano (page 96), or Cheesy Parmesan (page 116).

- Serve cold over the following pastas: Broccoli (page 70), Bugs's Carrot (page 72), Beet (page 73), Jalapeño Pepper (page 75), Pesto (page 64), Sage Thyme (page 88), Parsley (page 90), Buckwheat With Cilantro (page 92), Garlic (page 62), Spinach Basil (page 94), Carrot Dill (page 98), Curry (page 102), Chili Powder (page 109), or Sweet Paprika (page 105).

Olive Oils for Every Taste

The oil of preference in our recipes is olive oil. It is a monosaturated fat, which means that it is relatively healthy. It is also tasty, adding a wonderful flavor to any recipe.

So many different oils abound on our supermarket shelves that picking the correct oil can be confusing. Olive oil is graded according to how it is processed. Olives are cold-pressed in circular stone presses without chemicals or additives. The first pressing results in the finest and most expensive olive oil, called *extra virgin*. This oil has a strong aroma and an intense flavor. Heating this oil changes its taste, so it should only be used in recipes that call for very short cooking times. Extra virgin olive oil is best used on salads, or drizzled directly over warm food.

The second cold-pressing of the olives results in *virgin* olive oil. This oil is less expensive than extra virgin, but its flavor is also less intense. Because its taste is lighter, heating will not change the taste as much. Still, the best use of virgin oil is also on salads or over warm food.

After the second pressing, the olives are mixed with solvents and cold-pressed again to produce *pure* olive oil. Finally, the olive pulp is heated with water to extract the last bit of flavor, which results in *plain* olive oil. Both pure and plain olive oil are very mild-tasting, and are the best oils for cooking.

While images of the Italian countryside come to mind when thinking about olive oils, it is actually produced in many countries. Spain, Greece, France, and even the United States produce exceptional oils. The oil of each country has its own unique flavor. Experiment to find the ones you like best.

Sautéed Garlic and Bread Crumbs

This delicious pasta topping from Italy's Tuscany region is a variation of Aglio e Olio. We have cut down on the oil needed with the addition of some vegetable broth. This topping can be added to the top layer of white sauce in Vegetable Lasagna With White Sauce (page 208), or served over Tortellini With Fresh Spinach Filling (page 217).

Preparation Time: *15 Minutes*
Yield: *1 Cup*

1 cup fresh whole grain bread crumbs

¼ cup Vegetable Broth (page 200)

½ cup extra virgin olive oil

4 garlic cloves, crushed

⅛ teaspoon freshly ground black pepper

¼ cup chopped fresh Italian parsley

1. Place the bread crumbs in a small saucepan over medium heat. Stir constantly for 1 to 2 minutes, until the crumbs begin to toast. Remove the pan from the heat. Place the bread crumbs in a small dish, and set aside.

2. Place the broth and the oil in the saucepan. Add the garlic, and sauté for 1 minute. Add the bread crumbs and pepper, and sauté for another 1 to 2 minutes.

3. Remove the pan from the heat, and add the parsley.

4. Spoon over the pasta. Serve hot.

Take a Chance:

• Use ¼ cup soy margarine instead of the oil, and serve over egg noodles.

Suggested Pastas:

• Serve over the following pastas or noodles: Spinach (page 66), Whole Wheat Spinach (page 68), Garlic (page 62), Spinach Basil (page 94), Curry Spinach (page 114), or Cheesy Parmesan (page 116).

Quick Olive Sauce

Preparation Time: 20 Minutes
Yield: 1 Cup

¼ cup Vegetable Broth (page 200)

¼ cup extra virgin olive oil

4 garlic cloves, finely chopped

1 cup pitted and finely chopped black olives

Once the olives have been pitted, this sauce is a breeze to make.

1. Place the broth and the oil in a small saucepan over medium heat. Add the garlic, and sauté for 2 minutes. Add the olives, and continue to sauté for another minute.

2. Spoon over the pasta. Serve hot or cold. If serving cold, cool the pasta and the sauce together.

Take a Chance:

• Use a combination of black and green olives.
• Add ½ teaspoon grated orange zest with the olives.

Suggested Pastas:

• Serve hot over Broccoli Pasta (page 70) or Tomato Oregano Pasta (page 96).

• Serve hot or cold over Garlic Pasta (page 62) or Cheesy Parmesan Noodles (page 116).

• Serve cold over the following pastas: Basil (page 82), Whole Wheat Basil (page 84), Lemon Basil (page 86), Pesto (page 64), Parsley (page 90), Buckwheat With Cilantro (page 92), or Whole Wheat Lemon Pepper (page 107).

Puttanesca Sauce

One Italian legend says that ladies of the evening would send the delicious aroma of this sauce wafting through the streets to attract customers. Use Puttanesca Sauce on Whole Wheat Chicken Mushroom Pizza (page 214).

1. Place the oil in a large skillet over medium heat. Add the garlic and oregano, and sauté for 1 minute.

2. Add the anchovy fillets, and stir the mixture constantly until the fillets dissolve, about 1 minute.

3. Add the tomatoes, olives, and capers. Cook, uncovered, over medium heat for 45 minutes, stirring occasionally.

4. Spoon over the pasta. Serve hot.

Preparation Time: *1 Hour*
Yield: *3 Cups*

3 tablespoons olive oil

4 garlic cloves, finely minced

1 teaspoon dried oregano, or about 1 tablespoon fresh

8 anchovy fillets

2 pounds tomatoes, peeled and coarsely chopped (about 4 cups)

$\frac{1}{2}$ cup pitted and chopped black olives

1 tablespoon capers

Take a Chance:

• Add 1 teaspoon crushed red pepper with the anchovy fillets.

Suggested Pastas:

• Serve over Garlic Pasta (page 62), Whole Wheat Lemon Pepper Pasta (page 107), Red Wine Pasta (page 111), or Cheesy Parmesan Noodles (page 116).

A World of Olives

Olives trace their heritage back into antiquity. Their popularity in the United States as something other than a side dish at buffets has soared as we experiment more and more with cross-cultural cooking.

Green olives are picked from the tree just before they ripen and are cured in brine. Black olives are actually ripe olives. These tasty gems are also cured in brine and then either dried, pickled, or packed in oil.

Whatever type of olive you favor, try to buy them fresh at the local deli or supermarket. The quality of these olives is superior to those from a can.

Olives in many colors and sizes are increasingly easy to find. Some of the most frequently used olives include:

• **Gaeta.** This Italian olive is small and wrinkled, and is either black or mahogany in color. It has a mild, somewhat earthy taste.

• **Kalamata.** This plump Greek olive is a shiny purplish-black. It is among the easiest olives to find, and the tastiest.

• **Moroccan.** This tiny, shriveled, olive from Morocco is very black, and resembles a raisin.

• **Nicoise.** This small, classic olive from France ranges in color from a purplish-brown to black. Its smooth but pungent taste will remind you of the fields of Provence, where it is grown.

Chunky Marinara Sauce

Preparation Time: *30 Minutes*
Yield: *3½ Cups*

3 tablespoons olive oil

3 garlic cloves, coarsely chopped

2 pounds tomatoes, peeled and
   coarsely chopped (about 4
   cups)

A useful tip: putting the tomatoes in a hot skillet allows them to cook faster. This sauce goes well with many of the pasta dishes in Chapter 14.

1. Place the oil in a large skillet over medium heat. Add the garlic, and stir constantly until you can just smell the garlic.

2. Reduce the heat to low, and add the tomatoes. Stir the mixture until well blended. Cover and cook for 20 minutes, stirring occasionally. Add more oil or some water to the tomatoes if they become too thick.

3. Stir the sauce well, and spoon over the pasta. Serve hot.

Take a Chance:

- Add ½ teaspoon dried oregano with the garlic.
- Add ½ cup dry red wine with the tomatoes.

Suggested Pastas:

- Serve over the following pastas or noodles: Basil (page 82), Whole Wheat Basil (page 84), Lemon Basil (page 86), Pesto (page 64), Sage Thyme (page 88), Parsley (page 90), Buckwheat With Cilantro (page 92), Garlic (page 62), Spinach Basil (page 94), Whole Wheat Lemon Pepper (page 107), Red Wine (page 111), or Cheesy Parmesan (page 116).

Italian Meatballs

Preparation Time: *45 Minutes*
Yield: *12 Meatballs*

1 pound ground turkey or 96%
   lean ground beef
½ cup bread crumbs
⅓ cup grated Parmesan cheese
2 egg whites
1 onion, finely chopped
1 teaspoon crushed garlic
1½ teaspoons finely chopped
   fresh oregano
Nonstick cooking spray

Serve these low-fat, high-taste delights with any of the cooked tomato sauces.

1. Place the ingredients in a medium-sized bowl, and mix thoroughly. Shape into 12 meatballs.

2. Coat a baking sheet with nonstick cooking spray. Place the meatballs on the baking sheet and bake at 350°F for about 35 minutes, or until thoroughly cooked. Add the meatballs to the sauce just before the sauce finishes cooking.

Top: Blue Corn Pasta (page 80)
with Hot Citrus Sauce (page 175)
Bottom: Tomato Chili Pasta (page 112)
with Wild Mushroom Sauce (page 186)

Top: Whole Wheat Lemon Pepper Pasta (page 107)
 with White Clam Sauce (page 164)
Bottom: Garlic Pasta (page 62)
 with Pescatore Sauce (page 167)

Pesto Sauce

This wonderful sauce is sharp with the fresh taste of basil, Parmesan cheese, and pine nuts. Traditionally, all the ingredients are ground together with a mortar and pestle. You can serve pesto as a sauce over *Classic Cheese Ravioli (page 209)*, *Tortellini With Fresh Spinach Filling (page 217)*, or *Plain Potato Gnocchi (page 220)*. You can also freeze pesto in ice cube trays. Cubes can be used during the long winter months when fresh basil is not available, unless you store basil in oil (page 83).

Preparation Time: 10 Minutes
Yield: 1¼ Cups

3 garlic cloves

½ cup extra virgin olive oil

½ cup Vegetable Broth (page 200)

3 cups loosely packed fresh basil leaves

¼ cup freshly grated Parmesan cheese

3 tablespoons pine nuts

1. Place the garlic in a food processor, and pulse 3 times. You can use a blender, but if you do, be sure to make the pesto in small batches. Otherwise, the material on the bottom may liquefy before the material on the top is blended.

2. Add the remaining ingredients, and pulse 5 to 6 times, or until the pesto has a smooth consistency. If the pesto is too stiff, add more oil or broth, or some of the water used to cook the pasta.

3. Spoon over the pasta. Serve hot or cold. If serving cold, cool the pasta and the sauce together.

Take a Chance:

• Use walnuts or almonds instead of pine nuts.

• Cut down on the amount of oil used by making Pesto Sauce With Lemon. Reduce the amount of olive oil to ¼ cup, and mix with ¼ cup lemon juice.

Suggested Pastas:

• Serve hot or cold over the following pastas or noodles: Spinach (page 66), Whole Wheat Spinach (page 68), Garlic (page 62), Whole Wheat Lemon Pepper (page 107), or Cheesy Parmesan (page 116).

• Serve cold over the following pastas or noodles: Broccoli (page 70), Bugs's Carrot (page 72), Tomato (page 77), Corn (page 79), Blue Corn (page 80), Spinach Basil (page 94), Tomato Oregano (page 96), Tomato Chili (page 112), Curry Spinach (page 114), Red Wine (page 111), Udon (page 118), or Soba (page 120).

Tomatoes Fresh and Canned

In a perfect world, everyone would have access to wonderful fresh, ripe tomatoes every day. Unfortunately, most of us buy our tomatoes from the supermarket. For much of the year, they are hard and mealy, with almost no taste. If you are lucky enough to grow tomatoes in a summer garden, you can preserve your crop for use during the colder months.

For the rest of us, buying canned tomatoes is the only solution. There are many good brands on the market. If possible, choose an imported Italian plum tomato. These contain less acid and are meatier than regular tomatoes. Most of the recipes that use tomatoes call for fresh. Except where noted, canned can be used in their place. One 28-ounce can of plum tomatoes equals approximately 4 cups of fresh tomatoes. Of course, recipes that call for tomato sauce or tomato paste are calling for canned products.

Many of our recipes call for peeled tomatoes. This is mainly a matter of preference. If you don't mind the skins, then don't bother peeling. If you do want to peel the tomatoes, dip them in boiling water for 1 minute. Then plunge into cold water, drain, and peel.

Don't put fresh tomatoes in the food processor until they are partially cooked, as they can become mushy. Canned tomatoes can be processed at any time.

Smooth Tomato Marinara Sauce With Basil

Preparation Time: *45 Minutes*
Yield: *3½ Cups*

3 tablespoons olive oil

3 garlic cloves, coarsely chopped

2 pounds tomatoes, peeled and coarsely chopped (about 4 cups)

½ cup sliced fresh basil

Fresh basil adds a summery taste to any pasta. Serve with Traditional Lasagna (page 206) or over Classic Cheese Ravioli (page 209).

1. Place the oil in a large skillet over medium heat. Add the garlic, and sauté until you can just smell the garlic.

2. Lower the heat to medium, and add the tomatoes. Stir well. Cover and cook for 20 minutes, stirring occasionally.

3. Remove the skillet from the heat, and cool for 5 minutes. Using a large spoon or a ladle, place the contents of the skillet in a food processor or blender. Pulse 3 to 4 times, or until the tomatoes become smooth.

4. Pour the tomato sauce back into the skillet, cover, and continue cooking over medium heat for 20 minutes. Add more oil or some water if the tomatoes become too thick.

5. Remove from the heat, and stir in the basil.

6. Spoon over the pasta. Serve hot.

Take a Chance:

- Use fresh oregano or rosemary instead of basil.
- If fresh basil is not available, stir in some basil in oil (page 83).
- Add ½ cup red wine with the tomatoes.

Suggested Pastas:

- Serve over the following pastas or noodles: Garlic (page 62), Whole Wheat Lemon Pepper (page 107), Chili Powder (page 109), Sweet Paprika (page 105), Red Wine (page 111), or Cheesy Parmesan (page 116).

Arrabbiata Sauce

This normally mild-mannered sauce turns fiery with the addition of crushed red pepper. Serve with Traditional Lasagna (page 206) or over Classic Cheese Ravioli (page 209).

Preparation Time: *1 Hour*
Yield: *3 Cups*

3 tablespoons olive oil

1 garlic clove, cut in half

2 teaspoons crushed red pepper

2 pounds tomatoes, peeled, seeded, and coarsely chopped (about 4 cups)

3 tablespoons chopped fresh Italian parsley

1. Place the oil in a large skillet over medium heat. Add the garlic and sauté for 1 minute, or until you can just smell the garlic. Remove the garlic with a slotted spoon and discard.

2. Add the red pepper to the oil, and stir for 30 seconds. Add the tomatoes and cook, uncovered, for 15 minutes.

3. Remove the skillet from the heat. Using a large spoon or a ladle, put the tomatoes in a food processor or blender. Pulse 5 to 6 times, or until the tomatoes are smooth. Return the tomatoes to the skillet and cook, uncovered, over medium heat for 20 minutes.

4. Spoon over the pasta, and garnish with the parsley. Serve hot.

Take a Chance:

- Use 4 cups tomato sauce instead of whole tomatoes. Omit Step 3 and cook the sauce for 35 minutes.

Suggested Pastas:

- Serve over the following pastas or noodles: Basil (page 82), Whole Wheat Basil (page 84), Lemon Basil (page 86), Pesto (page 64), Garlic (page 62), Spinach Basil (page 94), Cheesy Parmesan (page 116), Udon (page 118), or Soba (page 120).

Round Up Those Free-Range Chickens

Free-range chickens, unlike those raised on factory farms, are allowed to roam over a relatively open area. That reduces the rates of disease and deformity. Many free-range chickens are also grown organically, that is, they are fed organic grains and are free from growth-producing hormones. Free-range chicken can be found in meat stores and gourmet shops, and in some supermarkets.

Slow-Cooked Spaghetti Sauce With Chicken

Preparation Time: *6 Hours*
Yield: *10 Cups*

¼ cup olive oil

1 3-pound free-range chicken, skin removed and cut into serving pieces

4 garlic cloves, coarsely chopped

8 cups (64 ounces) whole plum tomatoes (canned)

3½ cups (28 ounces) tomato purée

1 tablespoon dried oregano, or about 2 tablespoons fresh

This is an old family recipe (in the family, it's not called sauce but "gravy"). The original recipe calls for meatballs or hot Italian sausage, but it is also good meatless. Serve with Traditional Lasagna (page 206) or Baked Ziti (page 205), over Classic Cheese Ravioli (page 209), or on top of Whole Wheat Chicken Mushroom Pizza (page 214).

1. Place the oil in a large pot over medium heat. Add the chicken, and brown on each side for 5 minutes. During the last 2 minutes of browning, add the garlic.

2. Add the tomatoes, and stir well. Cook over low heat, partially covered, for 1 hour.

3. Remove the pot from the heat. Use a large fork to remove the chicken from the pot to a bowl. Cover the bowl, and cool for about 15 to 20 minutes. Refrigerate the chicken after the cooling period.

4. While the chicken cools, add the purée and the oregano to the pot. Continue cooking, partially covered, for 5 hours. Stir occasionally.

5. One hour before the sauce is finished cooking, remove the chicken from the refrigerator and bring to room temperature.

6. At the same time the water is put on for the pasta, add the chicken to the sauce to warm it up.

7. Remove the chicken from the sauce before serving. Spoon the sauce over the pasta with the chicken on the side. Serve hot.

Take a Chance:

• Use crushed tomatoes instead of whole tomatoes for a smoother sauce.

• Omit the chicken and use your favorite soy meat recipe to make meatballs.

Suggested Pastas:

• Serve over any of the pastas in Chapters 5, 6, and 7, except Beet, Jalapeño Pepper, Corn, Blue Corn, Carrot Dill, Curry, or Saffron.

Magnificent Mushroom Sauce

Slow cooking with just a hint of garlic brings out the taste of the mushrooms. Serve with Baked Ziti (page 205) or over Classic Cheese Ravioli (page 209), Lasagna Roll-Ups (page 213), Tortellini With Fresh Spinach Filling (page 217), or gnocchi (pages 220 and 223).

1. Place the broth in a large saucepan over medium heat. Add the mushrooms, cover, and cook over very low heat for 20 minutes, stirring occasionally. The mushrooms will release their own juices. If the mushrooms begin to stick, add a few tablespoons of water to the pan.

2. Add the tomatoes and black pepper, cover, and cook for 30 minutes over medium-low heat.

3. Stir in the garlic, and cook for 2 minutes.

4. Spoon over the pasta. Serve hot.

Preparation Time: *1 Hour*
Yield: *3$\frac{1}{2}$ Cups*

2 tablespoons Vegetable Broth (page 200)

1 cup thinly sliced fresh mushrooms

2 pounds tomatoes, peeled, seeded, and finely chopped (about 4 cups)

$\frac{1}{4}$ teaspoon freshly ground black pepper

1 garlic clove, crushed

Take a Chance:

• Add $\frac{1}{4}$ teaspoon chopped fresh rosemary with the mushrooms.

Suggested Pastas:

• Serve over the following pastas or noodles: Jalapeño Pepper (page 75), Corn (page 79), Sage Thyme (page 88), Parsley (page 90), Buckwheat With Cilantro (page 92), Garlic (page 62), Spinach Basil (page 94), Saffron (page 104), Red Wine (page 111), Cheesy Parmesan (page 116), Udon (page 118), or Soba (page 120).

White Clam Sauce

Preparation Time: *45 Minutes*
Yield: *2 Cups*

3 dozen cherrystone clams, in their shells

1 cup water

3 whole peppercorns

1/2 bay leaf

1/4 cup extra virgin olive oil

3 garlic cloves, coarsely chopped

1/4 teaspoon freshly ground black pepper

3 tablespoons chopped fresh Italian parsley

This clam sauce is a bit easier to make than the red, but is just as tasty. Steps 1 through 5 of the instructions can be done ahead of time, and the clams and their juices covered and refrigerated until needed. This sauce goes especially well with linguine.

1. Place the clams in a sink full of cold water. Using a small wire brush, clean each clam individually under cold running water. Discard any clams with open or cracked shells.

2. Place the water, peppercorns, and bay leaf in a large pot with a tight-fitting lid. Add the clams to the pot, and cover. Place the pot over high heat.

3. When the water comes to a boil, check the clams. If the shells are open, immediately uncover the pot and remove from the heat. If they are still closed, cover the pot again and return to the stove over medium-high heat. Check the clams after 1 minute. When all the shells are open, the clams are done. Do not overcook. Cool.

4. When the clams are cool enough to handle, remove the meat from each shell. Pour the clam juice into a small bowl, and set aside. Discard all the shells.

5. Using a sharp knife, coarsely chop the clams. Place the clams in another small bowl, and set aside.

6. Place the oil in a large skillet over medium heat. Add the garlic, and sauté for 1 minute. Add the clam juice and black pepper, and simmer over medium-low heat for 10 to 15 minutes.

7. At the same time the water is put on for the pasta, add the clams to the sauce.

8. Spoon over the pasta, and garnish with the parsley. Serve hot.

Take a Chance:

• Add 1/2 teaspoon crushed red pepper with the clam juice.

Suggested Pastas:

• Serve over the following pastas: Basil (page 82), Whole Wheat Basil (page 84), Lemon Basil (page 86), Pesto (page 64), Garlic (page 62), or Whole Wheat Lemon Pepper (page 107).

Red Clam Sauce

This family recipe for red sauce is Michelle's favorite meal of all time. Whether your favorite is red or white clam sauce, the only way to make it is with fresh clams. Steps 3 through 6 of the instructions can be done ahead of time, and the clams and their juices covered and refrigerated until needed. Like the white sauce, this sauce works especially well with linguine.

Preparation Time: *4 Hours*
Yield: *3 Cups*

¼ cup olive oil

3 garlic cloves, coarsely chopped

2 teaspoons dried oregano

4 cups (32 ounces) tomato sauce

4 dozen cherrystone clams, in their shells

1 cup water

½ teaspoon crushed red pepper

3 whole peppercorns

½ bay leaf

1. Place the oil in a large pot over medium heat. Add the garlic and oregano, and sauté for 1 to 2 minutes.

2. Add the tomato sauce, and stir well. Partially cover the pot, and continue to cook the sauce over very low heat for 4 hours, stirring occasionally. The sauce should reduce by one-third during cooking.

3. In the meantime, place the clams in a sink full of cold water. Using a small wire brush, clean each clam individually under cold running water. Discard any clams with open or cracked shells.

4. Place the water, red pepper, peppercorns, and bay leaf in a large pot with a tight-fitting lid. Add the clams to the pot, and cover. Place the pot over high heat.

5. When the water comes to a boil, check the clams. If the shells are open, immediately uncover the pot and remove from the heat. If they are still closed, cover the pot again and return to the stove over medium-high heat. Check the clams after 1 minute. When all the shells are open, the clams are done. Do not overcook. Cool.

6. When the clams are cool enough to handle, remove the meat from each shell. Pour the clam juice into a small bowl, and set aside. Discard all the shells.

7. Using a sharp knife, coarsely chop the clams. Place the clams in a another small bowl, and set aside.

8. After the sauce has been cooking for about 3 hours, add the clam juice to the sauce, stirring well. Partially cover and continue cooking.

9. At the same time the water is put on for the pasta, add the clams to the sauce.

10. Spoon over the pasta. Serve hot.

Take a Chance:

• Most of the taste of the clams comes from the juice. Discard the whole clams if you can't bear the thought of biting into them.

Suggested Pastas:

- Serve over the following pastas: Basil (page 82), Whole Wheat Basil (page 84), Lemon Basil (page 86), Pesto (page 64), or Garlic (page 62).

Herbed Butter Sauce

Preparation Time: *10 Minutes*
Yield: *¼ Cup*

¼ cup plus 2 tablespoons soy butter

2 garlic cloves, crushed

8 fresh sage leaves, thinly sliced, or 2 teaspoons dried

With so many sauces to choose from, we tend to forget one of the most simple—butter. With a touch of herbs, this makes a great side dish. Or, serve over Plain Potato Gnocchi (page 220).

1. Place the butter in a small saucepan over medium heat. After it melts, add the garlic, and sauté for 1 minute.

2. Remove the pan from the heat, and add the sage.

3. Spoon over the pasta. Serve hot.

Take a Chance:

- Use oregano, basil, rosemary, or dill instead of sage. Or use a combination of herbs.

Suggested Pastas:

- Serve over the following pastas or noodles: Broccoli (page 70), Bugs's Carrot (page 72), Beet (page 73), Tomato (page 77), Jalapeño Pepper (page 75), Corn (page 79), Blue Corn (page 80), Basil (page 82), Whole Wheat Basil (page 84), Lemon Basil (page 86), Pesto (page 64), Sage Thyme (page 88), Parsley (page 90), Buckwheat With Cilantro (page 92), Garlic (page 62), Carrot Dill (page 98), Curry (page 102), Saffron (page 104), Whole Wheat Lemon Pepper (page 107), Chili Powder (page 109), Sweet Paprika (page 105), Tomato Chili (page 112), Cheesy Parmesan (page 116), Udon (page 118), or Soba (page 120).

Pescatore Sauce

This delicate tomato sauce is filled with sweet morsels of fresh fish.

Preparation Time: *45 Minutes*
Yield: *4 Cups*

1. Place the clams and mussels in a sink full of cold water. Using a small wire brush, clean each clam and mussel individually under cold running water. Discard any with open or cracked shells. Set aside.

2. Place ¼ cup of the broth and 2 tablespoons of the oil in a large skillet over medium heat. Add the garlic and shallots, and sauté for 1 minute. Add the oregano, and sauté another minute.

3. Add the tomatoes and pepper, and mix well. Cover and cook for 25 to 30 minutes.

4. Place the remaining broth and oil in another large skillet over medium heat. Add the shrimp, and sauté until they just start to turn pink. Use a slotted spoon to remove the shrimp to a warmed dish.

5. Place the fish in the same skillet, and sauté for 1 to 2 minutes, or until the fish starts to turn opaque. Using a slotted spoon, place the fish in the same dish with the shrimp.

6. Place the clams and mussels in the same skillet. Add more broth or oil if necessary. Turn the heat to high, cover, and cook for 5 minutes, or until their shells are open. Discard any that do not open.

7. Add the shrimp, fish, clams, and mussels to the tomato sauce, and heat for 1 to 2 minutes. Do not overcook.

8. Spoon over the pasta. Serve hot.

8 small clams, in their shells

8 mussels, in their shells

½ cup Vegetable Broth (page 200), divided

¼ cup olive oil, divided

2 garlic cloves, finely minced

2 shallots, coarsely chopped

1 teaspoon dried oregano, or about 2 teaspoons fresh

2 pounds tomatoes, peeled and coarsely chopped (about 4 cups)

⅛ teaspoon freshly ground black pepper

8 ounces medium shrimp, shelled and deveined

8 ounces firm white fish, such as cod, flounder, or sole

Take a Chance:

• Omit the oregano, and add 3 tablespoons shredded fresh basil with the fish.

• Add ½ teaspoon crushed red pepper with the tomatoes.

Suggested Pastas:

• Serve over Garlic Pasta (page 62), Chili Powder Pasta (page 109), Sweet Paprika Pasta (page 105), or Red Wine Pasta (page 111).

Sinless Summer Cheese Sauce

Preparation Time: 5 Minutes
Yield: 2 Cups

2 cups low-fat ricotta or cottage
  cheese

2 green onions, thinly sliced

1 tablespoon chopped fresh
  oregano, or about 1 teaspoon
  dried

This is not exactly a traditional cheese sauce. But it is easy, and only the pasta needs to be cooked. This makes a quick lunch or a light summer dinner. You can also serve it as a dip with the chips in Chapter 9.

1. Place all the ingredients in a small bowl, and mix well.

2. Spoon over the pasta. Serve cold. Cool the pasta after adding the sauce.

Take a Chance:

- Use ¼ cup finely chopped onions or leeks instead of green onions.
- Add ½ cup seeded and chopped cucumber.

Suggested Pastas:

- Serve over the following pastas or noodles: Corn (page 79), Blue Corn (page 80), Basil (page 82), Whole Wheat Basil (page 84), Lemon Basil (page 86), Pesto (page 64), Parsley (page 90), Buckwheat With Cilantro (page 92), Garlic (page 62), Spinach Basil (page 94), Carrot Dill (page 98), Saffron (page 104), Whole Wheat Lemon Pepper (page 107), Chili Powder (page 109), Sweet Paprika (page 105), or Cheesy Parmesan (page 116).

Italian Cheese Medley

This is a wonderfully rich, creamy sauce. Use this as the sauce for Baked Ziti (page 205) or Festive Macaroni and Cheese (page 207), or on top of Whole Wheat Chicken Mushroom Pizza (page 214) or Lasagna Roll-Ups (page 213).

1. Place all the cheeses in a medium-sized saucepan. Cook over low heat until the cheese begins to melt, stirring constantly.

2. Add the milk 1 tablespoon at a time until the sauce is smooth.

3. Spoon over the pasta. Serve hot.

Take a Chance:

- Use low-fat cottage cheese instead of ricotta.

Suggested Pastas:

- Serve over the following pastas or noodles: Spinach (page 66), Whole Wheat Spinach (page 68), Broccoli (page 70), Tomato (page 77), Jalapeño Pepper (page 75), Parsley (page 90), Buckwheat With Cilantro (page 92), Garlic (page 62), Tomato Oregano (page 96), Chili Powder (page 109), Sweet Paprika (page 105), Tomato Chili (page 112), or Cheesy Parmesan (page 116).

Preparation Time: *20 Minutes*
Yield: *1 1/2 Cups*

1/4 cup shredded low-fat mozzarella cheese

1/4 cup diced Gruyère cheese

1/4 cup freshly grated Parmesan cheese

1/2 cup low-fat ricotta cheese

1/4 cup soy milk

11

Light Sauces

If you're like us, you are always looking for pasta meals that combine great taste with good nutrition, and that's the focus of the recipes provided in this chapter. Some are slimmed-down versions of classic recipes. Others are our own light, natural creations.

One way to cut down on calories is to use broth to replace all or most of the oil normally called for in a recipe. Most of our recipes use our very own Vegetable Broth (page 200) or Chicken Broth (page 200), but even commercial bouillon–either the little cubes, or the bottles or packets of powder–will do. If you do use store-bought bouillon, try to get a low-sodium variety.

Another way to lighten up even a traditionally calorie-laden recipe is to use the substitute ingredients called for in many of these recipes. Soybeans are used to create healthier versions of such animal-based products as milk, butter, and meat. There is also Parmesan cheese made from soybeans, which can be used in any recipe in this book that calls for Parmesan cheese. Soybeans are also the basic ingredient in tofu, a more traditional foodstuff borrowed from Asian cooking, that is used in a number of the recipes in this book.

Lavender-Scented Roasted Garlic Sauce

Preparation Time: *1¼ Hours*
Yield: *½ Cup*

1 large head of garlic

¼ cup olive oil, divided

¼ teaspoon dried lavender

¼ cup Vegetable Broth (page 200)

⅛ teaspoon freshly ground black pepper

Roasted garlic is naturally sweet, and just a sprinkle of lavender adds an intriguing taste.

1. Peel away most of the papery outer skin from the head of garlic.

2. Cut a 6-inch-square piece of aluminum foil and place the garlic in the middle. Drizzle 2 teaspoons of the oil over the garlic, and sprinkle with the lavender. Wrap the foil around the garlic. Using a fork, poke some holes into the foil. Place the garlic on a baking sheet, and bake at 350°F for 1 hour, or until the garlic is tender.

3. Squeeze the garlic from each clove, and set aside.

4. Place the remaining oil and the broth in a small saucepan over medium heat. Using a wire whisk, incorporate the garlic into the liquid. Add the pepper, and stir well.

5. Spoon over the pasta. Serve hot or cold. If serving cold, cool the pasta and the sauce together.

Take a Chance:

- Use thyme or rosemary instead of lavender.
- Add ½ teaspoon crushed red pepper with the oil.
- Add 1 cup steamed vegetables to the sauce.

Suggested Pastas:

- Serve hot over Corn Pasta (page 79).
- Serve hot or cold over Broccoli Pasta (page 70), Garlic Pasta (page 62), or Cheesy Parmesan Noodles (page 116).
- Serve cold over Blue Corn Pasta (page 80), Whole Wheat Lemon Pepper Pasta (page 107), or Red Wine Pasta (page 111).

Uncooked Tomato Sauce

This sauce is best during the summer, when tomatoes are at their juicy best. Use only fresh tomatoes in this recipe. Serve over Tortellini With Fresh Spinach Filling (page 217).

1. Place all the ingredients except the flowers in a large bowl. Mix well, cover, and set aside for at least 30 minutes, stirring occasionally.

2. Spoon over the pasta, and garnish with the flowers. Serve over hot or cold pasta.

Take a Chance:

• Add ½ cup zucchini or crookneck squash cut into matchstick-sized pieces.

Suggested Pastas:

• Serve over the following pastas or noodles: Spinach (page 66), Whole Wheat Spinach (page 68), Jalapeño Pepper (page 75), Corn (page 79), Blue Corn (page 80), Basil (page 82), Whole Wheat Basil (page 84), Lemon Basil (page 86), Pesto (page 64), Sage Thyme (page 88), Garlic (page 62), Saffron (page 104), Whole Wheat Lemon Pepper (page 107), Curry Spinach (page 114), Cheesy Parmesan (page 116), Udon (page 118), or Soba (page 120).

Preparation Time: *30 Minutes*
Yield: *4 Cups*

2 pounds tomatoes, coarsely chopped (about 4 cups)

2 garlic cloves, coarsely chopped

¼ cup coarsely chopped onion

3 tablespoons extra virgin olive oil

1 teaspoon chopped fresh oregano or basil, or about ½ teaspoon dried

¼ teaspoon freshly ground black pepper

¼ cup edible flowers, such as nasturtiums or calendulas

Onion Raisin Sauce

A handful of raisins enhances the naturally sweet taste of this slow-cooked sauce.

1. Place the butter in a large skillet over medium heat. After it melts, reduce the heat to low, and add the onions. Cover and cook for 30 minutes, stirring occasionally. Add additional butter or some of the vegetable broth, if necessary.

2. Add the vegetable broth and raisins. Continue cooking, uncovered, for 20 minutes. Stir in the pepper.

3. Spoon over the pasta. Serve hot.

Preparation Time: *60 Minutes*
Yield: *1¼ Cups*

2 tablespoons soy butter

1 pound white or yellow onions, peeled and thinly sliced

¾ cup Vegetable Broth (page 200)

½ cup dark raisins

⅛ teaspoon freshly ground black pepper

Take a Chance:

- Use golden raisins instead of dark.
- Omit the raisins, and add 1 teaspoon fennel seeds with the onions.

Suggested Pastas:

- Serve over the following pastas or noodles: Spinach (page 66), Whole Wheat Spinach (page 68), Corn (page 79), Sage Thyme (page 88), Garlic (page 62), Curry (page 102), Whole Wheat Lemon Pepper (page 107), Chili Powder (page 109), Sweet Paprika (page 105), Cheesy Parmesan (page 116), Udon (page 118), or Soba (page 120).

Amatriciana Sauce

Preparation Time: *45 Minutes*
Yield: *3 Cups*

8 turkey breakfast strips

2 tablespoons olive oil

½ cup coarsely chopped onion

1 garlic clove, coarsely chopped

3½ cups (28 ounces) crushed tomatoes (canned)

¼ teaspoon freshly ground black pepper

¼ cup freshly grated Romano cheese

The original recipe for this famous dish from the region just north of Rome calls for an Italian bacon called "pancetta." We have substituted turkey breakfast strips.

1. Place the breakfast strips in a large skillet, and cook until crisp. Drain on paper toweling, crumble, and set aside. Wipe out the skillet with paper toweling.

2. Place the oil in the skillet over medium heat. Add the onion, and sauté for 5 minutes. Add the garlic, and sauté for another 2 minutes.

3. Add the breakfast strips, tomatoes, and pepper, and cook, uncovered, for 30 minutes.

4. Spoon over the pasta, and garnish with the cheese. Serve hot.

Take a Chance:

- Use Parmesan cheese instead of Romano.
- Add ¼ teaspoon crushed red pepper with the garlic.

Suggested Pastas:

- Serve over the following pastas or noodles: Parsley (page 90), Buckwheat With Cilantro (page 92), Garlic (page 62), Saffron (page 104), Whole Wheat Lemon Pepper (page 107), or Cheesy Parmesan (page 116).

Hot Citrus Sauce

Each mouthful is a combination of hot peppers and cool citrus. This sauce works best with tubular pasta.

Preparation Time: *20 Minutes*
Yield: *4 Cups*

1. Place the broth in a large skillet, and sauté the garlic for 1 minute. Add the chili peppers, and both the lemon and orange zests, and sauté another minute.

2. Add the tomatoes and cook, uncovered, over medium heat for 25 minutes.

3. Remove from the heat. Add the lemon and orange juices. Stir well.

4. Spoon over the pasta, and garnish with the cilantro. Serve hot.

¼ cup Vegetable Broth (page 200)

3 large garlic cloves, minced

4 large red chili peppers, crushed (we suggest dried, but you could use fresh)

Grated zest and juice of 1 medium lemon

Grated zest and juice of 1 medium orange

2 pounds tomatoes, peeled, seeded, and diced (about 4 cups)

¼ cup fresh chopped cilantro

Take a Chance:

- Use 2 teaspoons cayenne pepper instead of the chili peppers.
- Add 2 teaspoons chopped fresh oregano with the tomatoes.

Suggested Pastas:

- Serve over the following pastas or noodles: Corn (page 79), Blue Corn (page 80), Garlic (page 62), Whole Wheat Lemon Pepper (page 107), Chili Powder (page 109), Sweet Paprika (page 105), Cheesy Parmesan (page 116), Udon (page 118), or Soba (page 120).

Adding Zest With Citrus

Some of the recipes in this book call for lemon or orange zest. Zest is the outermost layer of skin on citrus fruit, and contains the most aromatic oils.

There are several ways to zest a fruit. One is to use a hand grater. Another is to use a vegetable peeler, which will take the zest off in larger pieces that may then have to be chopped before adding to a recipe. A third method is to use a zester, which works like a vegetable peeler but is specifically designed to remove zest. Whatever method you use, be sure to not remove any of the pith, the white part underneath the colored outer surface. The pith is bitter.

If you don't grow your own citrus, or if you can't get organic fruit, be sure to wash your lemons and oranges very carefully before zesting them.

Creamy Natural Tomato Sauce

Preparation Time: 30 Minutes
Yield: 3 Cups

3 cups (24 ounces) tomato sauce

3 fresh basil leaves

¼ cup drained, mashed firm silken tofu

3 tablespoons chopped fresh garlic chives

The use of silken tofu makes for a light cream sauce.

1. Place the tomato sauce and basil in a medium-sized saucepan over medium heat. Cook, uncovered, for 20 minutes.

2. Add the tofu, and mix well. Continue cooking the sauce for 10 minutes.

3. Serve over the pasta, and garnish with the chives. Serve hot.

Take a Chance:

• Instead of using all silken tofu, use equal parts tofu and soy milk.

Suggested Pastas:

• Serve over the following pastas or noodles: Spinach (page 66), Whole Wheat Spinach (page 68), Broccoli (page 70), Bugs's Carrot (page 72), Jalapeño Pepper (page 75), Corn (page 79), Blue Corn (page 80), Parsley (page 90), Buckwheat With Cilantro (page 92), Garlic (page 62), Whole Wheat Lemon Pepper (page 107), Chili Powder (page 109), Sweet Paprika (page 105), Curry Spinach (page 114), Red Wine (page 111), Cheesy Parmesan (page 116), Udon (page 118), or Soba (page 120).

Carbonara Sauce

Preparation Time: 15 Minutes
Yield: ½ Cup

6 turkey breakfast strips

1 cup egg substitute, or enough to equal 4 whole eggs

¼ cup plus 1 tablespoon freshly grated Romano cheese

¼ teaspoon freshly ground black pepper

The Romano cheese used in this recipe gives it more of a bite than Parmesan cheese would. We've replaced the pancetta, *or Italian bacon, and whole eggs in the original recipe with turkey breakfast strips and an egg substitute.*

1. Place the breakfast strips in a large skillet, and cook until crisp. Drain on paper toweling, crumble, and set aside.

2. Place the egg substitute, cheese, and pepper in a small bowl, and whisk together.

3. Toss the egg mixture with the hot pasta, and garnish with the crumbled turkey strips. The pasta will cook the egg.

Take a Chance:

- Use 4 whole eggs or egg whites instead of the egg subsitute.
- Add ½ teaspoon crushed red pepper to the egg mixture.

Suggested Pastas:

- Serve over the following pastas or noodles: Broccoli (page 70), Tomato (page 77), Parsley (page 90), Garlic (page 62), or Cheesy Parmesan (page 116).

Feathery Light Alfredo Sauce

Even when made with healthy lifestyle ingredients, this sauce is something you may want to save for a special treat. It is traditionally served with fettuccine, or you can serve it over Tortellini With Fresh Spinach Filling (page 217).

Preparation Time: *25 Minutes*
Yield: *2 Cups*

2 tablespoons Vegetable Broth (page 200)

1 teaspoon soy margarine

2 garlic cloves, crushed

1 tablespoon arrowroot

1½ cups soy milk

½ cup Parmesan cheese*

½ cup drained, mashed firm silken tofu

⅛ teaspoon freshly ground black pepper

1 tablespoon chopped fresh Italian parsley

* For the healthiest sauce possible, we recommend the use of Parmesan made from soybeans.

1. Place the broth and margarine in a medium-sized skillet over medium heat. Add the garlic, and sauté for 1 minute.

2. Add the arrowroot and stir. Gradually add the milk, stirring constantly to blend the arrowroot. Simmer, uncovered, for 10 minutes, or until the liquid thickens. Stir constantly to keep the milk from burning.

3. Add the cheese, tofu, and pepper. Stir constantly, until the cheese melts.

4. Spoon over the pasta, and garnish with the parsley. Serve hot.

Take a Chance:

- Omit the parsley, and use chopped fresh basil.

Suggested Pastas:

- Serve over the following pastas or noodles: Jalapeño Pepper (page 75), Parsley (page 90), Buckwheat With Cilantro (page 92), Garlic (page 62), Tomato Oregano (page 96), Whole Wheat Lemon Pepper (page 107), Chili Powder (page 109), Sweet Paprika (page 105), or Cheesy Parmesan (page 116).

Spicy Steamed Vegetable Sauce

Preparation Time: *30 Minutes*
Yield: *3 Cups*

1 cup broccoli florets

1 cup cauliflower florets

1 medium carrot, sliced

8 ounces mushrooms, sliced

¼ cup Vegetable Broth (page 200)

3 tablespoons extra virgin olive oil

3 cloves garlic, minced

3 shallots, chopped

¼ teaspoon crushed red pepper

1 teaspoon arrowroot

The crisp taste of fresh vegetables is the perfect foil for spaghetti. Or you can serve this sauce over Tortellini With Fresh Spinach Filling (page 217) or Lasagna Roll-Ups (page 213).

1. Place the broccoli and cauliflower florets in a steamer, and steam for 3 minutes. Remove the florets to a large dish.

2. Place the carrot and mushrooms in the steamer for 2 minutes. Remove and add to the broccoli and cauliflower. All the vegetables should be crisp.

3. Place the broth and oil in a large skillet over medium heat. Add the garlic and the shallots, and sauté for 2 minutes. Add the red pepper, and sauté for an additional minute.

4. Add the arrowroot, and mix well. Cook 2 to 3 minutes, or until the broth begins to thicken.

5. Add all the vegetables to the skillet, and sauté for 2 minutes.

6. Spoon over the pasta. Serve hot or cold. If serving cold, cool the pasta and the sauce together.

Take a Chance:

• Omit the crushed red pepper and add 1 teaspoon garlic chili paste.*

• Add ½ cup tomato sauce after adding the crushed red pepper. Cook the sauce for 10 minutes before adding the vegetables.

Suggested Pastas:

• Serve hot over the following pastas: Broccoli (page 70), Beet (page 73), Tomato (page 77), Jalapeño Pepper (page 75), Corn (page 79), Blue Corn (page 80), Sage Thyme (page 88), Saffron (page 104), or Tomato Chili (page 112).

• Serve hot or cold over Garlic Pasta (page 62) or Cheesy Parmesan Noodles (page 116).

• Serve cold over with the following pastas: Basil (page 82), Whole Wheat Basil (page 84), Lemon Basil (page 86), Pesto (page 64), Parsley (page 90), Buckwheat With Cilantro (page 92), Tomato Oregano (page 96), Carrot Dill (page 98), Curry (page 102), or Red Wine (page 111).

*This delicious hot condiment consists of garlic mashed with red chili. Sometimes, a little vinegar is added. You can find it in Asian food markets.

Bolognese-Style Sauce

Traditional Bolognese sauce is made with beef and pork that has been ground or cut into cubes, along with heavy cream. It didn't take much effort to make this sauce fit into our healthier lifestyle. Use it in Baked Ziti (page 205).

1. Place the broth and margarine in a large skillet over medium heat. Add the onion, and sauté for 2 minutes. Add the carrot and celery, and sauté another 5 minutes. Add the meat, and cook for 2 minutes.

2. Increase the heat to medium-high, and add the tomatoes, nutmeg, and pepper. Bring the mixture almost to the boiling point, and then reduce the heat to medium-low. Cook, covered, for 20 minutes.

3. Add the milk, stir well, and continue cooking for an additional 20 minutes.

4. Remove the cover from the skillet and add the mashed tofu, stirring well. Simmer for 2 minutes.

5. Spoon over the pasta. Serve hot.

Take a Chance:

- Add ½ cup sliced white mushrooms with the vegetables.
- Add ½ cup dry red wine with the vegetables.

Suggested Pastas:

- Serve over the following pastas or noodles: Parsley (page 90), Buckwheat With Cilantro (page 92), Garlic (page 62), Carrot Dill (page 98), Saffron (page 104), Chili Powder (page 109), Sweet Paprika (page 105), or Cheesy Parmesan (page 116).

Preparation Time: *1¼ Hours*
Yield: *4½ Cups*

¼ cup Vegetable Broth (page 200)

3 tablespoons soy margarine

1 cup coarsely chopped onion

1 large carrot, coarsely chopped

1 large celery stalk, coarsely chopped

1 cup of your favorite meat substitute, such as Heartline

2 pounds tomatoes, peeled and finely chopped (about 4 cups)

Pinch of nutmeg

¼ teaspoon freshly ground black pepper

½ cup soy milk

½ cup drained, mashed firm silken tofu

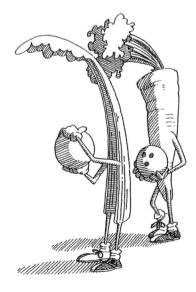

Garden Fresh Primavera

Preparation Time: *30 Minutes*
Yield: *3 Cups*

1 cup soy milk

¾ cup low-fat cottage cheese

¼ cup freshly grated Parmesan cheese

2 tablespoons soy margarine

2 shallots, finely chopped

½ cup sliced mushrooms

½ cup fresh green peas

8 ounces thin asparagus, trimmed, cut into 2-inch pieces, and steamed

2 tablespoons chopped fresh Italian parsley, or about 1 tablespoon dried

The Italian word "primavera" means "spring." Although fresh vegetables just popping up out of the ground are the best, use any fresh vegetable available during the year. Traditionally made with cream, we've lightened up this classic sauce with soy milk and low-fat cottage cheese. It goes well with spaghetti or fettuccine.

1. Place the milk, cottage cheese, and Parmesan cheese in a food processor or blender, and pulse 5 times or until smooth. Set aside.

2. Place the margarine in a large skillet over medium heat. After the margarine melts, add the shallots, and sauté for 2 minutes. Add the mushrooms and green peas, and sauté for 2 minutes. Remove the pan from the heat.

3. Place the cheese mixture in a medium-sized saucepan, and cook over medium heat for 10 minutes, or until the sauce thickens, stirring constantly.

4. Return the skillet with the vegetables to medium heat. Pour the cheese mixture into the skillet, and add the asparagus and the parsley. Mix well.

5. Spoon over the pasta. Serve hot.

Take a Chance:

• Add ½ cup sliced zucchini with the vegetables.

• Instead of steaming the asparagus, cut the stalks diagonally into ½-inch pieces and sauté with the mushrooms. Adjust the cooking time if necessary.

• Use low-fat ricotta cheese instead of cottage cheese.

Suggested Pastas:

• Serve over the following pastas or noodles: Spinach (page 66), Whole Wheat Spinach (page 68), Broccoli (page 70), Jalapeño Pepper (page 75), Sage Thyme (page 88), Garlic (page 62), Tomato Oregano (page 96), Carrot Dill (page 98), Whole Wheat Lemon Pepper (page 107), Chili Powder (page 109), Sweet Paprika (page 105), Curry Spinach (page 114), or Cheesy Parmesan (page 116).

12

International Sauces

These are the sauces you can turn to on those nights when you're in the mood for culinary adventure, with flavors that will take you from France to Thailand to Mexico. Get ready for some new taste experiences!

You might have to hunt a little for some of the ingredients, but we can promise that the results will be worth it. Truffles and wild mushrooms can be found in gourmet shops. Lemongrass and cilantro can be found in Asian food markets, along with condiments such as shoyu sauce. Cilantro can also be found in stores that specialize in Mexican food, as can tomatillos and a wide variety of chilies.

And don't forget your friendly local supermarket. Many supermarkets are trying to keep up with their customers' expanding tastes by stocking items that many Americans hadn't even heard of a few years ago. Why this interest in international food? There are many reasons, from the influx of different cusines through immigration to the popularity of TV cooking shows. Whatever the reason, a pasta lover couldn't be happier.

A Sauce of Truffles

Preparation Time: *20 Minutes*
Yield: *½ Cup*

¼ cup plus 2 tablespoons
  Chicken Broth (page 200)

¼ cup plus 2 tablespoons extra
  virgin olive oil

1 tablespoon dry sherry

1 ounce black truffles, fresh or
  canned, finely chopped

½ teaspoon freshly ground black
  pepper

Freshly grated Romano cheese

Truffles—those prized underground mushrooms—are not something we eat every day, so a gift of wonderful black truffles sent us scrambling. Not knowing exactly how to serve them, we made a very simple sauce and tossed it with pasta.

1. Place the chicken broth, oil, and sherry in a medium-sized skillet over medium heat. Add the truffles and pepper, and sauté for 1 minute.

2. Spoon over the pasta with the cheese on the side. Serve hot or cold. If serving cold, cool the pasta and the sauce together.

Take a Chance:

• Sauté 2 chopped garlic cloves with the chicken broth mixture. The garlic can either be left in the pan or removed before adding the truffles and pepper.

Suggested Pastas:

• Serve hot or cold with Garlic Pasta (page 62) or Cheesy Parmesan Noodles (page 116).
• Serve cold with Red Wine Pasta (page 111).

Cilantro Peanut Pesto

Preparation Time: *10 Minutes*
Yield: *3 Cups*

2 garlic cloves

½ cup dry-roasted peanuts

3 cups fresh cilantro, stems
  removed

½ cup lemon juice

½ cup extra virgin olive oil

¼ cup freshly grated Parmesan
  cheese

Why should basil and pine nuts have all the fun? Used extensively in both Asian and Mexican cooking, cilantro mixes well with peanuts. The lemon juice gives this pesto a sunny taste, and cuts down on the amount of oil needed. Serve over Classic Cheese Ravioli (page 209). This sauce also goes well with fettuccine, fusilli, shells, or penne.

1. Place the garlic cloves in a food processor or blender, and pulse 3 times. Add the peanuts, and process until the nuts are finely ground.

2. Add the cilantro, and pulse until it is finely chopped.

3. Add the lemon juice, and pulse until mixed. Add the oil in a slow stream. Add the cheese, and pulse until blended.

Top: **Bugs's Carrot Pasta (page 72)**
with Herbed Butter Sauce (page 166)
Center: **Lemon Basil Pasta (page 86)**
with Uncooked Tomato Sauce (page 173)
Bottom: **Parsley Pasta (page 90)**
with Featherly Light Alfredo Sauce (page 177)

Top: Corn Pasta (page 79)
*   with Confetti Sauce (page 187)*
Center: Beet Pasta (page 73)
*   with Spicy Steamed Vegetable Sauce (page 178)*
Bottom: Broccoli Pasta (page 70)
*   with Garden Fresh Primavera (page 180)*

4. Spoon over the pasta. Serve hot or cold. If serving cold, cool the pasta after adding the sauce.

Take a Chance:

• Add 2 chopped and seeded serrano or Thai peppers (see page 76) with the cilantro.

• Instead of cilantro, use parsley.

Suggested Pastas:

• Serve hot over Corn Pasta (page 79) or Blue Corn Pasta (page 80).

• Serve hot or cold over Garlic Pasta (page 62) or Cheesy Parmesan Noodles (page 116).

• Serve cold over Chili Powder Pasta (page 109), Sweet Paprika Pasta (page 105), Udon Noodles (page 118), or Soba Noodles (page 120).

Greek Tomato Sauce

A surprising amount of pasta is eaten in Greece, where all pasta except spaghetti itself is called macaroni. Serve over Classic Cheese Ravioli (page 209), or on top of Whole Wheat Chicken Mushroom Pizza (page 214), or use as a sauce for Traditional Lasagna (page 206).

Preparation Time: *1 Hour*
Yield: *3 Cups*

3 tablespoons olive oil, preferably Greek

3 garlic cloves, coarsely chopped

2 pounds tomatoes, peeled and coarsely chopped (about 4 cups)

¼ teaspoon ground cinnamon

¼ teaspoon freshly ground black pepper

3 teaspoons melted soy margarine

1. Place the oil in a large skillet over medium heat. Add the garlic, and sauté 1 minute.

2. Add the tomatoes, cinnamon, and pepper. Cover and cook over low heat for 45 minutes, stirring occasionally.

3. Toss the pasta with the melted margarine, and spoon the sauce over the pasta. Serve hot.

Take a Chance:

• Add 1 teaspoon of capers with the tomatoes.

Suggested Pastas:

• Serve over Sage Thyme Pasta (page 88), Garlic Pasta (page 62), Red Wine Pasta (page 111), or Cheesy Parmesan Noodles (page 116).

Curry Sauce With Chicken

Preparation Time: *1¹⁄₂ Hours*
Yield: *1¹⁄₂ Cups*

1 teaspoon ground coriander

¹⁄₂ teaspoon ground turmeric

¹⁄₈ teaspoon ground cumin

¹⁄₈ teaspoon cayenne pepper

¹⁄₈ teaspoon powdered mustard

¹⁄₈ teaspoon freshly ground black pepper

1 pound free-range chicken pieces, skin removed (see page 162)

3 teaspoons soy margarine

¹⁄₄ cup finely chopped onion

1 garlic clove, crushed

¹⁄₄ teaspoon grated fresh ginger

2 teaspoons distilled white vinegar

¹⁄₂ cup Chicken Broth (page 200)

¹⁄₄ cup water

1 tablespoon lemon juice

1 tablespoon finely chopped fresh cilantro

Never make more of the spice mixture than is needed, as it tends to lose its flavor when kept for any period of time.

1. Place all of the dry spices together in a small bowl, and mix. Set aside.

2. Place the chicken pieces in a large skillet, and cover with water. Bring the water to a boil over high heat. Reduce the heat to medium, and poach the chicken until it's cooked through, approximately 20 minutes. Drain. Cover and cool on the counter about 15 to 20 minutes, or until cool to the touch.

3. Place the cooked chicken on a cutting board and remove the bones. Using either your fingers or two forks, shred the chicken into ¹⁄₂-inch pieces. Set aside.

4. Place the margarine in a large skillet over medium heat. After it melts, add the onion, and sauté 2 minutes. Add the garlic, ginger, and the dry spices, and sauté another minute.

5. Add the vinegar, broth, and water, and simmer for 10 minutes. Add the chicken, and cook another 10 minutes.

6. Remove the pan from the heat, and stir in the lemon juice.

7. Spoon over the pasta, and garnish with the cilantro. Serve hot.

Take a Chance:

• Add ¹⁄₄ cup chopped almonds with the lemon juice.

• Eliminate the first six ingredients, and use 2 teaspoons of commercial curry powder.

Suggested Pastas:

• Serve over the following pastas or noodles: Spinach (page 66), Whole Wheat Spinach (page 68), Broccoli (page 70), Jalapeño Pepper (page 75), Garlic (page 62), Whole Wheat Lemon Pepper (page 107), Cheesy Parmesan (page 116), Udon (page 118), or Soba (page 120).

Fresh Lemongrass Sauce

Lemongrass is an herb that's popular in Southeast Asia. It gives this simple sauce a lemony tang.

Preparation Time: 10 Minutes
Yield: 1/2 Cup

1. Place the broth and the oil in a small saucepan, and warm over medium-low heat.

2. Place the lemongrass in a medium-sized bowl. Just before the pasta is finished cooking, pour the warm liquid over the lemongrass.

3. Spoon the sauce over the pasta, and sprinkle with the cheese. Serve warm.

1/4 cup plus 2 tablespoons
    Vegetable Broth (page 200)

1/4 cup plus 2 tablespoons extra
    virgin olive oil

2 stalks fresh lemongrass, finely
    chopped (only use the bottom
    third of each stalk)

2 teaspoons freshly grated
    Parmesan cheese

Take a Chance:

• Make Herb Sauce by using 1 cup of another fresh herb such as thyme, sage, basil, or mint, either by themselves or in various combinations, instead of the lemongrass.

Suggested Pastas:

• Serve over the following pastas or noodles: Jalapeño Pepper (page 75), Corn (page 79), Blue Corn (page 80), Garlic (page 62), Chili Powder (page 109), Sweet Paprika (page 105), Cheesy Parmesan (page 116), Udon (page 118), or Soba (page 120).

Wild Mushroom Sauce

Preparation Time: 45 Minutes
Yield: 1$\frac{1}{2}$ Cups

1 ounce dried black mushrooms

1 ounce dried porcini mushrooms

1 ounce dried oyster mushrooms

Water

$\frac{1}{2}$ cup Vegetable Broth (page 200)

$\frac{1}{4}$ cup plus 1 tablespoon extra virgin olive oil

2 garlic cloves, crushed

2 teaspoons finely chopped fresh chives

The robust taste of wild mushrooms goes well with the delicate strands of angel hair pasta. Serve over Classic Cheese Ravioli (page 209) or Herbed Gnocchi (page 223).

1. Place the mushrooms in a large bowl, and cover with water. Let them sit for 30 minutes. Reserve $\frac{1}{2}$ cup of the water, and drain the excess.

2. Using a sharp knife, finely cut all the mushrooms.

3. Place the reserved water, the broth, and the oil in a medium-sized saucepan over medium-high heat. Add the garlic, and sauté for 1 minute. Add the mushrooms, and sauté another 2 minutes.

4. Spoon over the pasta, and garnish with the chives. Serve hot.

Take a Chance:

• Make a Creamy Wild Mushroom Sauce by reducing the reserved water to $\frac{1}{4}$ cup, sautéing the garlic, and then adding $\frac{1}{2}$ cup soy milk and 1 teaspoon arrowroot. Stir until the liquid thickens, and then add the mushrooms.

Suggested Pastas:

• Serve over the following pastas or noodles: Spinach (page 66), Whole Wheat Spinach (page 68), Tomato (page 77), Jalapeño Pepper (page 75), Basil (page 82), Whole Wheat Basil (page 84), Lemon Basil (page 86), Pesto (page 64), Garlic (page 62), Tomato Oregano (page 96), Curry (page 102), Tomato Chili (page 112), Curry Spinach (page 114), or Cheesy Parmesan (page 116).

Confetti Sauce

The sweetness of bell pepper, in rainbow colors, adds an interesting taste and texture to pasta.

Preparation Time: *20 Minutes*
Yield: *2 Cups*

1. Place the broth and the oil in a large skillet over medium heat. Add the garlic and shallots, and sauté for 1 minute.

2. Add all the peppers, the corn, and the tomato, and sauté for 2 minutes.

3. Remove the skillet from the heat, and stir in the oregano and parsley.

4. Spoon over the pasta. Serve hot or cold. If serving cold, cool the pasta and the sauce together.

Take a Chance:

• Add 2 seeded and chopped serrano or habanero peppers (see page 76).

• For a sweeter sauce, use all red peppers.

Suggested Pastas:

• Serve hot over the following pastas: Tomato (page 77), Sage Thyme (page 88), Parsley (page 90), Buckwheat With Cilantro (page 92), Saffron (page 104), or Tomato Chili (page 112).

• Serve hot or cold over Garlic Pasta (page 62) or Cheesy Parmesan Noodles (page 116).

• Serve cold over the following pastas: Beet (page 73), Jalapeño Pepper (page 75), Corn (page 79), Blue Corn (page 80), or Red Wine (page 111).

¾ cup Vegetable Broth (page 200)

3 tablespoons olive oil

2 garlic cloves, coarsely chopped

3 shallots, coarsely chopped

¼ cup coarsely chopped red bell pepper

¼ cup coarsely chopped yellow bell pepper

¼ cup coarsely chopped orange bell pepper

½ cup corn kernels, fresh or frozen

1 medium tomato, peeled, seeded, and coarsely chopped

1 tablespoon chopped fresh oregano, or about 1 teaspoon dried

1 tablespoon chopped fresh parsley, or about 1 teaspoon dried

Green Yogurt Dressing

Preparation Time: *30 Minutes*
Yield: *3 Cups*

1 cup broccoli florets

8 ounces fresh spinach, cleaned and cut into ½-inch slices

⅓ cup trimmed and chopped snow peas

1 green onion, thinly sliced

2 cups plain yogurt

½ teaspoon ground cumin

⅛ teaspoon cayenne pepper

⅛ teaspoon freshly ground black pepper

This is a pretty sauce, with flecks of tasty green vegetables peeping out of the creamy yogurt. Mix with shaped pasta for a wonderfully cool summer salad.

1. Place the broccoli florets in the steamer, and steam for 1 minute. Remove them, and pat dry with paper toweling. Place the broccoli in a large bowl, and set aside.

2. Steam the spinach for 1 minute. Remove from the steamer, and pat dry with paper toweling. Add to the bowl containing the broccoli. Add the peas and green onion to the bowl.

3. Place the yogurt and the spices in a small bowl, mix, and pour over the vegetables. Mix well.

4. Spoon over the pasta. Serve cold. Cool the pasta after adding the sauce.

Take a Chance:

- Omit the snow peas, and add ¼ cup green peas.
- Use half yogurt and half drained, mashed firm silken tofu.

Suggested Pastas:

- Serve over the following pastas or noodles: Corn (page 79), Blue Corn (page 80), Basil (page 82), Whole Wheat Basil (page 84), Lemon Basil (page 86), Pesto (page 64), Sage Thyme (page 88), Garlic (page 62), Spinach Basil (page 94), Tomato Oregano (page 96), Curry (page 102), Saffron (page 104), or Cheesy Parmesan (page 116).

Spicy Ginger Sauce

Serve this tantalizing sauce over noodles for a refreshing lunch or light dinner.

Preparation Time: *45 Minutes*
Yield: *$^1/_2$ Cup*

1. Place all the ingredients except the cilantro together in a small bowl, mix, and let sit for 30 minutes.

2. Spoon over the pasta, and garnish with the cilantro. Serve hot or cold. If serving cold, cool the pasta after adding the sauce.

Take a Chance:

• For a hearty salad, add 1 cucumber, peeled, seeded, and cut into matchsticks; $^1/_2$ cup bean sprouts; 1 small carrot, grated; and $^1/_4$ cup trimmed snow peas.

• Add $^1/_2$ cup shredded cooked chicken.

• Garnish with $^1/_2$ cup chopped peanuts.

Suggested Pastas:

• Serve hot over Curry Pasta (page 102).

• Serve hot or cold over Garlic Pasta (page 62) or Cheesy Parmesan Noodles (page 116).

• Serve cold over the following pastas or noodles: Spinach (page 66), Whole Wheat Spinach (page 68), Jalapeño Pepper (page 75), Chili Powder (page 109), Sweet Paprika (page 105), Curry Spinach (page 114), Udon (page 118), or Soba (page 120).

2 teaspoons grated fresh ginger

1 green onion, coarsely chopped

2 garlic cloves, crushed

2 chili peppers, seeded and diced (Thai, serrano, or jalapeño; see page 76)

3 tablespoons canola oil

3 tablespoons rice vinegar

1 tablespoon hot chili oil

$^1/_4$ cup shoyu or tamari sauce

$^1/_8$ teaspoon freshly ground black pepper

3 tablespoons chopped fresh cilantro

Verde Sauce

Preparation Time: *30 Minutes*
Yield: *3 Cups*

1 pound tomatillos

3 tablespoons Vegetable Broth (page200)

¼ cup finely chopped onion

3 garlic cloves, coarsely chopped

2 large jalapeño or serrano peppers (see page 76), seeded and coarsely chopped

1 large tomato, seeded and coarsely chopped (about ½ cup)

4 teaspoons low-fat sour cream

Tomatillos are luscious green fruits from Mexico that come covered with a paper-thin husk. This sauce goes especially well with fettuccine or linguine. Serve as a dip for the chips in Chapter 9.

1. Run the tomatillos under cold running water. Remove the husks.

2. Place the tomatillos in a saucepan, and cover with water. Bring the water to a boil over high heat. Reduce the heat to medium, and simmer the tomatillos for 5 minutes, or until soft. Drain the tomatillos, and place them in a food processor or blender. Blend until smooth.

3. Place the broth in a large skillet over medium heat. Add the onion, garlic, and peppers, and sauté for 1 minute.

4. Add the tomatillos, and simmer for 5 minutes. Add the tomato, and simmer another 5 minutes.

5. Spoon over the pasta, and garnish with the sour cream. Serve hot.

Take a Chance:

• Stir 3 tablespoons finely chopped parsley or cilantro into the sauce before serving.

• Garnish with avocado slices.

Suggested Pastas:

• Serve over the following pastas or noodles: Spinach (page 66), Whole Wheat Spinach (page 68), Jalapeño Pepper (page 75), Corn (page 79), Blue Corn (page 80), Garlic (page 62), Saffron (page 104), or Cheesy Parmesan (page 116).

Gingered Chickpeas With Garlic

In Indian cuisine, "dal" is a dish made with any legume, such as peas or beans. It's unusual to serve an authentic dal without rice or the Indian bread "poori." But with neither on hand, we adapted the recipe to what we did have—pasta. Serve over Herbed Gnocchi (page 223).

Preparation Time: *45 Minutes*
Yield: *4 Cups*

¼ cup canola oil

1 tablespoon grated fresh ginger

8 garlic cloves, finely chopped

¼ teaspoon turmeric

½ teaspoon cayenne pepper

¼ teaspoon freshly ground black pepper

1 cup (8 ounces) tomato sauce

½ cup water

2 potatoes, peeled and cut into ½-inch cubes

2 cups chickpeas, canned, or dry, cooked according to the package instructions

1. Place the oil in a large skillet over medium heat. Add the ginger and garlic, and sauté for 1 minute. Add the turmeric, cayenne pepper, and black pepper, and sauté another minute.

2. Add the tomato sauce and water, and bring the sauce to a boil over high heat. Reduce the heat to medium and cook, uncovered, for 10 minutes.

3. Add the potatoes and chickpeas, and cook for 20 minutes.

4. Spoon over the pasta. Serve hot.

Take a Chance:

• Omit the cayenne pepper, and use 4 seeded and chopped jalapeño peppers.

Suggested Pastas:

• Serve over the following pastas or noodles: Broccoli (page 70), Bugs's Carrot (page 72), Garlic (page 62), Carrot Dill (page 98), Curry (page 102), Whole Wheat Lemon Pepper (page 107), Curry Spinach (page 114), Cheesy Parmesan (page 116), Udon (page 118), or Soba (page 120).

13

Dessert Toppings

Looking for a grand finale to a fancy dinner party? Or maybe just a simple ending to a family meal? One of these deliciously sweet sauces–along with your favorite dessert pasta from Chapter 8–is the perfect answer. The dessert will taste different when these toppings are used on plain pasta, but try it for a change of pace from your usual dessert. Or sprinkle some raisins, nuts, and cinnamon over plain lasagna noodles for a delightful taste treat.

The best pasta shape for dessert is a wide, flat noodle, such as linguine or fettuccine. These noodles allow toppings to cling, but won't break easily.

One advantage of these pasta desserts: Because they are not loaded with heavy, fatty ingredients, you can indulge in them more often than you might indulge in dessert normally. Pasta's easy digestibility means that you won't suffer from that "I ate too much!" feeling, while the choice of ingredients–fruits, yogurt, tofu, spices–means that you'll be getting nutrients along with your sweets, and not just empty calories. Good health, good taste–
the best of both worlds.

Raisin Nut Sauce

Preparation Time: *20 Minutes*
Yield: *1¼ Cups*

½ cup water

½ cup fruit juice concentrate
    (juice blend)

2 tablespoons soy margarine

2 tablespoons arrowroot

½ cup dark raisins

¼ cup chopped walnuts

This sauce is crunchy and sweet at the same time.

1. Place the water, concentrate, and margarine in a small saucepan over medium-high heat, and cook until the margarine melts.

2. Add the arrowroot, and stir constantly until the sauce begins to thicken, about 5 minutes.

3. Reduce the heat to medium-low, and add the raisins. Cook the sauce for 5 minutes.

4. Stir in the walnuts, and spoon over the pasta. Serve hot.

Take a Chance:

• Add ¼ teaspoon ground cinnamon with the arrowroot.

Suggested Pastas:

• Serve over the following pastas: Cinnamon (page 125), Oatmeal Cookie (page 127), Apple Pie (page 128), Lemon (page 130), or Whole Wheat Almond (page 131).

Pasta Sweet, Pasta Healthy

Who doesn't like dessert? We tend to forget all about fat and sugar when thinking about dessert. Now, we don't have to worry. It is possible to be kind to your sweet tooth and to your body at the same time. Pasta itself is a low-fat food, and there are alternatives to sugar. They include:

• **Barley Malt Syrup.** This sweetener, made from partially sprouted barley grains, can be found at health food stores. Barley malt syrup can be used like honey.

• **Fruit Juice Concentrate.** The frozen concentrate that you use to make your morning juice can also be used in dessert recipes. White grape juice and the juice blends are neutral flavors, while orange and apple juices give your recipes a flavor kick. Make sure, though, that you're buying juice concentrate, and not a juice *drink*, since the latter consists mainly of water and sugar.

• **Honey.** Honey isn't much more nutritious than table sugar. But since it's very sweet, you can use less of it.

• **Sucanat.** These granules of evaporated sugarcane juice can also be found in health food stores. Sucanat can be used like granulated sugar.

Tart Cherry Sauce

Dried cherries give this sauce a piquant flavor.

1. Place the water and barley syrup in a small saucepan, and bring to a boil over medium-high heat. Add the arrowroot, and simmer for 2 minutes, or until the liquid begins to thicken.

2. Add the cherries. Reduce the heat, and cook for 5 minutes.

3. Spoon over the pasta. Serve hot.

Take a Chance:

- Use dried cranberries instead of the cherries.

Suggested Pastas:

- Serve over the following pastas: Carob (page 124), Oatmeal Cookie (page 127), Apple Pie (page 128), Lemon (page 130), or Whole Wheat Almond (page 131).

Preparation Time: *15 Minutes*
Yield: *1 Cup*

½ cup water

¼ cup plus 2 tablespoons barley malt syrup

1 tablespoon arrowroot

½ cup dried cherries

Ricotta Cheese Dessert Topping

The slightly sweet taste of ricotta cheese makes this delicious!

1. Place all the ingredients in a bowl, and stir well.

2. Spoon over cooled pasta.

Take a Chance:

- Use dark raisins or currants instead of golden raisins.
- Use nutmeg instead of cinnamon.

Suggested Pastas:

- Serve over any of the following pastas: Carob (page 124), Cinnamon (page 125), Oatmeal Cookie (page 127), Lemon (page 130), Strawberry (page 133), Whole Wheat Almond (page 131), or Apricot-Peach (page 135).

Preparation Time: *10 Minutes*
Yield: *2 Cups*

2 cups low-fat ricotta cheese

½ teaspoon ground cinnamon

¼ cup golden raisins

Luscious Lemon Sauce

Preparation Time: *1¼ Hours*
Yield: *1½ Cups*

1 tablespoon grated lemon zest
(see page 175)

1 tablespoon fresh lemon juice

10½ ounces extra-firm silken tofu

¼ cup honey

1 teaspoon vanilla

This lemony sauce is light and refreshing.

1. Place all the ingredients in a blender or food processor, and blend until smooth and creamy. Scrape the sides occasionally to make sure everything is well blended.

2. Place the topping in a small bowl, cover, and chill for 1 hour.

3. Spoon over cooled pasta.

Take a Chance:

• Use 1¼ cups strained yogurt (see below) instead of the tofu.

• Use half honey and half concentrated fruit sweetener, such as fruit juice concentrate.

• To make Orange Sauce, omit the lemon zest and juice, and use orange zest and juice.

Suggested Pastas:

• Serve over Apple Pie Pasta (page 128), Lemon Pasta (page 130), Strawberry Pasta (page 133), or Whole Wheat Almond Pasta (page 131).

Sticky Sweet Honey Yogurt Sauce

Preparation Time: *5 Hours*
Yield: *1 Cup*

2 cups plain yogurt

3 tablespoons honey

This sauce is smooth, creamy, and delicious.

1. Place the yogurt in a yogurt strainer or a piece of cheesecloth set in a fine mesh food strainer. Cover the yogurt, and refrigerate at least 5 hours, or overnight. The yogurt will become thicker the longer it is strained.

2. Place the strained yogurt in a small bowl, and stir in the honey.

3. Spoon over cooled pasta. Or, if you wish, cover the sauce and refrigerate up to 1 week.

Take a Chance:

- Add ¼ cup crushed walnuts with the honey.
- Use a flavored yogurt instead of the plain.

Suggested Pastas:

- Serve over any of the following pastas: Carob (page 124), Cinnamon (page 125), Oatmeal Cookie (page 127), Apple Pie (page 128), Lemon (page 130), or Apricot-Peach (page 135).

Cinnamon Orange Cranberry Topping

Don't limit the tart goodness of cranberries to holiday turkey dinners. Sprinkle them with cinnamon and serve with pasta for a fanciful dessert.

1. Place all the ingredients except the orange zest in a medium-sized saucepan, and simmer over medium heat for 10 minutes, stirring occasionally.

2. Stir in the orange zest, and continue to cook for another minute.

3. Spoon over the pasta. Serve hot or cold. If serving cold, cool the pasta and the sauce together.

Preparation Time: *15 Minutes*
Yield: *1½ Cups*

2 cups fresh cranberries, cleaned

3 tablespoons barley malt syrup

½ teaspoon ground cinnamon

¼ cup orange juice (fresh or from concentrate)

Grated zest of 1 large orange (see page 175)

Take a Chance:

- Use lemon juice and zest instead of orange.
- Instead of using preground cinnamon, grind your own by rubbing a cinnamon stick over a grater.

Suggested Pastas:

- Serve over Cinnamon Pasta (page 125), Oatmeal Cookie Pasta (page 127), Apple Pie Pasta (page 128), or Lemon Pasta (page 130).

Apple Pear Compote

Preparation Time: *30 Minutes*
Yield: *3 Cups*

1 cup water

¼ cup apple juice concentrate

1 small cinnamon stick

3 apples, peeled, cored, and cut into thick slices

2 pears, peeled, cored, and cut into thick slices

½ cup currants

½ teaspoon ground cinnamon

This is good by itself, but it's even better when served over pasta.

1. Place the water, concentrate, and cinnamon stick in a large skillet, and bring to a boil over high heat. Lower the heat to medium, and simmer for 5 minutes.

2. Discard the cinnamon stick, and add the fruit. Simmer for 10 to 15 minutes, or until the fruit is softened.

3. Spoon over the pasta, and sprinkle with the ground cinnamon. Serve warm.

Take a Chance:

• Use raisins instead of currants.

Suggested Pastas:

• Serve over any of the following pastas: Cinnamon (page 125), Oatmeal Cookie (page 127), Apple Pie (page 128), Lemon (page 130), or Strawberry (page 133).

Fresh Berry Medley

Preparation Time: *1½ Hours*
Yield: *2½ Cups*

1 cup cleaned and thinly sliced fresh strawberries

½ cup fresh blueberries, cleaned

½ cup fresh raspberries, cleaned

½ cup fresh blackberries, cleaned

1 teaspoon Sucanat

Put the fresh fruit of summer over your favorite pasta.

1. Mix all the ingredients in a large bowl. Cover and refrigerate at least 1 hour.

2. Spoon over cooled pasta.

Take a Chance:

• Instead of Sucanat, use 2 tablespoons orange juice.

Suggested Pastas:

• Serve over Cinnamon Pasta (page 125), Lemon Pasta (page 130), Strawberry Pasta (page 133), or Whole Wheat Almond Pasta (page 131), or Apricot-Peach Pasta (page 135).

14

Pasta Dishes

There are hundreds of dishes that can be made using pasta. This chapter presents some of the classic soups, such as minestrone, made with our own broth and brimming with tender vegetables and pasta, or pasta e fagioli, a hearty soup with tomatoes, pasta, and cannellini beans. We also include some of the classic entrées, such as lasagna, made with both a traditional tomato sauce and a delicate white sauce, and tortellini, stuffed with spinach, ricotta cheese, and our pesto sauce. You'll notice that some of the entrées use premade pasta, whether homemade or store-bought, while others allow you to use your pasta machine in new and exciting ways. Of course, you shouldn't limit yourself to these recipes alone. Experiment and create your own classics!

If you use a hand-cranked machine, you should note that these recipes require a roller machine, not an extrusion machine. You should also note that the gnocchi cannot be made on a hand-cranked machine at all. You'll need an electric machine to make gnocchi, or you'll have to make them by hand (we give directions for both methods).

Two Versatile Broths

A good soup—and many another good dish—starts with a good broth. And while you can use commercially prepared broth (available in either cube or powder form), why not make it yourself? Either of these hearty broths can be made ahead of time and frozen in meal-sized amounts for quick weeknight dinners.

Chicken Broth

Preparation Time: *8 Hours*
Yield: *8 Cups*

1 3-pound free-range chicken (see page 162)

Water

1 large celery stalk, with leaves attached

1 large carrot, peeled

1 small onion, skin removed and left whole

$\frac{1}{2}$ teaspoon freshly ground black pepper

This rich broth can be used in any recipe in this book that calls for broth.

1. Place the chicken in a large pot and completely cover with water. Heat to boiling. Reduce the heat to low, and skim any foam off the top.

2. Add the vegetables and the pepper to the pot, cover, and simmer for $1\frac{1}{2}$ hours, or until the chicken is tender.

3. Remove the chicken, which can be used in any recipe that calls for boiled chicken. Remove and discard the vegetables.

4. Cool the broth, cover, and refrigerate for 6 hours.

5. Skim the fat off the top of the cooled broth.

Vegetable Broth

Preparation Time: *1 Hour*
Yield: *6 Cups*

1 teaspoon oil

1 medium onion, peeled and left whole

1 large garlic clove, quartered

8 cups of water

1 small carrot, peeled and quartered

1 small celery stalk with leaves, trimmed

2 medium potatoes, peeled and diced

6 peppercorns

This satisfying and nourishing broth is the basis for most of the recipes in this book. It can also be served over Udon Noodles (page 118) or Soba Noodles (page 120).

1. Place the oil in a large pot. Add the onion, and sauté for 2 minutes. Add the garlic, and sauté for another minute.

2. Add the remaining ingredients, and simmer, uncovered, for 1 hour.

3. Using a slotted spoon, remove the vegetables and discard.

SOUPS

Minestrone Soup

This soup is even more delicious when made early in the day and allowed to sit, covered, in the refrigerator. Don't go overboard on the noodles, especially if the soup is being made in advance, as they can make the broth very thick.

Preparation Time: *1 Hour*
Yield: *12 Cups*

8 cups Vegetable Broth

1 medium onion, coarsely chopped

1 large carrot, peeled and sliced

1 large tomato, peeled, seeded, and chopped

2 medium potatoes, peeled and diced small

2 small zucchini, trimmed and diced small

2 medium-sized celery stalks, trimmed and sliced thin (leaves optional)

½ cup chickpeas, canned, or dry, cooked according to the package instructions

1 cup small shells or elbow macaroni

Freshly grated Parmesan cheese

1. Place the broth in a large pot over medium heat, and heat for 5 minutes. Add the vegetables, and simmer for 25 minutes.

2. Add the chickpeas, and cook for 5 minutes. Add the macaroni. Simmer for 2 to 4 minutes if using fresh pasta or 5 to 7 minutes if using dried pasta, or until the noodles are al dente.

3. Serve hot with the grated cheese on the side.

Take a Chance:

• Use cooked cannellini beans instead of chickpeas.

• Omit the shells or macaroni, and use thin spaghetti that has been broken into 1-inch pieces.

Suggested Pastas:

• Serve with the following pastas or noodles: Tomato (page 77), Basil (page 82), Whole Wheat Basil (page 84), Parsley (page 90), Cheesy Parmesan (page 116), Udon (page 118), or Soba (page 120).

Chicken Soup With Noodles

Preparation Time: *20 Minutes*
Yield: *7 Cups*

6 cups Chicken Broth

1 3-pound free-range chicken, cooked (see page 162; use the chicken used to create the broth, if possible)

2 cups small egg noodles

We know that chicken soup is good for anything that ails you. Is it the broth or the noodles that contain the healing properties?

1. Place the broth in a large pot over medium-low heat.

2. Skin and bone the chicken. Shred the meat, using either two forks or your fingers.

3. When the broth is warm, add the chicken and the noodles. Simmer for 2 to 4 minutes if using fresh pasta or 6 to 8 minutes if using dried pasta, or until the noodles are al dente. Serve hot.

Take a Chance:

- Add a grated carrot along with the meat and the noodles.
- Add $\frac{1}{4}$ cup chopped fresh parsley or cilantro just before serving.
- Use Tortellini With Fresh Spinach Filling (page 217) or Chicken Won Tons (page 146) in place of the egg noodles.

Suggested Pastas:

- Use any of the brown rice pastas (page 56), Udon Noodles (page 118), or Soba Noodles (page 120).

Spinach Lasagna Noodle Soup

Preparation Time: *20 Minutes*
Yield: *6 Cups*

4 cups Chicken Broth

8 ounces fresh spinach, cleaned and chopped

$\frac{1}{4}$ teaspoon freshly ground black pepper

$\frac{3}{4}$ pound lasagna noodles

Freshly grated Parmesan cheese

If you like lasagna noodles, but don't have time to make lasagna, this is the recipe for you. If you are using fresh pasta, don't totally submerge the noodles in the broth.

1. Place the chicken broth in a large pot over medium heat. Add the spinach and pepper, and cook for 2 minutes.

2. Add the noodles. Simmer for 2 to 4 minutes if using fresh pasta or 6 to 8 minutes if using dried pasta, or until the noodles are al dente.

3. Serve hot with the grated cheese on the side.

Take a Chance:

- Use Tortellini With Fresh Spinach Filling (page 217) or Chicken Won Tons (page 146) in place of the lasagna noodles.

Suggested Pastas:

- Serve with the following pastas or noodles: Spinach (page 66), Lemon Basil (page 86), Buckwheat With Cilantro (page 92), Garlic (page 62), Chili Powder (page 109), or Cheesy Parmesan (page 116).

Pasta e Fagioli

This simple soup of pasta and beans is as delicious as it is nutritious.

1. Place the broth in a large pot over medium heat. Add the onion, and sauté for 2 minutes. Add the garlic, and sauté another minute.

2. Add the tomatoes, parsley, and pepper. Simmer, uncovered, over medium-high heat for 10 minutes, stirring occasionally.

3. Add the water and the beans to the pot and simmer, uncovered, for 20 minutes.

4. Add the pasta. Simmer for 2 to 3 minutes if using fresh pasta or 5 to 7 minutes if using dry pasta, or until the noodles are al dente.

5. Serve hot with the grated cheese on the side.

Take a Chance:

- Coarsely chop 2 stalks of celery and add with the tomatoes.
- Use elbow macaroni instead of the shells.

Suggested Pastas:

- Serve with the following pastas: any of the whole wheat pastas (page 50), Tomato (page 77), Parsley (page 90), Garlic (page 62), or Tomato Oregano (page 96).

Preparation Time: *45 Minutes*
Yield: *12 Cups*

$\frac{1}{4}$ cup Vegetable Broth

$\frac{1}{2}$ cup finely chopped onion

3 garlic cloves, finely chopped

1$\frac{1}{2}$ pounds tomatoes, peeled, seeded, and finely chopped (about 3 cups)

3 tablespoons chopped fresh Italian parsley

$\frac{1}{8}$ teaspoon freshly ground black pepper

8 cups water

3 cups cannellini beans, dry, cooked according to the package instructions*

1 cup pasta shells

Freshly grated Romano cheese

*Cannellini beans are large white beans. If you can't find them, use Great Northern beans.

ENTREES

Versatile Vegetable and Pasta Stew

Preparation Time: *45 Minutes*
Yield: *4 Cups*

3 tablespoons Vegetable Broth

1 small onion, coarsely chopped

3 garlic cloves, coarsely chopped

$\frac{1}{2}$ teaspoon dried oregano

2 green bell peppers, seeded and cut into $\frac{1}{2}$-inch slices

1 red bell pepper, seeded and cut into $\frac{1}{2}$-inch slices

2 small zucchini, trimmed and cut into $\frac{1}{2}$-inch slices

2 small crookneck squash, trimmed and cut into $\frac{1}{2}$-inch slices

8 ounces mushrooms, trimmed and sliced

1 cup (8 ounces) tomato sauce

$\frac{1}{2}$ cup water

$\frac{1}{4}$ teaspoon freshly ground black pepper

$1\frac{1}{2}$ pounds cooked fettuccine or spaghetti

Pasta can be used in everyday stew and chili dishes. One of our favorites is this incredibly simple vegetable stew.

1. Place the broth in a large skillet over medium heat. Add the onion, and sauté for 2 minutes. Add the garlic and oregano, and sauté another minute. Add the vegetables, and sauté for 5 minutes. Add more broth or a tablespoon of oil if the skillet becomes too dry.

2. Turn the heat to high and add the tomato sauce, the water, and the black pepper. Bring to a boil, and then reduce the heat to medium. Simmer, uncovered, for 25 to 30 minutes, or until the vegetables are tender, stirring occasionally.

3. Mix with the pasta, and serve hot.

Take a Chance:

- Add 1 small eggplant, cut into $\frac{1}{2}$-inch cubes, with the vegetables.
- Add 1 teaspoon hot sauce with the tomato sauce.

Suggested Pastas:

- Serve with the following pastas or noodles: any of the whole wheat pastas (page 50), Broccoli (page 70), Sage Thyme (page 88), Parsley (page 90), Whole Wheat Lemon Pepper (page 107), Chili Powder (page 109), Udon (page 118), or Soba (page 120).

Baked Ziti

This recipe is delicious whether served as a simple family dinner or as a party favorite. If your extrusion machine does not have a ziti die, use a die for penne or any other large tubular pasta. But you can bend the rules by using lasagna or fettuccine noodles, or even elbow macaroni.

Preparation Time: *40 Minutes*
Yield: *6 Cups*

1 pound ziti

2 cups low-fat ricotta cheese

4 cups Chunky Marinara Sauce (page 158)

1 cup shredded mozzarella cheese

1. Cook the pasta according to the directions on page 12. If you are using fresh pasta, decrease the cooking time by 2 minutes. If you are using dried pasta, decrease the cooking time by 3 to 4 minutes. The pasta should be slightly undercooked to keep it from becoming mushy while baking. Drain.

2. Place the cooked pasta in a baking pan large enough to hold all the pasta without spilling over.

3. Mix the pasta with the ricotta cheese.

4. Pour 2 cups of the sauce over the pasta mixture. Mix well, and level the pasta in the pan.

5. Pour another cup of sauce over the pasta mixture. Reserve the remaining sauce.

6. Sprinkle the mozzarella cheese over the top of the sauce and bake, uncovered, at 350°F for 25 minutes, or until cheese is bubbly and brown.

7. Serve immediately, with the heated reserved sauce on the side.

Take a Chance:

• Mix in 1 cup chopped cooked broccoli or zucchini with the ricotta cheese.

• Mix in 1 cup chopped cooked chicken.

• Sprinkle 2 tablespoons freshly grated Parmesan or Romano cheese over the mozzarella before baking.

• Instead of the marinara, use Slow-Cooked Spaghetti Sauce With Chicken (page 162), Magnificent Mushroom Sauce (page 163), Italian Cheese Medley (page 169), or Bolognese-Style Sauce (page 179).

Suggested Pastas:

• Serve with the following pastas or noodles: any of the whole wheat pastas (page 50), Broccoli (page 70), Garlic (page 62), Spinach (page 66) Spinach Basil (page 94), Tomato Oregano (page 96), or Cheesy Parmesan (page 116).

Traditional Lasagna

Preparation Time: *2 Hours*
Yield: *12 Cups*

3 tablespoons Vegetable Broth

½ cup finely chopped onion

3 garlic cloves, finely minced

1 tablespoon dried oregano

1 pound tomatoes, peeled and finely chopped (2 cups)

2 cups tomato sauce

1 cup freshly grated Parmesan cheese

3 cups low-fat ricotta cheese

8 ounces mozzarella cheese, shredded

3 tablespoons chopped fresh Italian parsley

¼ teaspoon freshly ground black pepper

1 pound lasagna noodles (either fresh pasta or cooked dry pasta)

There are many different recipes for lasagna. This is one of our favorites, a traditional lasagna smothered in a tomato-based sauce.

If you are cutting your own noodles by hand, place the ribbons of pasta on a large cutting board and cut the dough to the desired length and width with a fluted-edge pasta wheel. The wheel will cut the curly edges normally seen on lasagna noodles. A sharp knife can be used if you want straight edges.

1. To make the sauce, place the vegetable broth in a large skillet over medium heat. Add the onion and garlic, and sauté 1 minute.

2. Add the oregano, tomatoes, and tomato sauce, and stir. Heat until the sauce is almost boiling, then reduce the heat to medium-low and simmer, uncovered, for 30 minutes.

3. Place ½ cup of the Parmesan cheese with the ricotta, mozzarella, parsley, and pepper in a small bowl. Mix and set aside.

4. To assemble the lasagna, spread 2 tablespoons of the sauce on the bottom of an ungreased 13-x-9-x-2-inch baking pan.

5. Place overlapping lasagna noodles on the bottom of the pan until it is covered. Spread ½ cup of the sauce over the noodles. Spread one third of the cheese mixture over the sauce, and add another layer of noodles. Repeat this process two more times, ending with a layer of noodles.

6. Spread ½ cup of sauce over the top, and sprinkle with the remaining Parmesan cheese. Bake, uncovered, at 350°F for 45 minutes.

7. Remove the lasagna from the oven, and cool for 5 to 10 minutes. Cut and serve with the remaining sauce.

Take a Chance:

• Sauté 1 pound of your favorite meat substitute and add it to the tomatoes when making the sauce.

• Add 1 pound of cooked, chopped spinach to the cheese mixture.

• Omit the lasagna noodles and mix the cheese with cooked elbow macaroni, shells, or rigatoni. Put the mixture in a casserole dish and bake as stated above. The sauce can be served on the side or omitted altogether.

• Prepare the lasagna with any of the tomato sauces listed in Chapter 10 (except Red Clam and Pescatore) or Greek Tomato Sauce (page 183).

Top: Chicken Soup With Noodles (page 202)
Center: Potato Gnocchi (page 220)
with Magnificent Mushroom Sauce (page 163)
Bottom: Red Wine Pasta (page 111)
with Spaghetti Sauce with Chicken (page 162)

Top: Apple Pie Pasta (page 128) with
 Cinnamon Orange Cranberry Topping (page 197)
Left: Strawberry Pasta (page 133) with
 Luscious Lemon Sauce (page 196)
Right: Cinnamon Pasta (page 125) with
 Fresh Berry Medley (page 198)

Suggested Pastas:

- Serve with the following pastas or noodles: Spinach (page 66), Corn (page 79), Basil (page 82), Whole Wheat Basil (page 84), Pesto (page 64), Parsley (page 90), Red Wine (page 111), or Cheesy Parmesan (page 116).

Festive Macaroni and Cheese

This classic American dish, gooey with cheese, is everyone's favorite. We've added green and red peppers to give it a distinctive touch.

1. Place the butter in a large saucepan over medium heat. After it melts, add the flour and cook until thoroughly blended, approximately 2 minutes.

2. Gradually add the milk to the saucepan, stirring constantly. When all the milk has been added, turn the heat to medium-high and cook for 10 minutes, or until the sauce begins to thicken, stirring constantly.

3. Remove the saucepan from the heat, and add the bell peppers and the black pepper. Stir in 3 cups of the cheese.

4. Spray a 13-x-9-x-2-inch baking pan with the nonstick spray. Add the cooked pasta to the baking pan, and combine with the sauce. Sprinkle the top with the remaining cheese and bake, uncovered, at 350°F for 40 minutes, or until the top is browned. Serve hot.

Preparation Time: *1 Hour*
Yield: *8 Cups*

3 tablespoons soy butter

4 tablespoons unbleached white flour

3 cups soy milk, at room temperature

¼ cup diced green bell pepper

¼ cup diced red bell pepper

¼ teaspoon freshly ground black pepper

3½ cups shredded sharp cheddar cheese

Nonstick cooking spray

1 pound fresh or cooked dried whole wheat elbow, penne, or ziti

Take a Chance:

- Add 1 teaspoon chili powder or hot sauce to the cheese mixture.
- Add ½ cup sliced mushrooms with the bell peppers.
- Make Macaroni and Cheese Con Queso by adding 3 seeded and chopped jalapeño peppers with the bell peppers.
- Use Italian Cheese Medley (page 169) as the sauce.

Suggested Pastas:

- Pour the cheese sauce over Spinach Pasta (page 66) or Broccoli Pasta (page 70), and serve as a side dish.
- Serve the cheese sauce over Corn Tortilla Chips (page 143).

Vegetable Lasagna With White Sauce

Preparation Time: *2 Hours*
Yield: *12 Cups*

5 tablespoons soy margarine

4 tablespoons unbleached white flour

⅛ teaspoon freshly ground black pepper

2 cups soy milk, at room temperature

1 cup freshly grated Parmesan cheese, divided

3 cups low-fat ricotta cheese

8 ounces mozzarella cheese, shredded

3 tablespoons chopped fresh Italian parsley

¼ teaspoon freshly ground black pepper

3 tablespoons olive oil

3 garlic cloves, finely minced

1 onion, finely chopped

1 teaspoon dried oregano

1½ cups broccoli florets

3 leeks, trimmed and cut into ¼-inch slices

2 carrots, thinly sliced

1 pound spinach, chopped

1 cup trimmed and thinly sliced fresh mushrooms

1 pound lasagna noodles (either fresh pasta or cooked dry pasta)

This lasagna is loaded with the goodness of fresh vegetables. It may look different, but it tastes delicious. You can use this sauce over Lasagna Roll-Ups (page 213).

1. To make the sauce, place the margarine in a medium-sized saucepan over low heat. After it melts, add the flour and pepper, and stir until the flour absorbs the liquid. Remove the saucepan from the heat.

2. Slowly add the milk, stirring constantly to blend it with flour mixture.

3. Return the saucepan to the heat and cook over high heat until boiling, stirring constantly. Boil for 1 minute. Remove from the heat, and set aside.

4. Place ½ cup of the Parmesan cheese, along with the ricotta, mozzarella, parsley, and pepper, in a small bowl. Mix and set aside.

5. Place the oil in a large skillet over medium-high heat. Add garlic and onion, and sauté for 1 minute. Add oregano, and sauté another minute.

6. Add the broccoli, leeks, and carrots, and sauté for 3 minutes. Add the remaining vegetables, and sauté for 2 more minutes.

7. To assemble the lasagna, place 2 tablespoons of the sauce on the bottom of an ungreased 13-x-9-x-2-inch baking pan.

8. Line the bottom of the pan with overlapping lasagna noodles until it is covered. Spread ½ cup the sauce over the noodles. Spread one third of the cheese mixture over the sauce. Evenly distribute one third of the vegetables over the cheese, and cover with another layer of noodles. Repeat this process two more times, ending with a layer of noodles.

9. Spread ½ cup of sauce over the top and sprinkle with the remaining Parmesan cheese. Bake, uncovered, at 350°F for 45 minutes.

10. Remove the lasagna from the oven, and cool for 5 to 10 minutes. Cut and serve with the remaining sauce.

Take a Chance:

• Add 1 cup thinly sliced zucchini or crookneck squash with the vegetables.

• Use low-fat cottage cheese instead of the ricotta.

• Omit the lasagna noodles, and mix the cheese with cooked elbow macaroni, shells, or rigatoni. Put the mixture in a casserole dish and bake as stated above. The sauce can be served on the side, or omitted altogether.

- Add Sautéed Garlic and Bread Crumbs (page 155) to the top sauce layer.

Suggested Pastas:

- Serve with the following pastas: Spinach (page 66), Broccoli (page 70), Bugs's Carrot (page 72), Corn (page 79), Basil (page 82), Whole Wheat Basil (page 84), or Parsley (page 90).

Classic Cheese Ravioli

These popular little dumplings are available commercially with several types of fillings. But it's more fun to make your own!

Note that the directions for using a hand-cranked machine call for the use of a ravioli tray (page 23). If you don't have a ravioli tray, you can certainly follow the steps for filling and cutting the ravioli included in the electric extrusion machine directions. Conversely, dough from an electric extrusion machine can also be used on a ravioli tray, but only six can be made at one time, instead of a dozen, because the pieces are not wide enough.

Preparation Time: *2 Hours*
Yield: *4 Dozen*

RAVIOLI SKINS

3½ cups unbleached white flour

1 cup water

FILLING

3 cups low-fat ricotta cheese

¼ teaspoon freshly ground black pepper

FOR ELECTRIC EXTRUSION MACHINES:

1. Place the flour in the pasta machine. With the machine running, slowly add the water. Process until the dough reaches the consistency specified in the instruction booklet. If the dough is too dry or too wet, add more water or flour per the instruction booklet.

2. Extrude the pasta, following the directions in the instruction booklet. Use the lasagna die, and be sure to extrude the dough in even lengths.

3. Lay the pieces of dough on a work surface.

4. Place the cheese and the pepper together in a small bowl, and mix. Then place a teaspoon of the cheese filling in evenly spaced mounds on the dough, leaving a ½-inch border at each end.

5. Dip your finger or a pastry brush in water, and run it along the edges of the dough and between the mounds. Place the a second strip of dough on top of the first.

6. To close, use your finger to gently press the edges and the area between the mounds.

7. Using a sharp knife or a pastry cutter, cut the squares apart. Gently press the edges together again with your finger to make sure the ravioli are sealed, or use the tines of a fork to make a decorative edge.

FOR HAND-CRANKED ROLLER MACHINES:

1. Place the flour in the food processor. With the machine running, slowly add the water. Pulse until a ball begins to form, about 10 to 15 seconds.

2. If the dough is too dry when all the liquid has been added, add 1 teaspoon of water, and pulse until a ball begins to form. If the dough is too wet, add 1 tablespoon of flour, and pulse until a ball begins to form. Repeat either process as necessary.

3. Remove the dough from the food processor and place it on a lightly floured pastry board or work surface. Knead the dough, incorporating additional flour into the ball of dough until it becomes smooth and shiny. The dough should be kneaded for 2 minutes.

4. Cover the dough with plastic wrap and let it rest for 5 minutes on the counter, or refrigerate it for up to 2 days.

5. Roll the dough through the roller attachment according to the instructions on page 25. The dough needs to be thin. Setting 6 should be used for the final rolling. Cut the dough using the lasagna attachment. The dough can also be used directly off the rollers, without going through the cutting attachment.

6. Lay the ribbons of pasta on the counter and cut them to fit the ravioli tray. Lay a ribbon over the tray. Place the pocket former that comes with the tray on top of the dough, and press down gently. Remove the pocket former. There will be pockets in the dough for the filling.

7. Place the cheese and the pepper together in a small bowl, and mix. Then place approximately ½ teaspoon of filling in each pocket. Don't overfill, or the pockets will break during cooking.

8. Dip your finger or a pastry brush in water, and run it along the edges and between the pockets. Place another sheet of rolled dough over the top of the ravioli tray.

9. Using the rolling pin or glass, gently press down on the tray, running the rolling pin over the dough. Press the rolling pin again, pushing harder, until the dough around the edges begins to break, and the individual ravioli are formed.

10. Gently turn the tray over and shake the ravioli loose. Continue this process until all the ingredients are used.

COOKING INSTRUCTIONS:

1. Ravioli will stick to each other if piled together before cooking. Because the dough is rolled so thin, the pockets will tear while you're trying to pull them apart. The easiest way to prevent this is to sprinkle some whole wheat flour or cornmeal over the ravioli before cooking.

They will be very easy to pick up, and the flour or corn meal sinks to the bottom of the pot during cooking.

2. To cook the ravioli, bring 6 to 8 quarts of water to a full boil in a large pot. Add the ravioli a few at a time and cook. The ravioli are done when they float to the surface. Serve hot.

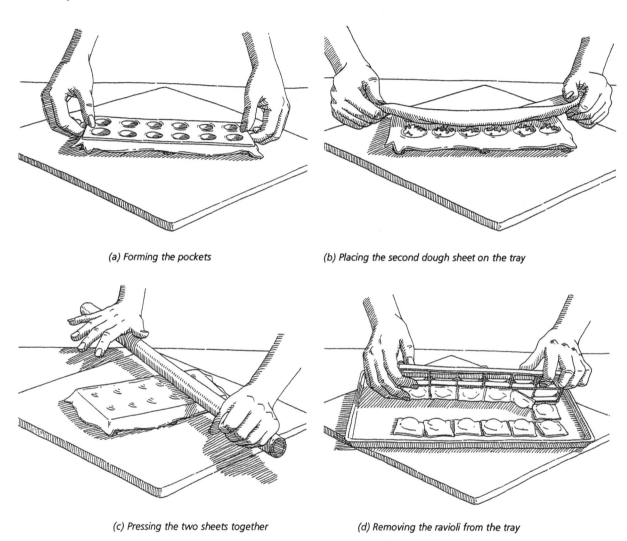

(a) Forming the pockets

(b) Placing the second dough sheet on the tray

(c) Pressing the two sheets together

(d) Removing the ravioli from the tray

Making Ravioli Using a Ravioli Tray

Take a Chance:

- Add ¼ cup finely chopped spinach to the ravioli filling.

- Omit the ricotta cheese and use low-fat cottage cheese.

- Use any of the following pastas: Spinach (page 66), Corn (page 79), Blue Corn (page 80), Basil (page 82), Whole Wheat Basil (page 84), Sage Thyme (page 88), or Parsley (page 90).

Suggested Sauces:

- Serve with the following sauces: Pesto (page 159), Chunky Marinara (page 158), Smooth Tomato Marinara With Basil (page 160), Slow-Cooked Spaghetti With Chicken (page 162), Arrabbiata (page 161), Magnificent Mushroom (page 163), Wild Mushroom (page 186), Greek Tomato (page 183), or Cilantro Peanut Pesto (page 182).

Lasagna Roll-Ups
With Chunky Marinara Sauce

Give lasagna a whole new look by rolling noodles instead of layering them.

Preparation Time: *45 Minutes*
Yield: *12 Roll-Ups*

1. Place ricotta cheese, 1 cup of the Parmesan cheese, and ½ cup of mozzarella cheese in a small bowl. Add parsley and pepper, and mix well.

2. Place a noodle on a flat working surface. Spread a tablespoon of the cheese mixture over the noodle to within ½ inch of each end.

3. Starting at one end, roll the noodle to form a little bundle. Repeat with the remaining noodles.

4. Place ½ cup of marinara sauce on bottom of a baking pan. Place roll-ups in the baking pan, seam sides down, and cover with remaining sauce.

5. Sprinkle the remaining mozzarella and Parmesan cheese on top, and bake at 350°F for 30 minutes, or until the cheese is bubbly.

3 cups low-fat ricotta cheese

1¼ cups freshly grated Parmesan cheese

1 cup shredded mozzarella cheese

3 tablespoons chopped fresh Italian parsley

¼ teaspoon freshly ground black pepper

1 pound lasagna noodles (either fresh pasta or cooked dry pasta)

Chunky Marinara Sauce (page 158)

Take a Chance:

• Instead of the marinara sauce, use the white sauce from Vegetable Lasagna With White Sauce (page 208), Magnificent Mushroom Sauce (page 163), Italian Cheese Medley (page 169), Spicy Steamed Vegetable Sauce (page 178), or Greek Tomato Sauce (page 183).

Suggested Pastas:

• Serve with the following pastas: Spinach (page 66), Broccoli (page 70), Corn (page 79), Basil (page 82), Whole Wheat Basil (page 84), Parsley (page 90), Garlic (page 62), or Red Wine (page 111).

Making a Lasagna Roll-Up

Whole Wheat Chicken Mushroom Pizza

***Preparation Time:** 2½ Hours*
***Yield:** 2 Pizzas*

PIZZA DOUGH

1 package dry yeast (¼ ounce)

1 tablespoon sugar or Sucanat
(see page 194)

Water

2 cups whole wheat flour

1½ cups unbleached white flour

1 tablespoon olive oil

TOPPING

Smooth Tomato Marinara Sauce
With Basil (page 160)

1 cup thinly sliced fresh
mushrooms

1 cup shredded cooked chicken

1½ cups shredded mozzarella
cheese

One of the optional dies available for the Simac PastaMatic machine is for pizza. So we thought, why not create a recipe for other machines? Using the hand-cranked Atlas was easy—we just had to make the dough thicker as we put it through the rollers. The other electric extrusion machines took a bit more ingenuity. We finally made a thinner pizza crust by rolling together two strips of extruded lasagna dough and overlapping the strips on a baking pan.

FOR ELECTRIC EXTRUSION MACHINES:

1. To make the dough, place the yeast and sugar or Sucanat in a large measuring cup. Add enough water to make 1 cup of liquid, and set aside for 10 minutes.

2. Place the flours in the pasta machine. With the machine running, slowly add the liquid. Process until the dough reaches the consistency specified in the instruction booklet. If the dough is too dry or too wet, add more water or flour per the instruction booklet.

3. Extrude the pasta, following the directions in the instruction booklet. Use the lasagna die.

4. Measure the size of the pan being used, and cut the dough to that length. If using a Simac PastaMatic, skip steps 5 and 6.

5. Place one piece of the cut dough on a work surface, and wet the edges of the dough with your fingers.

6. Place another piece of cut dough on top, and press the pieces together. Use a rolling pin with a very light touch to help the pieces stick together and create a thicker piece of dough.

7. Place the completed strips of dough on the lightly oiled baking pan with the edges slightly overlapping. Using your finger, wet the overlapping edges with water. Press the edges together to form as smooth a surface as possible.

8. Using your fingers, form a raised border around the outside edge.

9. Brush the dough with the olive oil. Cover the dough with a kitchen towel, and let it rise for 1 hour.

FOR HAND-CRANKED MACHINES
OR FOR HAND CUTTING:

1. To make the dough, place the yeast and sugar or Sucanat in a large measuring cup. Add enough water to make 1 cup of liquid, and set aside for 10 minutes.

2. Place the flours in a food processor, and pulse 3 times to mix. With the machine running, slowly add the liquid. Pulse until a ball begins to form, about 10 to 15 seconds.

3. If the dough is too dry when all the liquid has been added, add 1 teaspoon of water, and pulse until a ball begins to form. If the dough is too wet, add 1 tablespoon of flour, and pulse until a ball begins to form. Repeat either process as necessary.

4. Remove the dough from the food processor and place it on a lightly floured pastry board or work surface. Knead the dough, incorporating additional flour into the ball of dough until it becomes smooth and shiny. The dough should be kneaded for 2 minutes if it is being cut on a hand-cranked machine, or 20 minutes if it is being cut by hand.

5. Cover the dough with plastic wrap and let it rest for 20 minutes, or refrigerate it for up to 2 days.

6. If using a hand-cranked machine, roll the dough according to the instructions on page 25. Leave the dough thick by only rolling it out to setting 3 or 4. Don't put the dough through the cutting attachment. If cutting by hand, see page 28.

7. Measure the size of the pan being used, and cut the dough to that length.

8. Place the strips of dough on the lightly oiled baking pan with the edges slightly overlapping. Using your finger, wet the overlapping edges with water. Press the edges together to form as smooth a surface as possible.

9. Using your fingers, form a raised border around the outside edge.

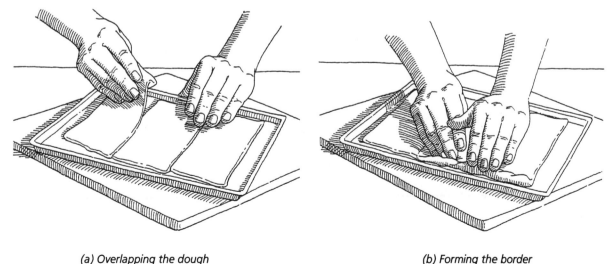

(a) Overlapping the dough   (b) Forming the border

Forming a Pizza Crust

The Pasta Gourmet

10. Brush the dough with the olive oil. Cover the dough with a kitchen towel, and let it rise for 1 hour.

ASSEMBLING AND BAKING INSTRUCTIONS:

1. To assemble the pizza, spread the marinara sauce on the dough, and cover with the chicken and the mushrooms. Evenly distribute the cheese over the chicken and mushrooms.

2. Bake at 400°F for 20 to 30 minutes, or until the crust is brown and the cheese is melted.

Take a Chance:

• Make Vegetarian Pizza by omitting the chicken, reducing the mushrooms to ¼ cup, and adding ¼ cup diced red or green bell peppers, ¼ cup cooked chopped spinach, ¼ cup steamed broccoli florets, and 3 tablespoons chopped black olives.

Suggested Sauces:

• Serve with the following sauces: Chunky Marinara (page 158), Slow-Cooked Spaghetti With Chicken (page 162), Puttanesca (page 157), Italian Cheese Medley (page 169), or Greek Tomato (page 183).

Tortellini with Fresh Spinach Filling

These tiny dumplings can be hard to form. Our first tries ended up looking like little hats. No one cared what they looked like when they tasted them. You can use tortellini in Chicken Soup With Noodles (page 202) or Spinach Lasagna Noodle Soup (page 202).

Preparation Time: *2 Hours*
Yield: *4 Dozen*

TORTELLINI DOUGH

$3\frac{1}{2}$ cups unbleached white flour

1 cup water

FILLING

8 ounces chopped, cooked spinach

$1\frac{1}{2}$ cups low-fat ricotta cheese

$\frac{1}{4}$ cup Pesto Sauce (page 159)

FOR ELECTRIC EXTRUSION MACHINES:

1. Place the flour in the pasta machine. With the machine running, slowly add the water. Process until the dough reaches the consistency specified in the instruction booklet. If the dough is too dry or too wet, add more water or flour per the instruction booklet.

2. Extrude the pasta, following the directions in the instruction booklet. Use the lasagna die, and be sure to extrude the dough in even lengths.

FOR HAND-CRANKED MACHINES:

1. Place the flour in food processor. With the machine running, slowly add the water. Pulse until a ball begins to form, about 10 to 15 seconds.

2. If the dough is too dry when all the liquid has been added, add 1 teaspoon of water, and pulse until a ball begins to form. If the dough is too wet, add 1 tablespoon of flour, and pulse until a ball begins to form. Repeat either process as necessary.

3. Remove the dough from the food processor and place it on a lightly floured pastry board or work surface. Knead the dough, incorporating additional flour into the ball of dough until it becomes smooth and shiny. The dough should be kneaded for 2 minutes.

4. Cover the dough with plastic wrap and let it rest for 5 minutes on the counter, or refrigerate it for up to 2 days.

5. Using the lasagna attachment, cut the dough according to the instructions on page 25. The dough can also be used directly off the rollers, without going through the cutting attachment.

ASSEMBLY AND COOKING INSTRUCTIONS:

1. Lay the dough on a lightly floured work surface. Using either a round tortellini stamp (page 23) or the rim of a glass dipped in flour, stamp out circles in the dough.

2. Place the spinach, cheese, and pesto sauce in a medium-sized bowl, and mix. Then place a scant $\frac{1}{2}$ teaspoon of filling in the center of each circle.

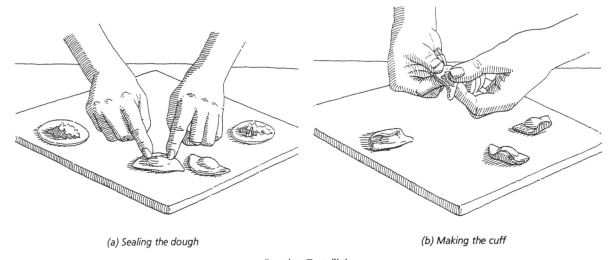

(a) Sealing the dough   (b) Making the cuff

Forming Tortellini

3.   Dip your finger or a pastry brush in water, and run it along the edge of each circle. Fold the dough over the filling, and press the edges together to seal.

4.   Make a cuff along the curved end of the tortillini by bending the dough lengthwise.

5.   Bend the straight edges of the tortillini toward each other until the corners meet. Seal the corners with a drop of water.

6.   If the dough is not wide enough to cut into the traditional tortellini shape, cut the dough into 2-inch squares. Place the filling in the center of the square, and fold the square into a triangle shape. Moisten the ends to seal. Moisten the bottom tips of the triangle, and bring them forward so they touch each other. Pinch to seal.

7.   To cook, bring 6 quarts of water to a full boil. Add a few tortellini at a time to the pot. Cook until they float to the top of the pot, about 2 minutes. Serve hot or cold.

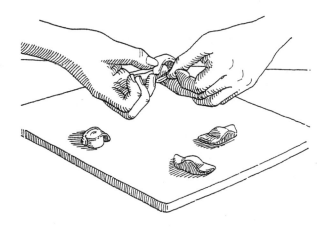

(c) Joining the corners

Take a Chance:

- Omit the spinach.
- Omit the Pesto Sauce, and add $\frac{1}{4}$ cup freshly grated Parmesan cheese.
- Use Spinach Pasta (page 66).

Suggested Sauces:

- Serve hot with Sautéed Garlic and Bread Crumbs (page 155), Chunky Marinara Sauce (page 158), Magnificent Mushroom Sauce (page 163), or Feathery Light Alfredo Sauce (page 177).

- Serve cold with Aglio e Olio (page 154), Pesto Sauce (page 159), Uncooked Tomato Sauce (page 173), or Spicy Steamed Vegetable Sauce (page 178).

Plain Potato Gnocchi

Preparation Time: *1¹/₂ Hours*
Yield: *4 Dozen*

1 pound potatoes, peeled and quartered

1 cup unbleached white flour

¼ teaspoon freshly ground black pepper

4 tablespoons soy margarine

3 tablespoons freshly grated Parmesan or Romano cheese

These richly satisfying morsels are made with potatoes. They are easy to make, especially with those electric extrusion machines that provide a suitable die. If you don't have such a machine, these treats are easy to make by hand.

FOR ELECTRIC EXTRUSION MACHINES:

1. Place the potatoes in a large pot, and cover with water. Bring the pot to a boil over high heat, and cook the potatoes until they are tender when pierced with a fork. Drain.

2. Place the potatoes in a food processor, and process until they are mashed. Place the mashed potatoes in a large bowl, and cool to room temperature. Or you can place the potatoes in the bowl, mash by hand, and allow them to cool.

3. Place the potatoes, flour, and pepper in the pasta machine. Process until the dough reaches the consistency specified in the instruction booklet. If the dough is too dry or too wet, add water or flour per the instruction booklet.

4. Extrude gnocchi, following the directions in the instruction booklet.

FOR HAND CUTTING:

1. Place the potatoes in a large pot, and cover with water. Bring the pot to a boil over high heat, and cook the potatoes until they are tender when pierced with a fork. Drain.

(a) Rolling the dough

2. Place the potatoes in a food processor, and process until they are mashed. Add the flour and pepper, and pulse until mixed. Place the potatoes in a large bowl, and cool to room temperature. Or you can place the potatoes in the bowl, mash by hand with the flour and pepper, and allow them to cool.

3. Transfer the dough to a lightly floured pastry board or work surface and knead for 5 minutes. The dough will be sticky, so keep a cup of flour nearby to flour your hands.

4. Flour your hands again, and pull off a piece of dough about 2 inches round. Roll the dough into a long rope about ½-inch round. Using a sharp knife, cut the rope into 1-inch pieces.

ASSEMBLY AND COOKING INSTRUCTIONS:

1. If making the gnocchi by hand, make a diagonal indentation in the middle of each piece (the pasta machine does this automatically). Fold the ends of the dough toward the indentation. Repeat with the remaining dough.

2. Bring a large pot of water to boil over high heat. Drop enough gnocchi in the water to form a single layer. Cook the gnocchi until they float to the surface. Using a slotted spoon, remove to a casserole dish. Repeat this step until all the gnocchi are cooked.

3. Place the margarine in a small saucepan over low heat. After it melts, pour over the gnocchi in the casserole dish and sprinkle with the grated cheese. Bake at 350°F for 10 to 15 minutes, or until the cheese melts.

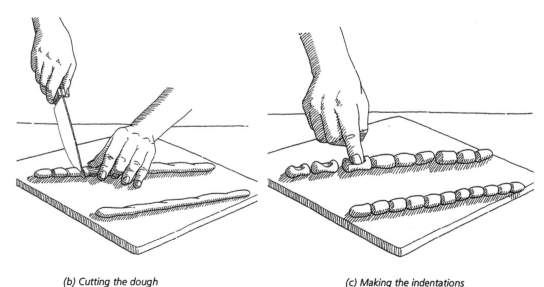

(b) Cutting the dough   *(c) Making the indentations*

Making Gnocchi by Hand

Take a Chance:

• Add ¼ cup freshly grated Parmesan cheese with the flour. Adjust the liquid as necessary.

Suggested Sauces:

• Serve with Pesto Sauce (page 159), Chunky Marinara Sauce (page 158), Magnificent Mushroom Sauce (page 163), or Herbed Butter Sauce (page 166).

Herbed Gnocchi

This is a delicious variation on regular gnocchi.

Preparation Time: 1$\frac{1}{2}$ Hours
Yield: 4 Dozen

1 pound potatoes, peeled and
  quartered

$\frac{3}{4}$ cup unbleached white flour

$\frac{1}{3}$ cup finely minced fresh basil

Chunky Marinara Sauce (page 158)

FOR ELECTRIC EXTRUSION MACHINES:

1. Place the potatoes in a large pot, and cover with water. Bring the pot to a boil over high heat, and cook the potatoes until they are tender when pierced with a fork. Drain.

2. Place the potatoes in a food processor, and process until they are mashed. Place the mashed potatoes in a large bowl, and cool to room temperature. Or you can place the potatoes in the bowl, mash by hand, and allow them to cool.

3. Place the potatoes, flour, and basil in the pasta machine. Process until the dough reaches the consistency specified in the instruction booklet. If the dough is too dry or too wet, add water or flour per the instruction booklet.

4. Extrude the gnocchi, following the directions in the instruction booklet.

FOR HAND CUTTING:

1. Place the potatoes in a large pot, and cover with water. Bring the pot to a boil over high heat, and cook the potatoes until they are tender when pierced with a fork. Drain.

2. Place the potatoes in a food processor, and process until they are mashed. Add the flour and basil, and pulse until mixed. Place the potatoes in a large bowl, and cool to room temperature. Or you can place the potatoes in the bowl, mash by hand with the flour and basil, and allow them to cool.

3. Transfer the dough to a lightly floured pastry board or work surface and knead for 5 minutes. The dough will be sticky, so keep a cup of flour nearby to flour your hands.

4. Flour your hands again and pull off a piece of dough about 2 inches round. Roll the dough into a long rope about $\frac{1}{2}$-inch round. Using a sharp knife, cut the rope into 1-inch pieces.

ASSEMBLY AND COOKING INSTRUCTIONS:

1. If making the gnocchi by hand, make a diagonal indentation in the middle of each piece (see page 221; the pasta machine does this automatically). Fold the ends of the dough toward the indentation. Repeat with the remaining dough.

2. Bring a large pot of water to boil over high heat. Drop enough gnocchi in the water to form a single layer. Cook the gnocchi until they float to the surface. Using a slotted spoon, remove to a serving dish. Repeat this step until all the gnocchi are cooked.

3. Serve hot with the heated marinara sauce over the top.

Take a Chance:

• Use fresh oregano or marjoram instead of basil.

• Mix the gnocchi with the sauce in a medium-sized baking pan. Cover with ½ cup shredded mozzarella cheese. Bake at 350°F for 25 minutes, or until the cheese begins to brown.

Suggested Sauces:

• Serve with Magnificent Mushroom Sauce (page 163), Wild Mushroom Sauce (page 186), or Gingered Chickpeas With Garlic (page 191).

Index

Aglio e Olio, 154
Al dente, 12
Alfredo Sauce, Feathery Light, 177
Almond Pasta, Whole Wheat, 131–132
Amatriciana Sauce, 174
Angel hair pasta. *See* Capellini pasta.
Apple Pear Compote, 198
Apple Pie Pasta, 128–129
Apricot-Peach Pasta, 135–136
Arrabbiata Sauce, 161
Atlas machine, 18–20

Baked Ziti, 205
Barley malt syrup, 194
Basil, preserving, 83
Basil Pasta, 82–83
Basil Pasta, Lemon, 86–87
Basil Pasta, Spinach, 94–95
Basil Pasta, Whole Wheat, 84–85
Beet Pasta, 73–74
Berry Medley, Fresh, 198
Bialetti machine, 18
Blender, drawbacks in pasta-making, 21
Blue Corn Pasta, 80–81
Bolognese-Style Sauce, 179

Bowtie pasta. *See* Farfelle pasta.
Bread Crumbs, Sautéed Garlic and, 155–156
Breadsticks, Whole Wheat, 138–139
Bridegroom pasta. *See* Ziti pasta.
Broccoli Pasta, 70–71
Broths, 200
Brown rice flour, 46–47
Brown Rice Pasta With Water, 56–57
Bucatini pasta, 7
Bucatino pasta, 38
Bucato pasta, 38
Buckwheat flour, 46
Buckwheat Pasta With Cilantro, 92–93
Buckwheat Pasta With Water, 54–55
Bugs's Carrot Pasta, 72–73
Butter Sauce, Herbed, 166
Butterfly pasta. *See* Farfelle pasta.

Calories, pasta and, 6
Capellini pasta, 7
Carbohydrates, pasta and, 6
Carbonara Sauce, 176–177
Carob Pasta, 124–125
Carrot Dill Pasta, 98–99
Carrot Pasta, Bugs's, 72–73

Cavatelli pasta, 9
Cayenne pepper, 76
Cheddar cheese, 13
Cheese, tips for using, 13
Cheese Medley, Italian, 169
Cheese Ravioli, Classic, 209–212
Cheese Sauce, Sinless Summer, 168
Cheesy Parmesan Noodles, 116–117
Cherry Sauce, Tart, 195
Chicken, Curry Sauce With, 184
Chicken, Slow-Cooked Spaghetti Sauce With,
    162–163
Chicken Broth, 200
Chicken Mushroom Pizza, Whole Wheat, 214–216
Chicken Soup With Noodles, 202
Chicken Won Tons, 146–147
Chickens, free-range, 162
Chickpeas With Garlic, Gingered, 191
Chili Pasta, Tomato, 112–113
Chili Powder Pasta, 109–110
Chips
    Corn Tortilla Chips, 143–144
    dips for, 145
    Whole Wheat Pasta Chips, 142–143
Chitarre pasta, 38
Chunky Marinara Sauce, 158
Cilantro, Buckwheat Pasta With, 92–93
Cilantro Peanut Pesto, 182–183
Cinnamon Orange Cranberry Topping, 197
Cinnamon Pasta, 125–126
Citrus Sauce, Hot, 175
Citrus zest, 175
Clam Sauce, Red, 165–166
Clam Sauce, White, 164
Classic Cheese Ravioli, 209–212
Conchiglie pasta, 9
Conchigliette pasta, 9
Confetti Sauce, 187
Corn meals, 47
Corn Pasta, 79–80
Corn Tortilla Chips, 143–144
Cottage Cheese Pesto Dip, 145
Creamy Natural Tomato Sauce, 176
Creative Technologies Corporation, 35
Cuisinart Deluxe Pasta Maker machine, 36–38

Cuisinarts Corporation, 36
Curry Pasta, 102–103
Curry Sauce With Chicken, 184
Curry Spinach Pasta, 114–115
Cutters, pasta, 22

Digestibility coefficient, 6
Dill Pasta, Carrot, 98–99
Dips, 145
Ditali pasta, 8
Dough
    dry, mixing, 41
    extruding, 41–42
    rolling, 19–21
    sticky, remixing, 41
Dry pasta, 10
Drying rack, 22

Eggs, leftover pasta with, 14
Egg Rolls, Shrimp, 148–150
Electric extrusion machines. *See* Pasta machines,
    electric extrusion.

Farfelle pasta, 9
Farmer's pasta, 38
Feathery Light Alfredo Sauce, 177
Festive Macaroni and Cheese, 207
Feta cheese, 13
Fettuccine noodles, 7
Fili d'oro pasta, 38
Flavor, pasta and, 9
Flour
    and flavor, 9
    types of, 46–47
Food processor, uses for, 21, 25
Free-range chickens, 162
Fresh Berry Medley, 198
Fresh Lemongrass Sauce, 185
Fresh pasta, 10
Fruit juice concentrate, 194
Fusilli pasta
    long, 7
    short, 8

Gaeta olives, 157

Garden Fresh Primavera, 180
Garlic, using, 63
Garlic and Bread Crumbs, Sautéed, 155–156
Garlic Pasta, 62–63
Garlic Sauce, Lavender-Scented Roasted, 172
Ginger Sauce, Spicy, 189
Gingered Chickpeas With Garlic, 191
Gnocchi, Herbed, 223–224
Gnocchi, making, 220–221 (f)
Gnocchi, Plain Potato, 220–222
Gouda cheese, 13
Greek Tomato Sauce, 183
Green Yogurt Dressing, 188

Habanero pepper, 76
Hand cutting pasta, 28–29
Hand-cranked pasta machines. *See* Pasta machines, hand-cranked.
Herbed Butter Sauce, 166
Herbed Gnocchi, 223–224
Honey, 194
Honey Yogurt Sauce, Sticky Sweet, 196–197
Hot Citrus Sauce, 175

Italian Cheese Medley, 169
Italian Meatballs, 158

Jalapeño pepper, 76
Jalapeño Pepper Pasta, 75, 77

Kalamata olives, 157

Laganum, 5
Lasagna, Traditional, 206–207
Lasagna noodles, 7
Lasagna Noodle Soup, Spinach, 202–203
Lasagna Roll-Ups With Chunky Marinara Sauce, 213
Lasagna With White Sauce, Vegetable, 208–209
Lavender-Scented Roasted Garlic Sauce, 172
Leftover pasta, serving, 13–14
Lello Appliances Corporation, 38
Lemon Basil Pasta, 86–87
Lemon Pasta, 130–131
Lemon Pepper Pasta, Whole Wheat, 107–108
Lemon Sauce, Luscious, 196

Lemon zest, 175
Lemongrass Sauce, Fresh, 185
Linguine noodles, 7
Long fusilli pasta, 7
Luscious Lemon Sauce, 196

Macaroni and Cheese, Festive, 207
Maccheroni quadrati pasta, 38
Maccheroni quadrifoglio pasta, 38
Machines. *See* Pasta machines, electric extrusion; Pasta machines, hand-cranked.
Magnificent Mushroom Sauce, 163
Marinara Sauce, Chunky, 158
Marinara Sauce, Smooth Tomato, With Basil, 160–161
Maverick Industries, Inc., 34
Meatballs, Italian, 158
Minestrone Soup, 201
Moroccan olives, 157
Mostaccioli pasta, 8
Mushroom Pizza, Whole Wheat Chicken, 214–216
Mushroom Sauce, Magnificent, 163

Nicoise olives, 157
Nut Sauce, Raisin, 194

Oat flour, 47
Oat Pasta With Water, 58–59
Oatmeal Cookie Pasta, 127–128
Olive oil, types of, 155
Olive Sauce, Quick, 156
Olives, types of, 157
OMC Marcato, 18, 20
Onion Raisin Sauce, 173–174
Orange zest, 175
Oregano Pasta, Tomato, 96–97
Orzo, 8

Pappardella noodles, 38
Paprika Pasta, Sweet, 105–106
Parmesan cheese, 13
Parmesan Noodles, Cheesy, 116–117
Parsley Pasta, 90–91
Pasta
    cheese and, 13

cooking, 12–13
cutters, 22
directions for basic, 48–62
dry, buying, 10
drying, 47
flavors, 9–10
fresh, buying, 10
history of, 5–6
nutritional content of, 6
serving, 13
shapes, 6–9
storing, 13–14, 47
types of, 6–10
wheels, 22
See also individual listings.
Pasta de contadino, 38
Pasta e Fagioli, 203
Pasta machines, electric extrusion
brands of, 32–39
cleaning, 32
dough handling with, 32
evaluating, 39–40
pricing, 32
shopping for, 39–40
using, 40–42
Pasta machines, hand-cranked
brands of, 18–21
cleaning, 17
dough handling with, 17
pricing, 17
using, 24–28
Pasta-Del-Giorno machine, 34–35
PastaExpress X3000 machine, 35–36
PastaMatic MX700 machine, 38–39
Pastry board, 22
Pastry scraper, 22
Peach Pasta, Apricot-, 135
Peanut Pesto, Cilantro, 182–183
Pear Compote, Apple, 198
Pecorino cheese. *See* Romano cheese.
Penne pasta, 8
Peppers, varieties of, 76
Pescatore Sauce, 167
Pesto, Cilantro Peanut, 182–183
Pesto Dip, Cottage Cheese, 145

Pesto Pasta, 64–65
Pesto Sauce, 159
Pizza, Whole Wheat Chicken Mushroom, 214–216
Plain Potato Gnocchi, 220–222
Poblano pepper, 76
Potato Gnocchi, Plain, 220–222
Pretzels, 140–141
Primavera, Garden Fresh, 180
Primo Pasta machine, 32–34
Protein, pasta and, 6
Puttanesca Sauce, 157

Quick Olive Sauce, 156

Raisin Nut Sauce, 194
Raisin Sauce, Onion, 173–174
Ravioli, Classic Cheese, 209–212
Ravioli rolling pin, 23
Ravioli trays, 23
using, 211 (f)
Red Clam Sauce, 165–166
Red Wine Pasta, 111–112
Regina Atlas machine, 20–21
Ricotta Cheese Dessert Topping, 195
Rigati pasta. *See* Penne pasta.
Rigatoni pasta, 8
Ristra peppers, 76
Rolling pin, ravioli, 23
Rolling pin, standard, 24
Roll-Ups, Lasagna With Chunky Marinara Sauce, 213
Romano cheese, 13
Rotelle pasta. *See* Short fusilli pasta.

Saffron Pasta, 104–105
Sage Thyme Pasta, 88–89
Salsa Serrano, 145
Sauce of Truffles, A, 182
Sauces. *See* individual listings.
Sautéed Garlic and Bread Crumbs, 155–156
Semolina flour, 46
Semolina Pasta With Water, 52–53
Serrano, Salsa, 145
Serrano pepper, 76
Sfoglia large per ravioli, 38

Short fusilli pasta, 8
Shrimp Egg Rolls, 148–150
Simple Homemade Pasta With Water, 48–49
Sinless Summer Cheese Sauce, 168
Slow-Cooked Spaghetti Sauce With Chicken, 162–163
Smooth Tomato Marinara Sauce With Basil, 160–161
Soba Noodles, 120–121
Soups
    Chicken Broth, 200
    Chicken Soup With Noodles, 202
    Minestrone Soup, 201
    Pasta e Fagioli, 203
    Spinach Lasagna Noodle Soup, 202–203
    Vegetable Broth, 200
Spaghetti pasta, 8
Spaghetti Sauce, Slow-Cooked, With Chicken, 162–163
Spaghettini pasta, 38
Spicy Ginger Sauce, 189
Spicy Steamed Vegetable Sauce, 178
Spinach Basil Pasta, 94–95
Spinach Filling, Tortellini With Fresh, 217–219
Spinach Lasagna Noodle Soup, 202–203
Spinach Pasta, 66–67
Spinach Pasta, Curry, 114
Spinach Pasta, Whole Wheat, 68–69
Sticky Sweet Honey Yogurt Sauce, 196–197
Storing pasta
    drying, 47
    fresh, 47
    leftover cooked, 13
Strawberry Pasta, 133–134
Sucanat, 194
Sugar alternatives, 194
Sweet Paprika Pasta, 105–106
Swiss cheese, 13

Tagliatella pasta, 38
Tagliatelle pasta. *See* Fettuccine noodles.
Tart Cherry Sauce, 195
Thai pepper, 76
Thyme Pasta, Sage, 88–89
Tomato Chili Pasta, 112–113
Tomato Oregano Pasta, 96–97

Tomato Pasta, 77–78
Tomato Sauce, Creamy Natural, 176
Tomato Sauce, Greek, 183
Tomato Sauce, Uncooked, 173
Tomatoes, choosing, 160
Tortellini, forming, 218–219 (f)
Tortellini stamp, 23
Tortellini With Fresh Spinach Filling, 217–219
Tortilla Chips, Corn, 143–144
Traditional Lasagna, 206–207
Truffles, A Sauce of, 182

Udon Noodles, 118–119
Unbleached white flour, 46
Uncooked Tomato Sauce, 173

Vegetable and Pasta Stew, Versatile, 204
Vegetable Broth, 200
Vegetable Lasagna With White Sauce, 208–209
Vegetable Sauce, Spicy Steamed, 178
Verde Sauce, 190
Versatile Vegetable and Pasta Stew, 204
VillaWare Manufacturing Company, 20

Waring Products, 32
Wheels, pasta, 22
White Clam Sauce, 164
Whole Wheat Almond Pasta, 131–132
Whole Wheat Basil Pasta, 84–85
Whole Wheat Breadsticks, 138–139
Whole Wheat Chicken Mushroom Pizza, 214–216
Whole wheat flour, 46
Whole Wheat Lemon Pepper Pasta, 107–108
Whole Wheat Pasta Chips, 142–143
Whole Wheat Pasta With Water, 50–51
Whole Wheat Spinach Pasta, 68–69
Wild Mushroom Sauce, 186
Won Tons, Chicken, 146–147

Yogurt Dressing, Green, 188
Yogurt Sauce, Sticky Sweet Honey, 196–197

Zest, citrus, 175
Ziti, Baked, 205
Ziti pasta, 8